SACRED FIRE

Willa Cather's Novel Cycle

Evelyn Helmick Hively

UNIVERSITY
PRESS OF
AMERICA

Lanham • New York • London

Copyright © 1994 by
University Press of America®, Inc.
4720 Boston Way
Lanham, Maryland 20706

3 Henrietta Street
London WC2E 8LU England

Library of Congress Cataloging-in-Publication Data
Hively, Evelyn Helmick.
Sacred fire : Willa Cather's novel cycle / Evelyn Helmick Hively.
p.   cm.
Includes bibliographical references and index.
1. Cather, Willa, 1873-1947 — Criticism and interpretation.
2. Historical fiction, American — History and criticism.
3. Frontier and pioneer life in literature.
4. West (U.S.) — In literature.   I. Title.
PS3505.A87Z664   1993   813'.52—dc20   94-4183   CIP

ISBN 0-8191-9481-6 (cloth : alk. paper)

Photograph by Carl van Vechten courtesy of the Library of Congress

For Melinda, Jenny, and Jon

Contents

Acknowledgments

First, my thanks must be expressed for the help and support given me in this project, as in everything else, by my husband, Robert Hively. Others who informed and encouraged my work were G. K. Smart, who introduced me to myth criticism and remains for me professor *par excellence*; William Dismukes, who shared his dissertation and his knowledge of Vico; and Joseph Campbell, who helped me to explore the mysteries. All three are, sadly, now beyond my expressions of gratitude. David Stouck, who has given so much to Cather scholarship, read the completed manuscript and made many valuable suggestions.

Early in my research the University of Colorado at Boulder permitted access to the many books on religion published before 1912 that were then uncatalogued--a treasure of information that made me aware of the material about the mystery religions that might have been available to Cather. In the final stages of manuscript preparation, Sam Fustukian, director of the library at the University of South Florida, arranged for special privileges in the Florida collections. Gracious assistance was given at the Houghton Library of Harvard University, the Boston Public Library, the Nebraska Historical Society, the Willa Cather Historical Center, The Beinecke Library of Yale University, and the library of the University of Rome. Several unnamed people provided information and materials at the Villa of the Mysteries at Pompeii.

I thank the editors of the following journals for permission to reprint in revised form several of my early articles on Cather: *Renascence* (Winter 1976) for "The Broken World: Medievalism in *A Lost Lady*,"; *Midwest Quarterly* (January 1976) for "The Mysteries of Ántonia"; *Midcontinent American Studies Journal* (Fall 1968) for "Myth in the Works of Willa Cather."

Acknowledgments

I am grateful to the University of Nebraska Press for permission to reprint quotations from Cather's *April Twilights, The Kingdom of Art, the World and the Parish;* David Stouck's *Willa Cather's Imagination;* Elizabeth Sergeant's *Willa Cather: A Memoir;* James Woodress' *Willa Cather: A Literary Life*; Bernice Slote and Virginia Faulkner's *The Art of Willa Cather;* Richard Giannone's *Music in Willa Cather's Fiction.*

Reprinted by permission of Alfred A. Knopf, Inc.: quotations from *One of Ours* by Willa Cather, copyright 1922 by Willa Cather, renewed 1950 by Edith Lewis and the City Bank Farmers Trust Company; from *A Lost Lady* by Willa Cather, copyright 1923 by Willa Cather, renewed 1951 by the executors of the estate of Willa Cather; from *The Professor's House* by Willa Cather, copyright 1925 by Willa Cather, renewed 1953 by Edith Lewis and the City Bank Farmers Trust Company; from *My Mortal Enemy* by Willa Cather, copyright 1926 by Willa Cather, renewed 1954 by Edith Lewis and the City Bank Farmers Trust Company; from *Death Comes for the Archbishop*, by Willa Cather, copyright 1927 by Willa Cather, renewed 1955 by the executors of the estate of Willa Cather; from *Shadows on the Rock* by Willa Cather, copyright 1931 by Willa Cather, renewed 1959 by the executors of the estate of Willa Cather; from *Not Under Forty* by Willa Cather, copyright 1936 by Willa Cather, renewed 1964 by Edith Lewis and the City Bank Farmers Trust Company; from *Willa Cather on Writing* by Willa Cather, copyright 1936 by Willa Cather, renewed 1949 by the executors of the estate of Willa Cather.

The frontispiece photograph of Willa Cather by Carl Van Vechten is reproduced through the courtesy of the Library of Congress.

Introduction

Today's literary criticism reflects a world view without a center, doubtful of the possibility of agreement about the very structure of civilization, not to mention literary texts. The deconstructionists of our postmodern era distrust grand designs, the "tyranny of wholes," universal truths. They deny the fundamental philosophies that have been the basis for thought in Western history.

Willa Cather, to the contrary, understood what she called the "whole of the higher artistic process" as one that sacrificed many individual conceptions, however good, for one that was "better and more universal." A British critic in 1926 praised her early novels for their "wholeness and harmony of narrative and feeling." Her understanding of the progression of historical eras and her global thinking about the way literature, music, and art relate to each other create much of the genius and individuality of her writing. In her time the command for awareness of one's world might well have been E. M. Forster's "Only connect."

Cather's connections do not result in a monolithic world view, but rather one that encompasses many philosophies, many cultures, many truths--and within them the possibility for the emergence of the exceptional human being. The scope of her vision can be seen in the varied scholarly analyses of her work in terms of romanticism, realism, naturalism, classicism, and modernism. All contribute to our understanding of her meaning, but she wished her writing not to be classified, even in terms of genre. When critics struggled to name the form of *Death Comes for the Archbishop*, "Why bother?" she asked, supplying instead "narrative," the broadest possible term for a story. Cather's formidable knowledge of literature, philosophy, history, and the arts permitted her to borrow and adapt forms, styles, settings, points of view, characters, plots, and phrases from a seemingly inexhaustible store. When she recombined them in a new, coherent whole, she presented the world with literature that was at once highly original and reminiscent of the best that centuries of Western culture had produced.

One of the reasons for the constant fascination of Cather's work for the contemporary mind may be exactly those qualities that reassure the human need for tradition, continuity, and humanistic values in our world, in spite of ever-increasing change, uncertainties, and ambiguities. She most intensely admired those writers who, in her phrase, were "large enough": Michelet and Parkman, with their multi-volume, sweeping histories; Bergson, with his sense of historical continuity; Mann, with his ambitious attempt to recreate biblical stories; William James, with his poetic sense of religious mystery. The intellectual milieu in which she worked as a mature writer was excited by the views of thinkers who had grand ideas of the wholeness of the world, and the role of the artist in it. Often, even as they found the intuitive understanding of the poet the most important characteristic of the human being, they hoped for a reconciliation between intuition and scientific reason. The historical views were accompanied by a new research into the myths that had been among the earliest known expressions of insight into metaphysical meaning. The first years of the twentieth century brought books by James Frazer, Jane Ellen Harrison, Gilbert Murray, Franz Cumont, and many other scholars who were replacing "bankrupt" classical mythology with the primitive myths and pagan mystery religions that excited writers such as Eliot, Pound, and Joyce. Cather, with her education and teaching experience in the classics, responded to the information and spirit of this new literature.

This study combines Cather's interest in the historians, the philosophers, and the mythographers, to examine nine of her novels on three levels. First, it postulates a cyclical design, beginning with *O Pioneers!* and ending with *Shadows on the Rock*, which traces a rise, maturity, and fall of the civilization of the American West, and presents a new beginning in the final books. The cycle follows the pattern developed in the philosophy of Giambattista Vico, although Cather may have derived much of the idea from both Michelet, Parkman, and Gibbon, among others. Some clues in the novels invite speculation that she may have consciously developed, at least in broad outline, such a design; it is evident in my view that much of her plan emerged from her study of the historians she admired.

The second level relates to Vico's theory that language follows and adapts to succeeding periods of civilization's cycle and that genre, a convention of language, has a connection with a particular age, expressing a relationship to the world view of the time. The many quotations in the study are there not only to savor the beauty of Cather's prose, but also to demonstrate the total appropriateness of the words to stages of the cycle. Readers of Cather will recognize that the the chapter titles are her own words; the first five phrases are from her poems, and the sixth is from *My Ántonia*, later used in Cather's epitaph. The analyses of literary forms in these chapters do not contradict contributive and significant work done by others; they are intended to add some insight into the relationship of the form to the historical period presented in the novel. Cather's use of genre is complex, and this study examines only one facet.

In addition to language, and closely allied in Vichian theory, is religion, specifically the mystery religions that pervaded the Roman world and marked the early stages of civilization. Those ancient mysteries, still the basis for much of religious ritual, were devoted to the worship of the goddess. They had, I believe, great significance for Cather. In using them for analysis of her novels, I have tried to restrict the sources to those which she might have been available to her before 1912.

Documentation here relies much on earlier critics, many of them contemporaries of Cather who, more often than do the modern critics, comment on the nationalist and religious themes of the novels, and thus have more relevance to my thesis. Literary scholars will recognize how much I owe to the criticism of Northrop Frye and Erich Auerbach, both ardent Vichians--Auerbach to the extent of translating Vico's *New Science* into his native German language. They have contributed a great deal to the understanding of Cather's meaning.

1

The Law Behind the Veil

When a writer means to accomplish anything noble and enduring, Willa Cather said, "he fades away into the land and people of his heart, he dies of love only to be born again" (*OW*,51). This statement reveals a key to her view of her role as novelist, artist, and interpreter of the culture of the American West. Her intentions to create noble, enduring, profound works of art were consistently expressed in exalted or even mystical terms. She meant to be the first to bring the Muse into her own country, and in order to do so she brought to bear all of her accumulated knowledge, her beliefs, and a finely tuned intuition. Handling such serious problems in a simple manner, she confessed in 1913, cost the writer "many births and deaths."[1] She thought that the writer's relation to literature carried religious overtones, as did all art for her.

Whether she set out in 1912 to write of a cycle of civilization or she developed the idea as she wrote, she achieved, beginning with *O Pioneers!*, a novel cycle that traces the rise and fall of the American West. A classical scholar, she followed the patterns of the great writers, and just as Virgil relied on Homer and Dante relied on Virgil, Cather followed the best of guides from the past. She turned to the frontier for inspiration because it dramatized universal moral problems. Her protagonists often evoke the gods and heroes of ancient civilizations. In her early novels, as important as in Virgil's time, loom the cycles of the seasons, the vegetation myths, the hostility or beneficence of a personified Nature. The magnitude of the Western landscape adds grandeur, and the historical background lends a sense of reality, but the stories are based on the few eternal conflicts of human existence and their attendant myths. Setting her stories in the past gave her the opportunity to depict the beginning of a civilization, with a stage stripped of many of the properties that would clutter it soon afterward. Stark drama could show the universal actions of man in an essentially timeless world.

Accepting the advice of her friend and mentor Sarah Orne Jewett to write about her own country, Cather began her work of narrating the story of the nation from the time of its true origins, the Western frontier, with her second novel, *O Pioneers!*. Instead of merely presenting yet another "figure of heroic innocence and vast potentialities, poised at the start of a new history" that R. W. B. Lewis in *The American Adam* found to be the dominating image of much of American literature,[2] she created a cycle of novels that would show the development of a civilization. Beginning with *O Pioneers!* and ending with *Shadows on the Rock*, her novels relate American history to the history of other cultures, using a progression of literary forms and devices to examine and reveal the people, their language, myth, and arts. The complete cycle is much more than the sum of its nine parts, and this segment of her work becomes an achievement offering "something complete and great" to be analyzed. The period between 1912 and 1931, the prime of Cather's artistic life, was a coherent, organic span of creativity which demonstrates that her mind, as Bernice Slote concluded in "The Secret Web," is more complex than has been acknowledged.[3] Wallace Stevens, Maxwell Geismar, and David Stouck express the same conviction.

Much of that complexity has to do with the amount of information she accumulated in her years of serious study, teaching, reading, attending as many artistic performances as time allowed. After her apprenticeship as music, art, and drama critic when she read voraciously and saw nearly every musical and dramatic presentation in Lincoln,[4] her choices were discriminating and provided her much material, of which she seemed to forget nothing. The forms, events, characters, and language of her novels are continuously evocative of the great literature, art, music, philosophy, and religion of the Western world. In order to decipher Cather, the reader would ideally know Greek, Latin, and French, be well acquainted with the works of major philosophers and historians, be familiar with much art and music, and be widely read in ancient and contemporary texts. Cather hungrily pursued this knowledge and then internalized it for her own uses. She built on what she had learned in order to construct for her own country a long corridor of history like those created by her classical models.

She then began the novel cycle that traced the rise and fall of the American West. Those who knew her best doubt that she planned a cycle at the outset. Her publisher, Alfred Knopf, wrote that the idea is "far from anything like her," as he knew her.[5] Her friend and literary confidante, Elizabeth Shepley Sergeant, thought that although her unconscious self may have had such a purpose all along, she was not aware of it when she began to write *O Pioneers!*.[6] Cather's own statements show a characteristic ambivalence about the possibilities of a design: although there were times when she told of her inspiration, those sudden explosions of insight, the novel that "just happened" to her, at other times she talked about the "thing that teases the mind" over the years, her fifteen-year plan to write *Death Comes for the Archbishop*, her sense that "America works on my mind like light on a photographic plate on a camera."[7] She was too complicated as a writer and too secretive as a public figure to be consistent in her own revelations of her method of work.

The idea of pattern, most of it related to Cather's own life and psychological states, does appeal to critics in confronting Cather's themes. Louis Kronenberger, in a review of *Shadows on the Rock*, divided her work into three periods: the first, with her three novels of the frontier--*O Pioneers!*, *The Song of the Lark*, and *My Ántonia*--was a time of affirmation; the period of the next four--*One of Ours* through *My Mortal Enemy*--signals a decline; the later period of *Death Comes for the Archbishop* and *Shadows on the Rock* was lifeless. James E. Miller, Jr. notes Cather's use of cyclical structures of nature in "*My Ántonia*: A Frontier Drama of Time," and found a kind of history of the American West in the works of Cather and Wright Morris.[8] Patricia Lee Yongue often connects Cather and American history; especially interesting are "*A Lost Lady*: The End of the First Cycle" and her doctoral dissertation, "The Immense Design."[9] Merrill Maguire Skaggs sees the novels from *One of Ours* to *Sapphira and the Slavegirl* as a sequence in which Cather was working out her own salvation.[10]

Leon Edel in his Library of Congress lecture, "Willa Cather: The Paradox of Success," treats the eight novels from *Alexander's Bridge* to *My Mortal Enemy* as a sequence, in which the subject of the first four is conquest, and the subject of the second phase is death. He is, in his analysis, proceeding from a critical assumption that says the individuality of a novel is a reflection of the novelist, and in this case of a woman who is overtaken by a despair which she herself does not understand and which arises in part from her difficulty with handling the success that came from her first four novels. His assumptions are firmly rooted in the school of psychological literary analysis that has directed the books on Cather from the 1953 memoir by Edith Lewis to the 1989 biography by Hermione Lee. (Two important exceptions are David Stouck's focus on her art and Richard Giannone's analysis of her use of music.) Edel goes beyond his eight-novel sequence to say that *Death Comes for the Archbishop* and *Shadows on the Rock* are Cather's escape from her inability to deal with the present and with change. For him the inner story illustrates the way in which Cather's creative consciousness keeps her personal world intact and prevents anything from altering it. He rejects the belief that a story can be found spontaneously outside the writer's consciousness.

For Cather, however, the material that lies at the bottom of the consciousness is what feeds the artistic impulse and becomes "the thing by which our feet find the road home on a dark night, accounting of themselves for roots and stone which we had never noticed by day" (*AB*,vii). It was when she began to focus on the places and people she had known in her youth that her writing became more spontaneous, beginning with the composition of *O Pioneers!*, which she said was like "taking a ride through a familiar country on a horse that knew the way, on a fine morning when you felt like riding" (*OW*,93). In the 1922 preface to *Alexander's Bridge* she cited Henri Bergson's concept of the wisdom of intuition, which he opposed to the wisdom of intellect, and told of her illumination that came "in flashes that are unreasoning, often unreasonable as life itself." She was suspicious of systematic analysis, says E. K. Brown, her early biographer, and her own criticism was "but purely personal response, unsupported by argument and occasionally veering into fantasy."[11] Her youthful criticism reprinted in *The Kingdom of Art* often mixes a rational approach with bursts of her strong, idiosyncratic style that jolts the reader to attention, most often because of her use of ancient literature to make a contemporary point. But in her criticism written when she was a mature, successful novelist, she chose to ignore standard modes and emphasize the intuitive, especially in her own work. Clearly she wanted her public to know her as an inspired writer.

Many writers have described the revelatory experience that Edel rejects in Cather's work. Do we discover or do we invent (or reinvent) our material? asks our contemporary, Annie Dillard.[12] Northrop Frye insists that whatever Plato's conscious mind was doing when he wrote the account of Atlantis, he was not inventing a myth so much as releasing it. Cather, in encouraging the public persona of the inspired writer, must have been aware that there would be doubters like Edel and Lee. For believers, however, Cather's statements of her intuitive approach help to translate a message that is complex, profound, and mystical. John Dewey's explanation in *Art as Experience* is that when excitement about art is deep it stirs up attitudes and meanings from prior experience.[13] Whether this is experience only in the individual past or, as Jung assumes, in the racial past, such evocation means a lessening of the rational, purely cognitive responses. Yeats has expressed the same idea more poetically than Dewey: "Whatever the passions of man have gathered about, becomes a symbol in Great Memory, and in the hands of him who has the secret it is a worker of wonders, a caller-up of angels or of devils."[14]

Inevitably, much of Cather's address to her work was a conscious choice of material and the attitude toward it, and as with most creative people, the content of her unconscious combined spontaneously with the conscious as she crafted her literature. Too much conscious writing in a style not her own produced the Jamesian *Alexander's Bridge*, a brief conventional work she later repudiated in an essay, "My First Novels: There Were Two" (*OW*,91-7). She began anew with *O Pioneers!* and found her own voice: "I wrote this book for myself," she declared in a Bunyanesque passage; "I found it a much more absorbing occupation than writing *Alexander's Bridge*, a different process altogether" (*OW*,92). She has turned her attention to the subject matter of the frontier and, by her own admission, allowed her subconscious to dictate much of her form and style. Her language illuminates her view of the role of the writer in her descriptions of a Jewett story as a "miracle" and Katherine Mansfield's stories as "magic." She speaks of Jewett's instinctive preference for her subject matter, her intuition, the temperament that allows her to see the deeper meaning of things. In an essay on Mann, Cather speaks of stories that "waken the deep vibrations of the soul," and in a letter titled "Escapism" in the collection *On Writing*, she insists that the usefulness of the true poet lies in his ability to recharge the spirit.

Much of the expression of Cather's intuitive approach to her writing could be a paraphrase of some of the philosophy of literary criticism published in the first decade of the twentieth century by Henri Bergson. In *Mind-Energy* of 1902 he declared that every artist first conceives his subject as a whole scheme, and only then moves to the specific image. Artistic creation, he said in *Creative Evolution*, comes after a painful effort to place oneself at the heart of the subject and to seek an impulse, after which the artist need only let himself go. The writer must immerse himself completely in the consciousness of his hero by use of his intuition, a kind of "intellectual sympathy." *Creative Evolution*, published in France in 1907 and in the United States in 1911, gave to philosophy the term *élan vital* to describe the creative power that moves through all living things, a term that Cather borrowed several times. Bergson's ideas were in the intellectual air at the beginning of the century and had influence on musicians and visual artists as well as on writers of the period. At the same time William James, whose work influenced Cather a great deal, wrote of many of the same principles. But the language of literary criticism that she uses, in assimilating these ideas along with many others, often matches Bergson's very closely. Further, we know that she read his work, from her 1922 introduction to *Alexander's Bridge*, from Elizabeth Sergeant's discussion of modern writers whom Cather admired, and from a letter in which Cather expresses enthusiasm for Bergson's *Creative Evolution*.[15]

She had much at the bottom of her consciousness to feed what Jung calls the "visionary mode of artistic creation." She is one of those writers on whom, in Henry James's words, no experience is lost; but in her hands, that experience of literature and life is transformed. Her literary vision, both universal and inclusive, is of interest because it is whole. As Bernice Slote says in commenting on Cather's poems and her critical statements before 1896, nothing in her work is unrelated to the whole (*AT*,v). That view seems especially applicable to her novels--at least through *Shadows on the Rock*--which, when considered together, reveal a coherent pattern.

She created, whether in its entirety in advance or a single book at a time, a novel cycle that echoes Virgil as it traces the rise, maturity, fall, and regeneration of the American West. At the same time she related that American experience to previous periods of history, identified her heroines with the goddesses of antiquity, and adapted earlier mythologies to contemporary life. Thus, the three early novels of the frontier--*O Pioneers!*, *The Song of the Lark,* and *My Ántonia*,--are placed in the age of gods, using agricultural settings, heroines with qualities of goddesses, myths of primitive and classical eras, and the pastoral and saga as literary structures. The inscription to *My Ántonia*-- "*Optima dies . . . prima fugit*"--is the keynote to the whole of her novel cycle. The second stage, a declining age of heroes, includes *One of Ours* and *A Lost Lady*. The myths are medieval, the literary forms are the epic and the courtly romance, civilization becomes urbanized and legalized, and the heroes are more fallible. The third stage, the age of men, is represented by *The Professor's House* and *My Mortal Enemy*. The civilization, language, and literary forms are complex and modern; the myths are sophisticated and buried deep within the structure of the novels. The final phase, after dissolution and death in the age of men, is a new beginning, a return to the theme of the founding of a new civilization--another age of gods in an ascending spiral. In these novels, *Death Comes for the Archbishop* and *Shadows on the Rock*, structure is again seemingly simplified, characters have a direct relation to the gods, and the civilizations depicted are new frontiers. Myths often have the qualities of early legends.

One of her guides in this ambitious project was undoubtedly Jules Michelet, whose *History of France* she had read by 1912 when *O Pioneers!* was completed. From Michelet she borrowed many ideas, structures, and even language. Michelet's nine-volume history was, in Edmund Wilson's words, "a great work of imagination and research of a kind perhaps never to occur again--the supreme effort in its time of a human being to enter into, to understand, to comprehend, the development of a modern nation."[16] But behind Michelet's work was the seminal mind of Giambattista Vico, a philosopher who lived in Italy from 1668 to 1744, but was little known outside of Italy until Michelet learned Italian in order to translate his works. Michelet wrote of Vico: "His principles of the living force of humanity creating itself, made both my book and my teaching."[17] At least two critics have seen Cather's awareness of the principle when they wrote that her theme is "man, and what he must do to 'create' himself."[18] In many other phrases Cather reveals her debt to Michelet, whose work inspired twentieth-century historians to reject positivism and bring a new method of study to modern history. Another source of information about Vico's philosophy might well have been Robert Flint, whose 1884 publication remains a standard. Vico's comprehensive theory proved fruitful for literature and philosophy as well, based as it is on a description of an eternal history whose course is run by the histories of all nations, leading to a universal pattern in the development of all creations of man. The course of history of one nation finds parallels in those of all nations. Thus, Vico's hypothesis about the culture of Rome describes all other civilizations as well. He saw two cycles in Western history up to his time: the first was in antiquity, ending with the fall of Rome; another had started in the Middle Ages and had reached its last phase in his own eighteenth

century. Willa Cather found parallels to the new start on the American
frontier in both of those cycles, and she structured the nine novels
beginning with *O Pioneers!* on the earlier patterns.

In addition to the parallelism of cultures, Vico found a cycle within
the history of every nation. Each nation's development goes through
succeeding ages of gods, heroes, and men from a state of barbaric
simplicity to one of reflective intelligence. To these three ages
correspond three stages of government, of law, customs, language,
myth, and even human nature itself. Thus, government in the age of
gods, when men believed they lived under divine rule and people were
commanded by auspices and oracles, became in the age of heroes a
government of aristocratic commonwealths, and in the age of men, a
process of men governing as equals. Jurisprudence in the age of gods
was mystic theology, with wise men as theological poets; it became in
the age of heroes verbal rigorousness, following precisely what is set
forth in words; in the age of men law developed a natural equity and a
demand for universal laws. Language in the age of gods was mute
language or signs, secret or sacred hieroglyphics; in the age of heroes
symbolic language develops, with emblems, comparisons, images; the
age of men uses words agreed upon by the people, becoming a vulgar
language. Similar evolutions take place in customs, myths, and human
nature. Vico, providing the philosophical base for comparative literature
with his theory, said that he read on successive days Cicero side by side
with Boccaccio, Virgil with Dante, and Horace with Petrarch. Each pair
represented the same stage in the cycles of their respective nations.

There were many cyclical systems of the evolution of nations known
to historians and philosophers before Vico, who admitted that his theory
was derived from the ancient Egyptians. Plato and Aristotle, among the
early Greeks, subscribed to the cyclical theory of history. Hesiod's
system included five periods, from the age of gold, with deathless gods
from Olympus, to the age of iron, with mortal men. Cicero's ages were
three: the dark time of the Egyptian gods, the fabulous time of heroes,
and the historic time of men. A traditional classical division was in four
parts: the creation and coming of gods; the pastoral life and ordering of
the seasons; the adventures and labors of heroes; and the time of war,
tragic tales, decline into history. There were others following Vico and
influenced by him whom Cather would have probably known in
addition to the earlier writers. Goethe, for example, formulated the
"ages of the spirit" as the poetic mythic period, the religious period, the
philosophical period, and the period of naturalistic prose. The

interpretations of the ages of man, however they are categorized and articulated, have in common a descent from a previous golden age. Gibbon, whose work is mentioned in *One of Ours*, and later Spengler and Toynbee, are among the historians who used the concept of national cycles and whose works support the claim that Vico's *New Science* foreshadowed the entire modern approach to the study of man's past. Although some critics see in Cather's view a kind of Spenglerian outline of a cycle of civilization, Spengler is not a likely source for Cather's cycle; his first volume in German was not published until 1918. Cather was influenced by Michelet, as were other precursors of Spengler.

Cather had long been interested in historical cycles, perhaps focused by her college semester on Heraclitus. Even her high school graduation speech began, "All human history is a record of an emigration, an exodus from barbarism to civilization."[19] Many of her reviews in her newspaper columns talked of the rise and fall of Rome, as in the 1896 reference to "the final decadence of the Roman empire, when old things, outworn and corrupt, were giving place to new, when nature was revenging herself." In another review she explains that when the Roman world became corrupt the barbarian races came to destroy and renew. Her use of the Roman historical cycle is so frequent in these newspaper pieces that Slote finds it one of two major themes during the apprentice years of 1883 to 1886 (*KA*,109). The historical references she made in this early period of her career as critic indicate an awareness of the strong advocates of the humanistic historiography after Vico and an acceptance of the cyclical principles of history. In analysis of her novels in this book, the term *Vichian* will refer to the general concepts described, no matter what Cather's sources.

The study of Michelet and a full understanding of Vico's principles add new moral and esthetic ideas, greater depth of cultural knowledge and a comprehensive vision to her awareness. Paramount to her purpose is the ideal of the universal cycle, which relates to the national historical evolution, to the movement of the seasons that structure so much of her work, and to the pattern of human life itself. Sharon O'Brien finds that "Cather's creative road was circular, leading into and out of the self, connecting inner and outer worlds."[20] That circular path had to do with more than self: it was a profound understanding of man's relation to nature, of the historical patterns of civilizations, as well as the psychological cycle of human existence. At the end of *My Ántonia* Jim Burden not only has a sense of coming home to himself, he also has found out that experience is a little circle. (*MA*,372). In her novels

Cather's world is the wider one of Vico and Michelet, Joyce and Mann. Bernice Slote's opinion is that "almost as if there *were* a design, the line of her creative will curves out from the first years, turns, and comes home" (*KA*,109).

Vico's system, more complex and complete than any of those that preceded it, offers insights into the structure of history that go beyond the normal confines of an academic discipline. The goal of both his "new science" and Michelet's *résurrection intégrale* is the uniting of all of the human sciences in an organic whole. Both historians proffer fertile ideas that nurtured many writers of the nineteenth and twentieth centuries. Perhaps most important is the idea of the *corsi* and *ricorsi*; that after the civilization has run its course from gods to heroes to men, the results of too much reason, introspection, and control produce a reaction of a return to passion and imagination and the beginning of a new cycle. Further, the *ricorso* is not merely the simple recurrence of a cycle, but rather a cycle within a spiral. The new beginning of civilization after the fall of Rome is thus a Christian time of the age of gods, superior to the pagan era that began the previous cycle.

One strong appeal of Vico to writers is his description of the intellectual life in heroic terms--the "divinity of the mind" that included the concept of humanity creating itself and the emphasis on myth as poetic truth. The poetic process that "divines," Vico says, is not rational, but "felt and imagined." With these principles, both the individual strength and the national genius can emerge in the hands of skillful poets. Those concepts led Northrop Frye to call Vico "one of the very few thinkers to understand anything of the historical role of the poetic impulse in civilization as a whole."[21] Learning Vico's principles enabled Michelet to carry through successfully a project he had contemplated, a history of the race considered as an individual. What Wilson calls the "collision of Michelet's mind with Vico's" led Michelet later to write in his journal: "1824. Vico. Effort, infernal shades, grandeur, the Golden Bough."[22] Other writers, searching for broad and intuitive poetic methods, had much the same response to the discovery of Vico's *New Science*. Elizabeth Sewell tells of Coleridge, who, recognizing Vico at once as kin, proposed an edition of Bacon's *Novum Organum* with parallel passages from the *Scienza Nuova*.[23] Better known in France than in England, Vico even appears in Balzac's novels and in Flaubert's *Bouvard et Pécuchet*.

James Joyce, who said that Vico's ideas had gradually forced themselves on him, declared, "My imagination grows when I read

Vico."[24] The cyclic structure of civilization found in *The New Science* influences the form of *Finnegan's Wake* as well as many of its rhythmic four-part sentences. Joyce studied Vico as he wrote *Finnegan's Wake*, but according to some scholars he probably got much of his information from Michelet's *Oeuvres choisies de Vico*, whose preface contains nearly everything that Joyce used from Vico for his last novel.

Herbert Read, looking back on his own writing, became conscious of a Vichian spirit: "The ideas that came to me, like filings to a magnet, I now recognize as ideas prefigured and often explicitly stated by Vico." Read had not encountered the work of Vico at first hand, but had studied closely those who were inspired by it--Goethe, Coleridge and the Romantic poets and philosophers, Whitehead, Freud, and Jung. His conclusion is that Vico is probably the most unacknowledged source of ideas in the history of philosophy. Read's experience is not unique. In the same collection of essays an Italian professor observes that many Anglo-American authors who have not read Vico demonstrate to an astonishing degree what we call a "Vichian mentality."[25] Cather, in her position as editor for a major New York magazine at the time, would have been aware of these ideas and of writers such as Benedetto Croce, whose *Aesthetics* in 1902 credited Vico with having discovered that "science," and whose *Philosophy of Giambattista Vico*, translated into English in 1913, was preceded by excerpts published in periodicals in 1912.

It is also undoubtedly true, as Alfred North Whitehead asserts, that there are certain fundamental assumptions that are unconsciously held by many thinkers in a given era. In our modern age of psychoanalysis, it may be easier for us to comprehend the Vichian ages in psychological terms, perhaps expressed best in Jung's four stages of consciousness: the first consists of merely "knowing," and is an anarchic state; the second, that of the developed ego-complex, is monarchic; the third increases consciousness and brings awareness of a divided, dualistic state; the fourth is similar to the initial stage.[26] Vico's theory, which itself used psychological interpretations, especially of myth (when speaking of Freud's theories, Joyce once remarked that they had been anticipated by Vico), gave historians, philosophers, and poets the vocabulary and structure to help articulate their experiences.

In spite of the traditional views of linear progress held by many Western historians of the nineteenth and early twentieth century, the emerging ideas of cyclical development that would culminate in the works of Spengler and Toynbee were in the intellectual air during this period of Cather's maturation as a writer. As she increased the emphasis in her own writing on the centrality of cultural values in literature, the historical perspective that underlies her fiction is essentially Vico's analysis of the forces that shape human nature and institutions.

Bergson's theories complemented Vico's, often lending support to the major ideas. Evolution, he said, implies a persistence of the past in the present; the *élan vital* in the individual can be traced back to his remotest ancestors; and the evolution of a consciousness resembles the evolution of the organic world. His lucid, poetic language must have appealed to Cather as much as his elegant argument distinguishing intuition from the intellect.[27] His linking of mysticism with creative effort matched Cather's own stated views. Bergson supplied some new ideas and a vocabulary of inspiration, but Vico's were the controlling principles of Cather's novel cycle. His was the broader, more complete philosophy, with its emphasis on the stages of civilizations, their rise, maturity and fall, the spiral that permitted new beginnings at higher levels, the prominence of mythology in a nation's development, and the primacy of the role of the poet. From Michelet, Vico, Bergson, and other sources of ideas, Cather chose what she needed to write very effective novels, and never attempted to develop a coherent literary theory. She was, perhaps above all, an eclectic scholar and writer who used all the methods available to create her art. But she also had found a model in Michelet's histories for the powerful work that could be written using Vico's theories. What is more, they fit well with her own, sometimes contradictory, artistic impulses. Vico's philosophy provided an ordered concept for Cather's work, even as she wrote of the dissolution of society. His analysis of the cultural content of poetry served as a framework for her mythopoeic vision. And the background of his--and Michelet's--scholarly approach allowed her to write in the simplest of language and form. She submerged these dualities in an art that most often seems uncomplicated and accessible.[28]

Incorporating her many sources, the mature Willa Cather viewed history in the Vichian manner; that is, she understood it as a comparative chronology of nations, each moving through stages of development called the ages of gods, heroes, and men. During this cultural process, man evolves from simple response to his world to conscious reflection about it, manifesting the changes in corresponding states of his language, his customs, his laws. Each emerging civilization, like each individual, undergoes comparable experiences in similar, if not identical, patterns. According to Michelet it is important for the human being to know of these recurring cycles and of earlier stages of evolution, for if one isolates himself from the ancient world from which one descends, the contemporary world can only be an incomprehensible enigma. Partly for that reason, Michelet saw his purpose as a social historian to be the resurrection of the life of the past. Another reason for his keeping the past alive was his despair of the machine age, shared with equal intensity by Cather. Both writers, however, saw momentarily the possibilities of a pure beginning of civilization on the American frontier; both hoped for the greater potential of America because of immigration and the resulting strength of a mixed population.

Cather was responding to more than Michelet's ideas and his adaptations of the principles of universal history; his enthusiasm was contagious for many who read him, and his language, an elegant French prose, was modern and accessible. Much of his work undoubtedly brought a shock of recognition and perhaps clarified her own direction for the novels she wrote after 1912. Perhaps the greatest affinity between the two, however, is their shared belief in the strong relation of religion and art. Michelet finds a godlike quality in all creative activity; Cather said many times and in many ways that, in the end, art and religion are the same thing. In the tradition of the classical poets, she began to write about an idealized past in which the divine and the human are often inseparable.

"All science is one," said Michelet in paraphrasing Vico, "language, literature and history, physics, mathematics and philosophy; subjects which seem the most remote from one another are in reality connected, or rather they all form a single system."[29] In order to achieve the necessary synthesis, Michelet brought to his research the same kind of acquisitiveness for information and experiences that Cather maintained throughout her life. Wilson says that we feel that Michelet "has read all the books, been to look at all the monuments and pictures, interviewed personally all the authorities, and explored all the libraries and archives of Europe; and that he has it all under his hat."[30] Michelet's own view of humanity was as a single person learning continually.

Willa Cather had the same kind of insatiable need to absorb the world of the arts, and then to translate to her literature whatever lent another dimension to the story she was telling. She culled from Michelet, as from all her sources, only as much as contributed to her own art, in the same way that Michelet had gone to the heart of Vico's theories, "enucleating" them, as one historian says. Her use of information ranged from casual mention of music or art to strengthen her theme, to the creation of artists as characters, to the structuring of a novel on a painting or a musical form. Memorable artistic characters include Thea Kronborg, who was patterned after Olive Fremstad, in *The Song of the Lark*; David Gerhardt, whom Cather knew as David Hochstein, in *One of Ours*, Helena Modjeska as herself in *My Mortal Enemy*; and the hero of "The Sculptor's Funeral," among her short stories. Cather envisioned Ántonia's place in the novel as a vase in the center of the table; she made the architecture of two houses and the Indian pueblos the focus of *The Professor's House*; she combined ideas from a painting and the sonata form in constructing *Death Comes for the Archbishop*. Her mixture of modes of art and appeals to the senses fulfills the requirements of *synesthesia* so valued by Keats and other romantic poets. And in a sophisticated way she expresses arts that normally move in time, like music, in spatial terms, and those that move in space, like painting, in rhythmic terms. All, of course, are expressed in terms of language in her novels. A friend had accused her, Cather wrote in her newspaper column in 1898, of "too great a tendency to interpret musical compositions into literal pictures, and of caring more for the pictures than the composition in itself" (*WP*,1:376).

But art in the novels of Willa Cather was more than merely a source of structure or an added level of meaning. In the Vichian theory of evolving artifacts with the rise and fall of nations, the arts would change along with religion, language, law, custom, and the nature of the people. Warren French has traced a developmental pattern in Cather's use of painting in her novels. He thinks that she conceived her major works from *O Pioneers!* through *Shadows on the Rock* as, among other things, a series of progressive experiments that can best be understood through the successive experiments of some outstanding painters of the late nineteenth and early twentieth century.[31] He compares techniques in her novels to those of Breughel, Cézanne, van Gogh, and Mondrian. French points out that some of the elements of design that have given problems to some literary critics are easily explained in terms of painterly technique. So often a Vichian principle can explain in Cather a repetition that is awkward, a cliché that is uncharacteristic, a puzzling reference that, when solved, illuminates much. Just by explaining the way in which Cather fuses foreground, middle ground, and background in the novels to create an integral whole, French adds to our understanding of individual novels as well as the cycle as a whole. Cather's ability to combine her "formidable learning" in European art and literature with unformed American subjects led A. S. Byatt to write the introductions to the Virago editions of Cather's novels in Great Britain.

Music had a similar influence on Cather's composition, says Edith Lewis, her companion of many years, who finds that music was an emotional, rather than an intellectual interest for Cather and that her cadence and rhythm were an almost unconscious result of a "sort of transposed musical feeling."[32] But in his comprehensive study, *Music in Willa Cather's Fiction*, Richard Giannone uses music, as Warren French uses painting, to show the evolution of Cather's own complex art. As sound, as allusion, as design, as moral and spiritual meaning, music, from hymns and folksongs to the great operas of the nineteenth century, pervades the novels and helps to structure this world of her imagination. Like the painting, the music of the novels alters to fit themes, tones, and styles of the individual works.

Cather's literary language and choice of genres to support the cycle of her novels are even more impressive than her manipulation of painting and music. She is, as Katherine Mansfield said, a virtuoso. In *Willa Cather's Imagination* David Stouck has analyzed the themes and forms of the novels, relating them to her development and to the evolution of her work. Finding a universal character and design in some of her books, he demonstrates the depth of her background in literature and the aptness of her application of the tools of her trade. Matching her characters and plots with genres and modes, tracing her many literary allusions and subtle appropriations from other sources, he, like French and Giannone, often clarifies the intention of a scene. Although Stouck's design is not chronological, his work can be used to structure a progression of literary forms within Cather's novels.

Her cycle follows closely the Vichian concept that man's language and literature evolve with each civilization, that literary forms, such as pastorals, tragedies, epics, and romances, are clusters of ideas that externalize collective psychological states. When a writer is concerned with the culture of a nation, the result is likely to be traditional literature; and as David Daiches points out, Cather's technique remained for the most part traditional.[33] The literary forms, with their accompanying conventions and syntax, follow the changes of consciousness in the stages of cultural development of the nation in which they are grounded. Cather in her essay on Sarah Orne Jewett best describes her own method as an artist who gave herself to her material: like the Greek writers and Jewett, she worked toward an "organic, living simplicity and directness" that came from designing each work for one purpose. In her novels there is no detail unrelated to the broader meaning of the whole, no name, event, or character arbitrarily chosen. When she wished for Jewett's novel to become "a message to the future, a message in a universal language," she was no doubt hoping for the same for her own novel cycle. That one purpose, for Cather, was to recreate in her novels the kind of relationship she found in earlier writers to their countries and their eras; the traditional modes of literature that express the very nature of a culture are a kind of universal language. The native idiom, the sayings and proverbs of a community, she says in the same essay, are its "characteristic comment upon life; they imply its history, suggest its attitude toward the world, and its way of accepting life" (*OW*,56-59).

Music, language and literature, art and architecture, all creations of the human mind, were vital to the analysis of the patterns of civilization, according to Vico. But most significant, because it arose so early in the development of nations and because it is so close to whatever is divine in man, is mythology. Cather relied strongly on mythology to express her own vision about the identification of art and religion, advancing Vico's theory of the common origin of all human manifestations of culture. An examination of the individual novels, especially in sequence, leaves no doubt of her conscious use of the mythological literature of Western man; a contemplation of her work as a whole reveals a larger dimension of mythopoeic thought, forming the themes of quest, death and rebirth, and transformation as the basis for her stories.

She had already acquired a knowledge of myth during the intellectually crucial years of adolescence. Her own opinion, voiced in an interview in 1921, was that the writer gathers his basic materials unconsciously in the years from eight to fifteen. In those years when her tastes were developing she found as mentor the Englishman William Drucker, with whom she read the *Iliad*, works of Virgil and Ovid, the odes of Anacreon. Later her courses at the University of Nebraska included the study of classical literature, three years of Greek language, and two of Latin.

From the beginning of her writing career, mythological references filled her newspaper columns, poems, and stories. An early column, "Concerning Thomas Carlyle," not only claimed that "the best traits of his character and the strongest powers of his mind belonged to other times and to other peoples," but also suggested that a great part of his genius lay in the ability to see the divine in everything. In the poems of her first book, *April Twilights*, titles such as *"Fides, Spes"* and *"In Media Vita"* reflect her interest in the language of classical myth, and "Winter at Delphi" and "Antinous" attest to her reliance on myth for her subject matter. Even more revealing are the references to ordinary experiences in classical terms: the dedicatory poem speaks of "odysseys of summer mornings"; a love is as lost as "the gold of Helen's vanished head"; pines on a mountain are "elder gods" and they form an "arc of some vast wreck of Titan state." Her study of ancient cultures taught her to place contemporary events in perspective to the ages, as in her reference to the London roses "perfumed with a thousand years," or in the comparison of birch trees with Brunhilda and her Valkyr sisters. Even when these classical allusions fail in Cather's early writing, they are indicative of the way her mind so often worked in her literature.

Her early fiction, too, alluded often to classical myth, although more superficially than in the later novels. Often the early references are no more than mere ornaments, like the names of the boat *The Silver Heel* in the story "Resurrection," and at other times their meanings are obscure, as the description of a couple in "Eleanor's House": "They heeded only eternity and each other. But whatever it was, it was Olympian." Frequently Cather uses myth to add dimension to a character through comparison with a classical deity, as in "Jack-a-boy" where the child is not human, but "one of the immortal children of Greek fable made flesh for a little while." In "The Namesake" the narrator says, "I thought of that sad one of the Destinies, who, as the Greeks believed, watch from birth over those marked for a violent or untimely death." Even her letters are sprinkled with mythological references applied to her own life: she wrote to a friend that she felt the impotence of the shadows who tried but failed to communicate with Ulysses in Hades. She thought of her writing often in terms of mythic struggle. Her extensive use of classical myth in this period is demonstrated in the introduction to *The Kingdom of Art*, in which Bernice Slote details the work of the early years when Cather was "caught in the ancient pull of the gods" (*KA*,81-103).

Her early writing begins an emphasis on mythic ideas and a connection of the past with the present that became more pronounced in her novels. Her basic theme is the age-old quest, in which the goal scarcely matters, in stories with echoes of Odysseus and Aeneas, Arthur and Siegfried. Cather repeated the phrase she ascribed to Michelet, *"Le but n'est rien; le chemin c'est tout,"* as a motto given to a young girl in the short story, "Old Mrs. Harris," and rephrased it in *My Mortal Enemy* to suit her religious theme: "In other searchings it might be the object of the quest that brought satisfaction, or it might be the something incidental that one got on the way; but in religion, desire was fulfillment, it was the seeking itself that was rewarded" (*MME*,94).[34] Caring little for novelty in literature, she understood that "there are only two or three stories, and they go on repeating themselves as fiercely as if they had never happened before" (*OP*,119). A model for this literary reductionism was Jacob Grimm, whose *Teutonic Mythology*, which she read as a child, followed Vico in finding unity among myriad stories of gods and goddesses. The few eternal conflicts of human existence and their attendant myths underlie much of Cather's art. Like Joyce, she understood the "eternal verities" and tapped into the archetypal themes that reveal those very basic patterns of thought used to organize a world that often seems chaotic. Because the human feels such reverence for the force of these thoughts, he accords them divine status, then creates deities to personify them, tells stories to exemplify them, and constructs rituals to enact them. That process forms the foundation of Cather's novels from *O Pioneers!* to *Shadows on the Rock*.

Critics, especially those writing soon after Cather's death, point to the myths found in her work, from the early, often superficial classical allusions in the short stories to the later, deeper adumbrations of pagan myth. Speaking of the youthful excitement in the protagonist of *Alexander's Bridge*, Howard Mumford Jones discovers a "tribute to universal Pan": "In view of the pagan mysticism of this passage, one almost expects Bartley to have sight of Proteus rising from the sea. He is the victim of the Dionysiac fascination, the Bacchic appeal, the illusion of youth, which create in him a new and overwhelming feeling of self, sensed in a series of mystical insights superior to his normal self and eventually controlling it."[35] In *The Last of the Provincials*, Maxwell Geismar says that there is no doubt that *The Professor's House* is "a novel of death and rebirth--of a spiritual purging and regeneration, and of that second coming, which formalized in the central ritual of religion, is actually part of the deepest experience of man."[36] David Daiches envisions Lesley, the young teacher of "The Best Years" (the last story that Cather completed), as the goddess Proserpine, a symbol of lost innocence; John H. Randall names Captain Forrester of *A Lost Lady* as a Fisher King. This criticism recognizes the psychological implications of the myths that become stronger in the mature novels.

According to Cather's own philosophy of literature, the emotional penumbra is the vital part of the artist's creation. In one of her often quoted passages--this one reflecting her knowledge of Mallarmé--she said, "Whatever is felt upon the page without being specifically named there--that, one might say, is created. It is the inexplicable presence of the thing not named, of the overtone divined by the ear, but not heard by it, the verbal mood, the emotional aura of the fact or the thing or the deed, that gives high quality to the novel or the drama, as well as to poetry itself" (*NUF*,50). Myth is a way of examining what is penumbral, not only in literature, but in the events of people's lives. As Stephen Tennant observed in "The Room Beyond," his introduction to Cather's *On Writing*, her art is essentially one of "gazing beyond the immediate scene to a timeless sky or a timeless room, in which the future and the past, the unspoken and the unknown, forever beckon the happy reader." She was writing for the reader who, like her, rejects the "overfurnished" novel, and who, like the child Cécile in *Shadows on the Rock*, preferring her own imaginative interpretation to the rational lesson she is about to receive, asks of the storyteller, "*N'expliquez pas.*" Cather thought that the same kind of personal imagination was responsible for her art--indeed, for all art. "A child's attitude toward everything is the artist's attitude," she said in *The Song of the Lark*, recalling the words of Wagner, whose art she intensely admired.

Her admiration for artists, both ancient and contemporary, depends in large measure on the extent to which they fulfill the role as Vico sees it; that is, they are the transmitters of the myths that instruct the people. Vico's chief tools in his examination of culture are linguistics and mythology, and for him poets are the historians of theology and culture. Because they are the receptors of secret wisdom, through them the expression of human imagination helps to create the language, the morals, the laws, and even the gods of the people. The poets bring to life what Northrop Frye has called "myths of concern," which have their roots in a specific culture and later expand to cover "a society's view of its past, present, and future, its relation to its gods and its neighbours, its traditions, its social and religious duties, and its ultimate destiny."[37] The central question of the cultural myth is, according to Frye, what must we do to be saved? The religious connotations of the question and the rhythm of death and rebirth that accompanies the cyclical pattern make clear the role of the inspired poet who writes as seer and prophet. The mature Willa Cather in 1912, midway on her life's journey, turned her attention to the myth of the frontier and her role as its inspired poet.

She was able to incorporate the use of myth into her ideas of the cycle of American literature easily, still following Vico, who has been described as a pioneer in the study of human imagination and mythmaking. Looking at Homer as not an individual, but as the expression of heroic Greece, Vico changed the perceptions of the meaning of mythology. For him mythology was a language that was the key to the meaning of ancient history, a time when the people spoke in poetic images. A task such as Cather assumed could not rely only on the classical Greek myths that were worn out even as they were passed to the Romans in the early years of the Empire. The Olympian religion was, in Hellenistic Greece, and even to a greater degree in Rome, "bankrupt" or "paralyzed," according to most scholars, even as the people continued to observe their rites. A select portion of the populace in the Mediterranean world became initiates into cults that promised purification and salvation in an age that was developing new patterns of thought. As Cather began her novels, she continued her allusions to the classical stories, but they remained on the surface, often simply as signposts for the direction the reader's interpretation should take. One critic makes much of her diffuse, often inexact, classical references;[38] but she is not teaching the classics in these novels (a job that was not to her liking), but rather calling up an appropriate emotional response to a scene. She alters Latin, and the Greek goddesses, and contemporary philosophers, and all the material of her art to suit her novelistic purpose. The classical myths add emphasis in the nine novels of her cycle; often they have only casual meaning, but at times they carry greater import. Therefore, when St. Peter in *The Professor's House*, thinking of his exasperating daughters, asks, "Was there no way but Medea's?" the reader can simply remember that Medea killed her children. In this context, the question is perhaps a small academic joke. Add that, however, to the citing of the Amys and Amilyon story whose ending involves Amilyon's sacrifice of his children to save his friend, and the meaning gathers force.

Cather recognized that the meanings of the Greek, Roman, medieval, and Renaissance myths have been codified and reduced to allegorical equivalents in the modern era. In *The Song of the Lark*, hearing Thea's interpretation of her "Rhinegold" role, her lover reflects that the role of *Fricka* had been interpreted as a jealous spouse for so long that her original meaning of wisdom had been forgotten, along with the fact that she had always been a goddess. The *Fricka* of that afternoon quite redeems for him the actions of the gods. The trivialization of especially the female divinities had left the classical religion without vitality, and like Thea, Cather intended to enlarge and ennoble the mythic background of her art. While she continued to sprinkle allusions to classical myths on the surface of her stories, beginning with *O Pioneers!* she buried deep within each novel myths that were, for a privileged few, revelations of transcendental mysteries.

The respective uses of classical myth and the mystery religions in the novels correspond to their positions in the life of the ancient civilizations where they were honored. The first was traditional, on the surface, and not taken too seriously; the second was exotic, deep beneath the surface, and considered by initiates to be the true means of redemption. Just as it is clear that Cather deliberately evokes the associations of her stories with the classical myths, the overwhelming number of times that she uses the language, symbols, actions, and characterizations of the mystery rituals leaves little doubt that she consciously embedded them in her novels. The mystery religions, little taught in American education and difficult to research in English texts until recently, would have been known by Cather with her training in classical languages and literature. As one scholar believes, "One cannot read the *Odes* of Pindar, devout Orphic that he was, or the prayers of a fervent Isiacist like Lucius, or the *Consolatio* of a serious-minded Plutarch, or the *encomia* or Aristides and Julian, without realizing that the mysteries were a real means of grace to many a convinced and sincere pagan. These cults had their apologists: Iamblicus, for example, and Porphyry, and Proclus."[39] He adds the names of more objective writers like Cicero and Epictetus, and to those can be appended many others, such as Aristotle, Plato, and Virgil.[40] The Christian fathers, in their attacks on the mystery rites, also revealed much that is known of them. St. Augustine, who knew first-hand the Manichaean and Neoplatonist beliefs, presents an interesting analysis in his *Confessions* and in *The City of God*.

Cather's novels were informed not only by the classical poets and historians she had studied as student and teacher, the great writers she read omnivorously, and the biblical passages she pondered each day before she wrote, but also by her contemporaries. As she was preparing to begin a full-time career as a writer of fiction, there were an extraordinary number of books published on myth, mysteries, and related subjects. The year that she began her frontier novels--1912--has been called a watershed for information on mythology. Jane Ellen Harrison, acknowledging her debt to Henri Bergson's *Creative Evolution*, published *Themis*, her study of the social origins of Greek religion, that year. Even more important was the third edition of her ground-breaking *Prolegomena to a Study of Greek Religion*, first published in 1903, which described the chthonic mystery rites and provided as evidence liturgical hymns and more than 175 pictures of paintings, friezes, sculptures, and urns revealing many details of the initiations. Others of the Cambridge School, especially Gilbert Murray, whom Cather read, and F. M. Cornford, brought out books on religious drama in the classical era. Sir James Frazer's *Golden Bough*, published in an expanded edition that year, inspired many, from T. S. Eliot to Jessie L. Weston, to think about custom and religion in new ways. Franz Cumont, whose *Mysteries of Mithra* appeared in 1903, followed that research with English editions of *Oriental Religions in Roman Paganism* in 1911 and *Astrology and Religion among the Greeks and Romans* in 1912, all seminal sources for mythographers. Other standard sources available at the time were W. W. Fowler, *The Religious Experience of the Roman People*, M. P. Foucart, *Eleusinian Mysteries*, and Andrew Lang, *Myth, Ritual, and Religion*. These are only a few of the works in English that excited the intellectual world in the early twentieth century. Even Bergson's *élan vital* was acknowledged to be descended from the Dionysian mysteries through the philosophy of Plotinus. The bibliography in Angus, *The Mystery-Religions*, is evidence that enough significant material published at this time is available for a critical study of the use of mystery religions in Cather's novels, without any need to refer to later religious, archaeological, and literary studies that have contributed so much to our knowledge in the past eighty years. Even the full accounts of the mystery religions and related philosophies in the eleventh edition of the *Encyclopaedia Britannica* demonstrate both the extent of scholarly interest and the availability of information at the time. This period saw an intense interest in these subjects that would go underground and not resurface until much later in the century.

Her incorporation of mystery religions into her cycle serves first to provide a dramatic background for the stories, in the same way that Stouck, Giannone, and French have demonstrated that she used literary form, music, and painting to emphasize the themes and strengthen the voices of her books. What we know of the mystery cults is a very small amount of literature, some philosophy, and a good deal of ritual. Cather's fictional scenes that re-enact mystery rites are highly charged with significance, often totally silent, related to the cycles of nature, and filled with the questions of death and rebirth that are her primary concern in the novels. They also create a counterpoint to the Vichian cycles, which focus on the cultural elements created by man and are therefore more easily understood by him. These scenes, like the mystery rites themselves, are stylized, obscured in some way, never named, and make their appearances at moments of great emotion in the protagonists' lives.

In addition to their contribution of dramatic structure to Cather's scenes, the mysteries serve to place the history of the frontier in a context of universal significance. The myths, in Vico's system, define social issues more than any other components of culture. The successive mystery cults form roughly a cycle of their own, showing a development parallel with the historical cycle that these novels describe and supporting the pattern of rise, fall, and regeneration. The themes of fertility and rebirth that are at the core of the mysteries help to create in these novels perhaps the strongest American expression of a holy quest at that time, even though the ideas were widespread in politics and literature. The ancient mysteries are tied to Vico's philosophy not only in the social purpose of religion; they reinforce the idea of the writer's place in the divine cyclical scheme. In Cather's crucial passages, the religious terminology and the high drama of the ritual lend a grandeur to the stories that, contrasted with the stark settings, elicits strong, at times inexplicable, responses.

A third reason for her insertion of the mystery rituals into the novels is, on Cather's part, a hidden and more personal one. The mystery religions, no matter what form or philosophy they embraced, were devoted to worship of a goddess. These novels--all of her books, in fact--were written for Isabelle McClung, a woman whom she had adored since their time together in Pittsburgh.[41] She wrote to a friend that she was there, *chez* the goddess, and described Isabelle, who had met her at the train station, looking as if the Parthenon ought to have been with her.[42] As the reader encounters in Cather's novels ceremonial scenes of the goddess robed in white, it is difficult to avoid picturing Isabelle in the role. The worship of the goddesses in the mystery rites was a way to satisfy a passionate approach to life, and writing about them may have been Cather's way to handle the "heat and abundance that surged up in her."[43] The question of Cather's sexual orientation has been only recently addressed in print, from Truman Capote's blunt assessment of her as lesbian on meeting her for the first time to Sharon O'Brien's comprehensive analysis in *Willa Cather: The Emerging Voice*. Less interesting than the answer is the impulse that Cather's emotion lent to her creative powers. Aside from this private and secret dedication of her novels, Cather used skillfully the power of the initiation rituals to touch forces deep within the unconscious life of the reader. Reason is great, explained Gilbert Murray in *Ancient Greek Literature*, but it is not everything.

> There are in the world things, not of reason, but both below and above it, causes of emotion which we cannot express, which we tend to worship, which we feel perhaps to be the precious things in life. These things are God or forms of God, not fabulous immortal men, but "Things which Are," things utterly non-human and non-moral which bring man bliss or tear life to shreds without a break in their own serenity.[44]

Around such things were the ineffable mysteries constructed and taught in ways that remained largely secret, because they were both sacred and incommunicable.

There were literally hundreds of mystery religions in the ancient world, springing from a rejection of scientific philosophy, a resurgence of chthonic conceptions, and an acknowledgment of the darker forces in man's nature. Closely related, at least in the early stages, to nature, the rituals had at their center the worship of some form of the Great Mother, centered around the goddess and her consort. Although each mystery religion had its own deities and rituals, they borrowed from each other and evolved during their time, some of them for 1,500 years and more. This religious syncretism has been traced to the intermingling of the races in the Hellenistic and Near Eastern countries after the triumph of Alexander the Great, who insisted on the equality in his empire of all peoples and their gods. And so the Roman world, in particular, welcomed the gods from Phrygia, Syria, Egypt, and Persia to place alongside the Olympian panoply that formed the state religion. "It was a proper melting pot," begins MacMullen's *Paganism in the Roman Empire*.[45] The new "Oriental" religions offered more to the individual than the impersonal official gods, which were, according to some writers, only tools used to control the masses. From the moment in 204 B.C. when the statue of Cybele, the *Magna Mater*, arrived in Rome in a great and solemn procession, the rulers, even when they tried, could not curb the enthusiasm for worship in the mystery rituals. Emperor Claudius, celebrating the rites of Isis and Attis, encouraged the people to adopt the many divinities from Asia Minor. Although there were bans from time to time, only the Druids were successfully eliminated, and later rulers--Julian, Diocletian, and Hadrian among them--participated in rites until Clement of Alexandria chose with finality Christianity as the state religion. In the meantime, the famous writers and philosophers of Rome underwent successive initiations and told as much of them as was possible, just as Plato, Aristophanes, Aeschylus and others had in Greece. Apuleius, whose *Metamorphoses*, or *The Golden Ass*, contains the most lyrical description of the rituals, boasted that he had been initiated into almost all of the mysteries, but nothing would compel him to tell the secrets to the uninitiated.[46]

Many writers connect the popularity of the Oriental mystery cults to a new consciousness developing among the people at the time that had suddenly enlarged to frightening proportions. The populace of the early Empire felt that the control of a disordered world was not in their own hands. In addition, there was a growing sense of sin, which was related to a belief that history was a process of degeneration, and which could find atonement only in union with the deity.[47] The rituals of the mystery cults satisfied both the needs of individuals in their emotional life and the collective need in expressing the anxieties of a culture. Further, the dawning of self-consciousness heightened awareness and fear of death; the mysteries, related as they were to the generative powers of nature, promised rebirth in addition to redemption. The primordial mysteries of the fertility rites could become a metaphor for the cosmic order and explain the whole mystery of life. In the words of Mircea Eliade, "In the religious history of humanity we constantly find this theme: the initiate, he who has experienced the mysteries, is he *who knows*."[48]

What the initiates, or *mystae*, knew when they completed one or more initiations is still being argued by scholars. All generally agree that the basic idea concerns death and rebirth. Mystery gods were savior gods who offered redemption and immortality, asserting the divine nature of the soul and assuring its fate. The mystery religions, says Cumont, "gave satisfaction first to the senses and the passions, second to the intelligence, finally, and above all to the conscience."[49] Thus, they gained hold on the entire person, inducing a state of ecstasy as the initiate emerged from "that most appalling and at the same time most entrancing spectacle," in the words of Aristides.

The rituals varied greatly from one cult to another, many originating in prehistory, but a general pattern can be described from elements agreed upon by most scholars. The first celebrations were public processions along a sacred road during the days devoted to the appropriate gods and goddesses. Dancers, mimes, and musicians playing all manner of instruments accompanied the parade, and actors often depicted the deities. Animals to be sacrificed were included in the festival. In some cults the procession was followed by a public ceremony in which all could participate. But those who were to be initiated into the deeper mysteries, usually the wealthy and the prominent, underwent a preparation that included purification rites of fasting of up to nine days, ritual bathing and cleansing, and abstinence from sexual intercourse. They withdrew to a smaller place of worship, sometimes a beautiful structure some distance from town and sometimes a subterranean cave serving as the sacred space, to take part in a nocturnal ritual that was private and so secret that much is still veiled. In some cults and at some times there was the ritual of the *taurobolium*, the sacrifice of the bull or another animal as substitute and the bathing of the initiate in its blood; in others the *hieros gamos*, or sacred marriage, took place; the use of hallucinogenic drugs has been suggested in others. Each mystery religion had its particular deity and accompanying rituals. But customarily initiation rites offered revelations concerning sacred stories or objects, death and rebirth, and sexuality; epiphanies were related to the moon or they emerged in some radiant light. For the initiates the ceremony ended with the feeling that they had found some mystic identification with the divinity who represented the great forces of the universe, and they had been born to a "new life," as Apuleius described it.

Of the hundreds of specific mystery religions that developed in the Mediterranean world, the strongest and most widespread are those that Willa Cather incorporated into her novels, approximately in the same chronological order as they appeared in the days of the Roman Republic and Empire. The cults have not been dated exactly, and much of the current knowledge of the syncretistic philosophies and practices of cults that existed for more than two thousand years was not available to Cather; but it is remarkable that a general outline of the pagan rites found in her novels move in the *corso* of rise, maturity, and fall from those of the Great Mother to the Gnostic mysteries. In the *ricorso*, or second rise, are included two periods of the Christian mysteries, which co-existed with the pagan cults and competed with them for followers.

The first of the pagan deities to gain acceptance in Roman culture was the Great Mother, an earth goddess also called Cybele or Mâ in her native Phrygia. After her temple was erected on the Palatine her arrival was celebrated each year in early April. She brought with her in 204 B.C. a primitive worship of trees, rocks, and certain animals, especially the lion. Hers were naïve and sometimes savage vegetation rites that from an early time included mystery initiations. Her rituals soon included the worship of Attis as her consort and as a powerful vegetation god in his own right, and then many other deities, first from Asia Minor, then from Egypt. Thus, from the beginning the mysteries were what one scholar has called "promiscuously eclectic."[50] Soon Isis and Osiris, Serapis, Astarte, and others were merged into a cult of nature that continued until A.D. 394. Book XI of *The Golden Ass* gives a clear picture of the syncretism in the mysteries. The goddess says to Apuleius: "Though I am worshipped in many aspects, known by countless names, and propitiated with all manner of different rites, yet the whole round earth venerates me."

In *O Pioneers!* primitive attitudes toward the natural world and the rituals of the Great Mother underlie much of the structure of the novel. *The Song of the Lark* uses a more defined mystery religion, that of Orpheus, the god who carried on the Dionysian mysteries in the Roman world. The rituals of Orphism were widely interpreted in religious and psychological terms after the discovery in 1910 of the *Villa Item*, or Villa of the Mysteries, just outside Pompeii. The magnificent wall paintings, the underground chambers, and the appalling *taurobolium* revealed important evidence for the understanding of the cult. The mysteries emphasized the joys of love, of wine, of song, in addition to the doctrines concerning the underworld and afterlife, as the frescoes of the villa and the Orphic hymns clearly illustrate. "Learn now," says Orpheus, "a rite mystic and most holy, a prayer which surely excels all others."[51] The stanzas then demonstrate the syncretism of the mysteries by calling on many other gods and goddesses to bring their particular powers to the initiates. The third of these fertility cults, the Eleusinian mysteries, became the most popular in the ancient world and are the best known today. Devoted to Demeter and her daughter Persephone, the cult promised agricultural fertility, cultural achievement, and rebirth to a nobler existence in the present and a happy afterlife. Established at Eleusis in pre-Hellenic times, the shrines eventually spread across Europe, and the cult of the grain goddesses was active long after the fall of Rome. *My Ántonia*, especially in the final chapter, contains many of the symbols and rituals of the Eleusinian mysteries. These three mystery religions, with their messages of generation and growth, are the appropriate background of the first stage of Willa Cather's story of the rise of culture in the American West.

The second stage of mature development moves away from the simpler fertility cults toward the philosophies that took on many of the characteristics of the mysteries. The dominant philosophy, Neoplatonism as taught by Plotinus, attempted to reconcile the ancient religions with more sophisticated moral and intellectual ideas. The same type of religious experience found in the mysteries lies behind the Gnostic belief and Neoplatonism.[52] Worship of the Oriental gods was so strong, according to Cumont, that philosophy moved toward mysticism and the Neoplatonist school became a theurgy,[53] accepting the sacred words of the Orphic religion and others to reinterpret the meaning of the ascent of the soul from the world of sense to the world of spirit. Cather's novel *One of Ours* has many elements of Neoplatonism. Another form of worship of the time that incorporated many of the mystery rites was the Roman Imperial cult, which hailed Julius Caesar as "God manifest and universal Saviour of human life," and Augustus as "Ancestral God and Saviour of the whole human race."[54] Deriving, like so much else in the world of this time, from Alexander the Great, the deification of the rulers was not much different from the identification of every initiate with his chosen deity, and the cult of emperor worship was often combined with those of mystery gods for increased power. Many of the concepts of the hero gods can be found in *A Lost Lady*.

The next stage in Cather's cycle moves further from the fertility goddesses to the Mithraic traditions, which present an intermediary between good and evil, divinity and humanity. The rites of Mithra do not include yearly death and rebirth, since he has conquered death. Mithraism, close to Christianity in many of its practices, was a powerful force in Roman life, especially among soldiers. The central section of *The Professor's House* repeats many of the ideas and rituals of the Mithraic mysteries. Related to these mysteries, to Orphism, to Neoplatonism, and to Christianity, Gnosticism was widespread and influential, with its fundamental dualism and its esoteric philosophy. *My Mortal Enemy* presents a picture of Gnostic ideas and rituals, which brings the Vichian *corso* to a fall from an age when humans could become the equal of the immortal gods in the mysteries to an age when alienated humans thought of the world as an illusion of a non-god.

The *ricorso* in this cycle of religions brings a spiral introducing Christianity as a mystery religion, just as Clement of Alexandria, in his *Exhortation to the Greeks* urging acceptance of the Christian gospel, offers the vision and the joys of truly sacred mysteries.[55] The new cycle had been foreshadowed at the end of both *The Professor's House* and *My Mortal Enemy*; now in *Death Comes for the Archbishop*, with the rituals of European, American Indian, and Mexican worship on a new frontier, a new syncretism begins and a renewed sense of affirmation is infused into the novel cycle. Even though *Shadows on the Rock* is set in an earlier period, the religious theme, which focuses on saints and legends, recounts more highly developed Christian mysteries.

In her use of the mysteries, Cather has not only enriched her narratives, she has reinforced the structure and principles of the Vichian cycle. The cyclical mythic structure matches the agricultural patterns that are beginnings of both the mystery religions and the frontier novels. Further, Cather intended that her novels should be permeated by the themes of the mystery religions in the search for answers to the questions of death and rebirth, redemption, and ultimate destiny of the soul. As Cicero--whose works were known well by Cather--says of the Eleusinian mysteries, among the many exceptional things Athens contributed to human life, "nothing is better than those mysteries. For by means of them we have been transformed from a rough and savage way of life to the state of humanity, and have been civilized. Just as they are called initiations, so in actual fact we have learned from them the fundamentals of life, and have grasped the basis not only for living with joy but also for dying with a better hope."[56] This vocabulary is similar to Cather's in her description of her art, indeed of all art, which for her equated with religion.

Some of the early critics of her novels recognized her holy quest, without identifying her means. Lionel Trilling in 1937 called her work a "march back toward the spiritual East . . . toward authority and permanence, toward Rome itself." He added that her later books are pervaded by the air of a "brooding ancient wisdom."[57] That was, very likely, the response she was working toward. Her youthful paean to Ruskin may be a clue--one of many--to the way she wished to be considered as a writer: for her, Ruskin is "perhaps the last of the great worshippers of beauty, perhaps the last man for many years to come who will ever kneel at the altar of Artemis, who will ever hear the oracle of Apollo. . . . This man's life has been one act of worship" (*KA*,400). Just a few years earlier, in an essay sprinkled with references to Orpheus, Ygdrasil, and Druids, Cather had written that Carlyle's "every act was a form of worship." She takes the religious imagery in that essay even further: "He says only, 'Thou shalt have no other gods before me.' Art, science, and letters cry, 'Thou shalt have no other gods at all.' They accept only human sacrifices" (*KA*,423). Cather chose Ruskin and Carlyle, along with Virgil and Dante, as literary models, and she read passages from the King James version of the Bible each day before beginning to write; there is little wonder that her work is filled with a transcendence--what Oliver Wendell Holmes called the "gift of the transfiguring touch."

One result of these models of literature and language is an almost inevitable use of allegory. Her earliest reading, especially *The Pilgrim's Progress*, had given her a predilection toward what Heraclitus had, in the first century A.D., first defined as something that says one thing but means something other than what it says.[58] He claimed to derive his principles from the practice of the mystery religions; indeed, the myths of those cults demand second interpretations beyond the narratives themselves. It is impossible, for example, not to connect Persephone to the grain and her story to the cycle of the seasons. The mysteries, as allegorized nature, easily lent themselves to incommunicable meanings that initiates nevertheless could share. The early crude nature allegory eventually becomes sophisticated metaphysics. Even in classical philosophy, allegory permeates the literature from the first stories onward.[59] The device suits Cather's purpose well, veiling the second meaning while allowing the narrative to remain solidly based in the tales of late nineteenth and early twentieth century America. Her allegory is not a simple matter of abstractions personified, but rather symbolic persons and events, and her use of allegory is modified in each novel to fit the other literary forms in operation.

Edward and Lillian Bloom recognized in her first novels the use of allegory to represent the quest of the individual;[60] her allegory, however, takes the quest beyond the individual to the universal. In the Vichian context the hero is merely the projection of the ideal character of the people, that collective force that impels the development of civilization. As Michelet said of heroic characters of primitive history, they are ideas, symbols. The concept of allegory in Cather's work should be extended not only beyond the individual as symbol, but also beyond the novels of the frontier. The nine novels in this analysis trace the cycle of the American West: the settings provide the historical and cultural background, the characters serve as symbols of the nation itself, and the accompanying mystery religions bring philosophical and spiritual depth. Thus, in *A Lost Lady*, among Cather's novels the one most often identified as an allegory, the world depicted, although set in the West, is a feudal, heroic world with many allusions to the Middle Ages. The lost lady, Marian, is at once a medieval noblewoman, a goddess, and an allegorical representation of the frontier; those around her are knights and consorts, villains and peasants; the appropriate mystery religion is that of the Imperial cult, which reinforces the many references to a secularized era that has fallen from a divine state. These levels of meaning, taken together, present a holistic world view in a remarkably compressed story. As the middle story in the nine-novel sequence, *A Lost Lady* is the end of the heroic stage in Vichian terms, a time of maturing just before the fall, and a stage in a repetition of the pattern of all cultures. The Blooms see this spiritual odyssey drawn by Cather as an eternal one that transcends time and place.

The allegorical context of her novels pulls together the many elements--the western migration and the sense of national rebirth, the cultural emphasis on music, painting, and literature, the pervasive religious connections with art and nature. In each novel, everything is related to the whole and integrated into a single theme. The casual reader will miss some of these elements or dismiss them as not significant to the literal story, but it is the accumulation of detail that builds the power of a Cather novel to a stunning whole. A great work of literature, says Northrop Frye, is a place in which "the whole cultural history of the nation that produced it comes into focus."[61] She is portraying a world that is ordered by the mind of the poet, and she gives the reader a clue to her method in her choice of *O Pioneers!*-- Whitman's title as well as his mystical vision--for the first book of her novel cycle. Hers was a less egocentric, less aggressive interpretation of the American experience: instead of a thrust of self, her approach is a dissolving of self into her material; instead of rejecting the past, she embraces the place of the present in the whole of history. But each poet is, in her or his own way, constructing on multiple levels of meaning the great myths that are the documents of the culture of the United States.

Both poets, like many others at crucial points in their writing careers, are thought to have undergone mystical experiences which led to dramatically new directions in their work. Cather, alone in the Southwest in 1912, found an inspiration for her later writing, a sense of the meaning of art, and an understanding of the artist's function. As E. K. Brown writes in the introduction to his biography, "The persistence and the diversity of the references to the Southwest suggest--what is indeed the truth--that the discovery of this region was the principal emotional experience of Willa Cather's mature life." She captured the moment in "The Ancient People" chapter of *The Song of the Lark*, in which Thea has "intuitions," "understanding," and feelings that were transmitted to her, not expressible in words. Cather left the Southwest in a new state of mind, Brown says, having discovered a lengthening of her past and an enlarging of her frame of reference.[62] She had brought into coherent wholeness her frontier upbringing, classical education, teaching and editing experiences, literary acquaintanceships, foreign travel, and remarkable range as a reader and discipline as a writer. An important coalescence of knowledge in philosophy, psychology, and anthropology was creating an intellectual climate in which she undoubtedly participated in her role as editor in a major publishing firm. That her work at *McClure's* was coming to a natural conclusion also contributed to this critical time of decision and direction.

From this time, her method of composition changed, and with it the scope and purpose of her writing. It has been said of Dante's writing of *The Divine Comedy* that from the moment of genesis were fixed the subject, architecture, structure, the role of imagination, the novelty and wealth of resources. At a turning point of her culture, Cather was attempting, like Dante, to represent the entire structure of her political, moral, and religious world, although her cosmology was quite different. In nine novels, with four stages of development, she created a cycle of Western culture that repeats the earlier cycles of the classical and Renaissance eras.

2

Prairie Dawn: The Age of Gods

It is at the beginning of a civilization that the basic questions of life's meanings are asked, identity is established, and national myths are born. In 1912 Willa Cather, realizing that colonial America had not truly begun a new cultural process, looked back at the setting of the West and related this nascent civilization to the others she had studied. Her first novel of the frontier is set in the dim, primordial past, "on the gray prairie, under a gray sky," where the characters participate in primitive man's awe of the powers of nature, his naïve ideas about the cosmos, and his belief in the need for human sacrifice.

The retreat to primitivism in the three novels of the first stage--*O Pioneers!*, *The Song of the Lark*, and *My Ántonia*--begins with the Nebraska frontier as setting, a choice "declassé" in the minds of critics, Cather admitted, but essential to her historical perspectives. Like the neolithic age, this is a feminine world, matriarchal in its design, led by strong women who bear conquerors' names, and full of the mysteries of fertility associated with female deities. In so many ways these first three novels signal the beginning of civilization. The territory chosen for much of the setting is newly born and as yet unformed. The minds of the heroines work in the ways of early human consciousness: Alexandra's intuitive understanding in *O Pioneers!*, so like man's first awareness of the forces of nature, for example, or Thea's realization in *The Song of the Lark*, which mirrors the primitive view that art is not play but a way to worship. The characters and their myths echo the earliest recorded moments in Western history. And finally the forms repeat those of early literature--the episodic, cyclical lyrics written and sung before the great epics of nations appear. The elements of this pattern work toward that organic simplicity of the writers of antiquity

whom the author recognized as her models in these stories of her
country.

The American frontier has long been recognized as a mythic force in
our social, governmental, and individual destinies. Frederick Jackson
Turner gave this thesis its most articulate definition in his essay, "The
Significance of the Frontier in American History," in 1893. He found
that the effects of the continuous advance of the frontier included a
more composite nationality, increased independence, stronger
government, and the individualistic character of the settlers. Each new
stage of the frontier meant a new beginning for the evolution of
civilization. In this idea he had been anticipated by St. John de
Crèvecoeur, who had written in his *Letters from an American Farmer*
of the 1770s that in order to have an idea of the "feeble beginnings" and
"barbarous rudiments" of America, one must visit the extended line of
frontiers. For Crèvecoeur as well as for Turner the Western settlements
were not only a historical fact; they were a spiritual force, and each new
frontier presented new opportunity, an escape from the bondage of the
past. Both of these writers were convinced that the frontier was a
possible foundation for an American mythology.

A civilization expresses its power in the form of its myths, using the
symbols, the legends, the idealized heroes that are significant in the
experience of its people. To the European mind, the American myth is
readily apparent; as far back as 1849, Carlyle wrote to Emerson: "There
is no *Myth* of Athene or Herakles equal to this fact." "This fact" was the
American frontier. Statesmen had been aware of its possibility to stir the
imagination: Franklin wrote pamphlets mapping the future of the
frontier; Jefferson authorized the Lewis and Clark expedition to exploit
the idea of a "passage to India"; Western figures--Daniel Boone, Kit
Carson, Buffalo Bill--became legendary heroes in American folklore.
American authors, however, with few exceptions, failed to use the raw
material of this myth for an interpretation of American life.

Willa Cather recognized the significance of the frontier; further, she
had both the literary skills and the historical awareness to devise and
develop the fictional treatment that the era deserved. She saw this new
beginning of the American West in its relation to the Rome of Virgil,
where much was similar in the rising stage of that civilization. Rome
under Augustus had all the hopes of a new world: following the
Hellenistic triumphs of Alexander the Great, a heterogeneous population
found itself in a state where, in the oratory of Aristides, "life and
politics were illumined by the dawn of an era of universal order." This

golden age found its rightful poet in Virgil, who was surely Cather's guide in the early part of her chronicle, just as he had been Dante's. His many literary forms and styles were available as the chief models for her own. Although in these three novels, as elsewhere, she is eclectic in her use of much of the literary past, she would have understood Michelet's comment, *"Je suis né de Virgil et Vico."* Both writers figure prominently in this first stage.

In the second book of *My Ántonia*, as Jim Burden becomes aware of the world about him through his study of Virgil's *Georgics*, he begins to understand the relation between life and art. Cather's discovery of her own destiny as a writer may well be reflected here; her debt to Virgil is much deeper than the use of a few phrases and the pastoral settings in these first novels. The links with his poetry are many, some of them operating profoundly in her work. The themes of pastoral poetry--the *Idylls* of Theocritus as well as the *Eclogues* and *Georgics* of Virgil-- repeat in her novels of the frontier; they include the acknowledgement of the difficulties of agrarian life, the celebration of its triumphs and joys, the personification of nature, the relation of agriculture to the social and political life of a country. Few serious novelists had dealt with such themes before Cather. In her novels as a whole she attempted to establish for the western United States the kind of historical background that the *Aeneid* had provided for Rome, and at the same time to heighten the significance of contemporary events by linking the present with the ancient past. In these novels, just as important as they had been to the Romans of Virgil's day, loom the cycles of the seasons, the hostility or beneficence of Nature personified. The immensity of the western landscape adds grandeur, and the historical facts lend a sense of reality, but the stories are based on the few eternal conflicts of human existence and their attendant myths. The emphasis is on the meaning of the Virgilian *patria*--country--as one's immediate neighborhood, an interpretation that Cather adopted after she considered the advice of Sarah Orne Jewett that she must understand her own region before she could learn to see her experiences in relation both to literature and to the world.

Cather's view of the frontier epoch as the golden age makes almost inevitable her choice of the pastoral as the literary form for the three novels of this first divine stage of her cycle.[1] She wrote of the worship of nature, specifically river gods, in "A Resurrection" (1897): that attitude toward nature, she says, gives "something of that intimate sympathy with inanimate nature that is the base of all poetry, something of that which the high-faced rocks of the gleaming Sicilian shore gave Theocritus" (*CSF*,433). It was Theocritus, and Virgil somewhat later, who developed the pastoral as a genre in the Hellenistic period. Only then, says Charles Segal, an interpreter of the genre, appears the combination of concerns, attitudes, and poetic expression that makes the pure form. Virgil refined the seemingly simple eclogue into the serious poem whose subjects include the relation of poetry to history, irrational violence, and the problem of order and disorder in human life.[2] Particularly important to Cather's work is the use of great mythic themes of an older tradition to clarify contemporary questions. In his discussion of the methods of Theocritus and Virgil, Segal might well include Cather's name:

> It is curious that so complex and difficult an art on conjoining dissimilars should ever have been regarded as primarily realistic in its aims and simple (or simplifying) in its spirit. The consummate poetic skill that creates a seamless elegance of surface distracts us from noticing the imaginative leaps across very distant realms. When one thinks of the ways in which both Theocritus and Virgil incorporate pieces of earlier poets, parts of other literary traditions, songs of varied poetic personae, one is tempted to apply Lévi-Strauss's notion of *bricolage*. These poets of melodious surface flow are also bold collagists of heterogeneous fragments.[3]

Cather's choice of the pastoral as form for *O Pioneers!*, *The Song of the Lark*, and *My Ántonia* is clearly in the tradition of the great poets who translated borrowed tales of a golden age into a nostalgic look at the beginnings of their own civilization. Like them she created stories in a unique voice to create new myths from old.

Not only did the pastoral form allow a coherence with the Vichian idea of the first part of a cultural cycle in its representation of the primitive awareness of simple opposites--planting and harvest, light and dark, life and death, it demanded the use of myth and mysteries as the content of the stories. The mysteries that appear in this first stage--those of Aphrodite and Adonis, Orpheus, and Demeter and Persephone--are all subjects of the pastorals of Theocritus and Virgil, not in their Olympian guise, but in the vegetation myths of the fertility rites. The magical connection between man and nature finds some of its greatest expression in the pairing of the religious rituals and the poetry that can bring their ineffable meanings to man's consciousness.

As Cather began the first phase of the cycle, she created a trio of female protagonists with strong intuitive powers in a neolithic-like setting. It is important to note the androgynous qualities of the heroines of the first three novels. Their names--Alexandra, Thea, and Ántonia-- are derivatives of masculine names, and images of them in masculine roles reinforce the sense of their completeness and wholeness, much like the early goddesses of the mysteries. This first, or divine, stage in the progress of the Cather version of the rise and fall of American civilization, then, is dominated by females whose sources of power are, for Alexandra and Ántonia, their close relation to and understanding of the land, and for Thea, that understanding plus her artistic genius. In this first divine age, action is controlled by sensation, instinct, imagination, and faith.[4] The protagonists are what Vico calls allegorical or collective beings. For him it is not the individual who makes history, but rather the collective force; those individuals whom we do find outstanding are really "poetical characters" of that force. Appropriately enough, as in classical art, the characters of these first novels are representations of the ideal of the norm. That status confers on Alexandra, Thea, and Ántonia a spiritual and sometimes magical power, a numinous value ascribed to archetypes by Jung. This whole primitive stage is an age described by Erich Neumann as one of "cosmic ritual," the epoch during which the great mythologies are created. In 1926 the British critic Alexander Porterfield perceived Cather's contribution to American literature, when he wrote in the *London Mercury* that her novels "convey the idea of mysterious and unwieldy forces operating, obscurely perhaps, somewhere underneath the surface of things which it would be impossible probably to treat in a directer manner. Miss Cather's Swedes and Germans have all the significance and symbolism which goes into the making of myths."[5]

O Pioneers!

The first novel of the frontier, *O Pioneers!*, was begun certainly with Whitman's poem in mind. The young Willa Cather thought Whitman somewhat ridiculous, but admired him because "there is a primitive elemental force about him." Alluding to him seems appropriate at the beginning of the first stage of the cycle for that reason and because, as she had said in the same essay, "He is so full of hardiness and of the joy of life. He looks at all nature in the delighted, admiring way in which the old Greeks and the primitive poets did" (*KA*,352). But for the classicist Erich Auerbach, the distinctive vocative form that the title uses recalls a construction that originates in the antique Roman verse of Virgil, Lucian, and Statius, and is not used again until the vernacular poetry of Dante.[6] With the title of the first book, then, there is reference to both the Virgilian aspect and the American.

O Pioneers! is, on one level, an examination of the relationship to the unsettled land of various types of people and ethnic groups. (The inscription, from the Polish writer Mickiewicz, a colleague of Michelet, is "Those fields, colored by various grain!") The land itself is pre-eminent; it is personified to such a degree that, like Hardy's heath, it seems a protagonist. In the words of the novel, "the great fact is the land itself." While the personalities of the human characters are static, the aspect of the land changes according to the temperament of the observer. The sentence introducing Alexandra's father is a significant one: "On one of the ridges of that winter waste stood the low log house in which John Bergson was dying." For old Mr. Bergson, watching his strength and finally his life being depleted by the struggle with the land, it was "still a wild thing that had its ugly moods; and no one knew when they were likely to come, or why. Mischance hung over it. Its Genius was unfriendly to man" (*OP*,12-13). Young Emil Bergson, never really a part of this untamed land, finds its meaning a grim one: the land

> seemed to overwhelm the little beginnings of human society that struggled in its sombre wastes. It was from facing this vast hardness that the boy's mouth had become so bitter; because he felt that men were too weak to make any mark here, that the land wanted to be let alone, to preserve its own fierce strength, its peculiar, savage kind of beauty, its uninterrupted mournfulness (*OP*,9).

Later, a three-year drought is called the "last struggle of a wild soil against the encroaching plowshare" (*OP*,28).[7]

Other archaic ideas persist in this stage of civilization in *O Pioneers!* to show the mind-set of an early people. The dawn in the east again seems to be "the light from some great fire that was burning under the edge of the world" (*OP*,74). Nature "sinks to sleep between the fruitfulness of autumn and the passion of spring" (*OP*,109). Like the ignorant primitive, the settler can "easily believe that in the dead landscape the germs of life and fruitfulness were extinct forever." Yet the woman-goddess knows intuitively what is not apparent, that "down under the frozen crusts, at the roots of the trees, the secret of life was still safe, warm as the blood in one's heart; and the spring would come again!" (*OP*,117). The many pathetic fallacies of the book heighten the direct address to nature, as when Marie thinks of time in terms of space: "The years seemed to stretch before her like the land; spring, summer, autumn, winter, spring; always the same patient fields, the patient little trees, the patient lives" (*OP*,144).

The older generation of males in this story and in *My Ántonia* fail to subdue the land; early in both novels the father dies, making way for the establishing of a matriarchal society. As in the early agricultural societies, the land is an enigma, and no one knows how to farm it properly. The sacrifice of the father is made to create a new order through the emergence of the female. Alexandra begins to play the dominant role that women held in primitive agricultural society. The description of the land changes dramatically at the beginning of the second part: the earth, with its power of growth and fertility,

> yields itself eagerly to the plow; rolls away from the shear, not even dimming the brightness of the metal, with a soft, deep sigh of happiness. . . . The grain is so heavy that it bends toward the blade and cuts like velvet. There is something frank and joyous and young in the open face of the country. It gives itself ungrudgingly to the moods of the season, holding nothing back. Like the plains of Lombardy, it seems to rise a little to meet the sun. The air and the earth are curiously mated and intermingled, as if the one were the breath of the other (*OP*,46).

The mating and intermingling of the air and earth point up Alexandra's dual role: she is at once identified with the feminine earth and appears wielding the masculine plow. Like the very earliest of fertility goddesses, she has the powers of both male and female. The wholeness of Alexandra, her capacity to encompass both masculine and feminine characteristics, is important to her role as goddess.[8] Michelet insists that in order to exert power even the later male heroes of civilization should always combine male and female qualities in a single person. Although Alexandra accepts her dual role with the same ease with which she wears a man's long ulster--"as if she were a young soldier," the maternal qualities of fruitfulness, imagination, and humanity are those that finally matter most, to her and to the world about her.[9]

Her strength, both physical and moral, is contrasted with the weakness of the men about her. "It is your fate to be always surrounded by little men," a friend tells her, reminding the reader of ancient friezes and urns picturing larger-than-life goddesses surrounded by smaller male figures. Her argument with her brothers about the ownership of the farm leaves no doubt about the relative importance of the male and female to agricultural society: if they have contributed labor, she has been the source of the rarer more vital needs--intuition, imagination, and drive. The first description of Alexandra and the men in her family reveal much. She walks "rapidly and resolutely, as if she knew where she was going and what she was going to do next." Emil is a little boy crying bitterly because of the cold. Her older brothers, Oscar and Lou, are physically strong but depend too much on their father and have little respect for nature. They become heads of families which neither honor the past nor presage the future. Alexandra alone is one of those creators whom Erich Neumann has described as forming the progressive element in a community at the same time that they retain the conservatism which links back to their origins.[10]

It is only Alexandra who can understand the land "and own it--for a little while." Her relationship with the earth is an intensely personal one, as she becomes more than an observer of nature and identifies with its colors, shapes, and creative force. As she feels the future stirring, she acts as intermediary between nature and the people who do not understand, like Oscar, who wants to plant at the same time each year, regardless of weather conditions. She can feel in her own body "the joyous germination in the soil," and the earth responds:

> For the first time, perhaps, since that land emerged from the waters of geologic ages, a human face was set toward it with love and yearning. It seemed beautiful to her, rich and strong and glorious. Her eyes drank in the breadth of it, until her tears blinded her. Then the Genius of the Divide, the great, free spirit which breathes across it, must have bent lower than it ever bent to a human will before (*OP*,37-38).

The Genius that had been so unfriendly to man in John Bergson's view, could also, according to early Romans, act as both a protecting companion and a sense of mission to be fulfilled. In the Vichian scheme, every age is dominated by a spirit, a genius of its own. Here in the first stage of civilization, the divine is identified with the natural world.

The religious connotations of the more lyrical descriptions of nature prepare us for the emergence of Alexandra as a form of the Great Mother. Her appearance suggests the earliest of grain goddesses, her thick reddish-yellow hair wound in a tiara-like braid, the fiery ends escaping to make her head look like a double sunflower. The goddess as flower is a striking theme in archaic sculpture. Marie Shabata, whose role moves her into the mythic realms later in the story, wears poppies on her hat, and even her face resembles a poppy, the flower more frequently associated with the fertility goddesses.[11]

In many realistic ways Alexandra excels as a farmer, acting on Crazy Ivar's suggestion that the pigs--those animals sacred to the goddess--be kept in a clean pen, constructing the first silo on the Divide, increasing her acreage when others are selling to speculators. Even these decisions involve imagination, demonstrating her belief that a pioneer should enjoy the idea of things more than the things themselves. But there is in Alexandra's decision a quality of mysticism that goes beyond mere imagination. When asked how she knows the price of land will rise, she says she can't explain it, "I *know*, that's all." Observing the transformation of the land from "wild beast" to fertile farmland, she says that the farmers had little to do with it. "The land did it. It had its little joke. It pretended to be poor because nobody knew how to work it right; and then, all at once, it worked itself." Even the structure of the novel supports the mystical interpretation of Alexandra's success. The first chapter, "The Wild Land," ends as she feels the future stirring; the second chapter, "Neighboring Fields," opens sixteen years later, success achieved.

The vital contribution to her success is made by the strength of her unconscious life. On two levels--as symbol in the allegory of frontier civilization and as fertility goddess--Alexandra depends on her unconscious as the operative force. Her ideas are all impersonal ones; her mind is "a white book, with clear writing about weather and beasts and growing things." She is a true chthonic deity in the early religious tradition in which, according to Vincent Scully, the land was not a picture--the landscape that the modern eye sees--but a "true force which physically embodied the powers that rule the world."[12] Alexandra's own realization of herself is described as almost a subconscious existence. One powerful drama of her unconscious life combines both her sense of herself as female and her personification of the primitive agricultural society. She has a recurring reverie of being carried across the fields by a large man who looks like the sunlight and smells like a ripe cornfield. What begins as a sexual fantasy when she is young turns into a kind of death wish as she grows older and tired, but the male figure remains consistently the consort of the goddess, representing fertility and resurrection.

As Great Mother, Alexandra is surrounded by other appropriate symbols. She lends religious significance to Crazy Ivar, the old man "touched by God" who lives in a clay bank so that he will not despoil nature, who reads from the Bible but interprets it in his own way, who knows instinctively how to tend both plants and animals. He is the archetypal figure of the "Wise Old Man" personifying the intuitive wisdom of the unconscious whose inspiration and secret advice guides the conscious personality of the hero. Ivar adds strength to the idea of Alexandra's divinity, calling her "Mistress," a translation of the Greek *Despoina*, the appellation of the earliest of Great Mother emanations, and making a ritual of washing his feet at night after he comes to live with her, as if he were entering a sacred temple. He is described not as washing, but as "making his ablutions." With his biblical attitudes, Ivar serves as a counterpoint, in his fear of temptation and his sense of evil, to the conviction of Emil that good was stronger than evil and was possible to men. The irony, of course, is that Ivar is a saintly figure and Emil, in the final view of his frontier community, is a man who has caused much evil.

The young Swedish women who work in the house have their origins in religious rituals, as well. They are always mentioned together as "the three," just as goddesses often came in trios. Alexandra keeps them in the house not for the work they do, but for their beauty and gaiety. Both the hermit and the three young dancing goddesses are standard figures in early accounts of the Great Mother and, moreover, they reappear in Cather's next two novels in this first part of her cycle, leaving no doubt that they are more than incidental. In *O Pioneers!* the three maidens are repeated in a scene with Alexandra and her three nieces in the flower garden.

Two standard characters in this sacred drama are Alexandra's younger brother Emil and his best friend Amédée. In early liturgy and art, the young men close to the goddess are identified with the ears of grain which she holds; in *O Pioneers!* the identification is no less explicit. As Emil compares his unhappy love with Amédée's new marriage,

> It seemed strange that now he should have to hide the thing that Amédée was so proud of, that the feeling which gave one of them such happiness should bring the other such despair. It was like that when Alexandra tested

her seed-corn in the spring, he mused. From two ears that had grown side by side, the grains of one shot up joyfully into the light, projected themselves into the future, and the grains from the other lay still in the earth and rotted; and nobody knew why (*OP*,95).

Like many passages in Cather, this recalls one from Shakespeare: "If you can look into the seeds of time/And say which grain will grow and which will not. . . (*Macbeth*,1.3.58), which recalls, in turn, John 12:24: "Except a corn of wheat fall into the ground and die, it abideth alone; but if it die, it bringeth forth much fruit." The concept was important to Cather; years later, she quoted the Shakespearean version in an essay on Thomas Mann.

Typical of final passages in the chapters of Cather's novels, this carries a heavy burden of meaning. It not only reinforces the idea of Alexandra as goddess, it also foreshadows the stories of Amédée and Emil as sacrificed gods. In the most primitive of the rituals of the Great Mother, the sacrifice of a beautiful vegetation god came at the time of the fall harvest to ensure the next year's grain. Just as primitive peoples chose the most virile of young men to propitiate the forces of fertility, Cather chooses to sacrifice Amédée, who not only is the head of a happy family, but also is the most productive farmer about. His fatal seizure comes in the wheat field on the first day of his harvest of the new crop.

Emil's love story, often interpreted as an almost unrelated episode, can be understood best in the terms of his relationship to Alexandra as fertility goddess. He appears only occasionally after he grows to manhood, since he lives on the Divide only during the summer; he disappears to the south, Mexico, for the winter and returns each June. He is the younger brother who is found frequently as a secondary figure in the cult of the Great Mother. His introduction as a young man compares him to a pine tree, the symbol of the vegetation god and his manhood; he is often seen wielding a scythe or a gun, to further signal the sexual scenes to come. Marie, the woman Emil loves, is presented in the first pages of the book as a young goddess in a circle of males to whom offerings of candy, pigs, and calves are made. As an adult her seductiveness, her constant smiles, and most of all, her need for love identify her with Aphrodite. Like that classical goddess, she is one of those women "who spread ruin around them through no fault of theirs, just by being too beautiful, too full of life and love"(*OP*,177). Aphrodite was borrowed by the Hellenic culture from the Asian chthonic religion, where she was related to Ishtar and Astarte and goddesses of many other names, and in the syncretistic world of the mysteries was worshipped as a fertility deity. One of her many emanations was as Mari in Paphos, her major center of worship. At other places her name was hyphenated as Aphrodite-Mari. Her aspect as a cruel goddess whose charms enslave men helps to explain the questions of Frank, the husband who has just killed Marie and Emil: "Why had Marie made him do this thing; why had she brought this upon him?" (*OP*,155). As in *My Ántonia*, the Aphrodite archetype is contrasted unfavorably with that of the older, wiser goddess, who is the Great Mother. In this drama, to Marie's Aphrodite, Emil plays Adonis, also an ancient Asian vegetation god who was adopted into the Greek Olympian panoply. His beauty, his seasonal wanderings, his sacrifice all point to the deliberate parallels. The deaths occur in late summer; as Emil leaves the church to find Marie the wheat stands ripe, and even the smell of ripeness has permeated the afternoon. The fertility god's usefulness for the season has ended.

Frank Shabata, Marie's husband, helps to establish the Adonis myth as the source of this story. Cather takes care to describe him both as the jealous war god Ares, who in some versions of the myth killed Adonis, and as the wild boar that Ares used as his disguise. His clenched fists, his savage energy, his constant "sense of injury and outrage," indicate the attitude of brutality and violence that characterizes the war god. Mentioned pointedly in three passages, Frank's yellow cane assumes significance as the counterpart to Ares' lance. He is also certainly the boar, always a part of the Adonis myth. Much is made of his white teeth, the heavy stubble on his face, and his sulking "as if he could eat everyone alive." Later, when Alexandra visits him in prison, his head is covered with bristles. His neck stiffens when he is angry to show that he is "one of those wild fellows," something "not altogether human."

The names of Aphrodite, Adonis, and Ares are used here because they are familiar names which emerged in both the fertility cults and classical mythology. However, in the syncretistic context of the myths and mysteries of the Hellenistic age, they can be exchanged for many other names of deities; the archetypal story of the earth mother and the divine son is universal in the religious rites of the time, and all of the myths are interrelated. In addition to the cross-fertilization of the myths of many regions, each myth had many versions, as might be expected of stories that spanned the entire Mediterranean area and eventually Europe during a period of two thousand years or more. Added to this incredibly rich and diverse background is Cather's own eclecticism--or syncretism--which makes hunting mythic patterns in her stories an adventure. Remarkably, patterns do appear, as in this consistent tale of a fertility god's sacrifice and resurrection, with characters, events, and symbols that are found in the earliest art and literature of the Western world.

After the deaths of Marie and Emil, two white butterflies, a symbol of resurrection, flutter in and out of the shadows, and "the last wild roses of the year opened their pink hearts to die." The two lovers have become a part of nature. Alexandra will one day join these two, to complete her mission of creating life on the divide: "Fortunate country, that is one day to receive hearts like Alexandra's into its bosom, to give them out again in the yellow wheat, in the rustling corn, in the shining eyes of youth!" (*OP*,180).

There are other interpretations of the story. L. V. Jacks explicates it as a version of the classical Pyramus and Thisbe myth.[13] The story mentions the white mulberry tree at least four times, but not all of the elements fit. Multiple explications are inevitable in light of the syncretism of Cather's sources in the Olympian and the Oriental mystery religions, as well as the "two or three human stories" that the world knows. Indeed, she may well have had more than one myth in mind for a single story.

The fertility myth, however, is undeniably the predominant theme of *O Pioneers!*, as it is the chief expression of the consciousness of early agricultural society. As part of that myth, one of the book's major symbols is the wild duck, important because it is one of the water birds sacred to the Great Mother as well as one of the natural symbols, able to be interpreted only by priests, that Vico places in the divine stage of culture. When Alexandra in several passages reveals her inexplicable joy in seeing a duck, the reader can recall that many vases from the Hellenistic period picture ducks alongside goddesses, identifying them in our awareness of the culture. At the beginning of Alexandra's story Emil, after learning much about the water birds at Ivar's pond, asks:

"And is that true, Ivar, about the head ducks falling back when they are tired, and the hind one taking their place?" "Yes. The point of the wedge gets the worst of it; they cut the wind. They can only stand it there a little while--half an hour, maybe. Then they fall back and the wedge splits a little while the rear ones come up the middle to the front. Then it closes up and they fly on, with a new edge" (*OP*,25).

This image shows the strength required of the pioneer leaders, of course; but throughout the book the stress is on the recurring cycles, the "little while" allotted to any human striving. Alexandra and Emil share a special day on the river watching a solitary duck swimming in the sunlight, an event that both find significant. Later Alexandra recalls that duck as a kind of enchanted bird that knew neither age nor change. But a darker, more portentous scene shows Marie's distress when Emil shoots five wild ducks--a scene that foreshadows the shooting of the lovers themselves, affirming the connection between the natural world and human events.

The connection between man and nature is what *O Pioneers!* is about, just as it is the heart of the mystery religions. The story of Aphrodite, Adonis, and Ares is part of the mythic content of the Great Mother mysteries. In some primitive versions, Aphrodite is also the Great Mother and both mother and lover of Adonis; Cather, however, follows the later versions such as that of Apollodorus in separating the roles of the goddess in the story in order to make it acceptable to public taste. In fact, in this ritual of the *hieros gamos*, or sacred marriage, and the resulting deaths of the lovers there are strong hints of their sacrifice as a couple: the terror of Marie's husband at sight of the mutilated and bleeding woman in his orchard, and Carl's comment in another context that maybe Marie was "cut to pieces, too." (*OP*,177). Both the male and the female are sacrificed because they are the best available.

That sacrifice, so terrible that much is hidden from view of even the assassin, was the climax in early accounts of mystery rites, such as those of Homer and Hesiod. But other elements of mysteries appear throughout *O Pioneers!*, often in juxtaposition with Christian rituals. As Emil, an unbeliever, sits through the mass for his dead friend, he responds to the singing of Gounod's *"Ave Maria"* by thinking of his own Marie: "He seemed to discover that there was a kind of rapture in which he could love forever without faltering and without sin. . . . The rapture was for those who could feel it; for people who could not, it was non-existent" (*OP*,148). Both the denial of sin and the exclusiveness of the experience of rapture differentiate the attitudes of the initiates into the mysteries from those of the Christian communicants. Emil's emotions as he goes to meet Marie are described in the language of the liturgy of the mysteries: "He was at that height of excitement from which everything is foreshortened, from which life seems short and simple, death very near, and the soul seems to soar like an eagle. . . . The heart, when it is too much alive, aches for that brown earth, and ecstasy has no fear of death" (*OP*,149). The smell of ripened grain and the sunlight bring the transformation scene necessary to the mystery rites: "When he reached the orchard the sun was hanging low over the wheatfield. Long fingers of light reached through the apple branches as through a net; the orchard was riddled and shot with gold; light was the reality, the trees were merely interferences that reflected and refracted light" (*OP*,150). As he sees Marie, Emil puts his hand over his mouth--a sign of the initiate related to the etymology of the word *mystery*, "to close the eyes or mouth." Marie's breast rises and falls--the primary symbol of the goddess, which is, as Segal shows, emphasized in the Theocritean idyll.

The scenes re-enacting the mystery rites involve only a few participants and take place in secluded natural settings. In contrast the Christian rituals in the novel--the cavalcade to greet the bishop, the combined funeral and confirmation service--are so public and open that only those who don't attend are noticed. From this first novel to the last in the cycle, Cather addresses the questions of comparative religion in subtle ways. In *O Pioneers!* Crazy Ivar is a link between the Christian and mystery religions. [14] He is the one to find the bodies of the lovers, and his judgment is a Christian one: "It is fallen!" he sobs, signalling the fall from innocence. "Sin and death for the young ones!" significantly puts sin ahead of death in his report and denies Emil's revelation at the church that he can love without sin. "God have mercy upon us!" he cries, expressing the sense later echoed by Alexandra's maid that everyone must be punished for the sins of Emil and Marie. Ivar later refuses to believe that Emil can be in Paradise. In spite of these Christian views, Ivar has a role in some of the mystery rites. Some of his locutions, sounding vaguely biblical, are in the language of mystery liturgy: "When the eyes of the flesh are shut, the eyes of the spirit are open," he says as he thinks of Alexandra. "She will have a message from those who are gone, and that will bring her peace" (*OP*,162).

Ivar's buggy ride to the graveyard to find Alexandra after a storm is another re-enactment of a ritual, with lanterns prominent in this nocturnal scene, a rain that obscures the distinction between earth and sky, and the sight of a white-robed Alexandra rising from a white gravestone. "When you get so near the dead," she instructs Ivar, "they seem more real than the living" (*OP*,164). The storm after the crisis, with Alexandra looking like a drowned woman and even Ivar's mare getting "a ducking," repeats the end of mystery rituals in which the final words were "Let it rain!" to complete the purification and insure the fertility resulting from the supposed "love-union" of the rain between heaven and earth.[15] Another of the novel's many ritual scenes occurs when Alexandra and Carl walk through the fields to plan their future. Alexandra wears ritual white for this journey with stops at important landmarks--the pond and the furthest ridge. Carl, remembering the young Alexandra who had looked "as if she had walked straight out of the morning itself," still sees her as integral with nature: gazing into the west, she has an expression of "exalted serenity" as the sinking sun shines in her eyes.

This language, combining the bucolic and the numinous, keeps an emphasis on Alexandra as goddess. But this story, like all pastorals, has two sides, and like the third *Idyll* of Theocritus, with the goatherd coming back to his mundane world, it brings the reader back to the realities of daily existence. In Lincoln to visit Frank Shabata in prison, Alexandra notes big brick buildings and an iron fence, hears sharp military commands to cadets, and talks to a young man from Cherry County, where the hay is fine and the coyotes find water easily. Frank's own reality is grim--he is called only 1037--and Alexandra shares his disgust with life, although she expresses the Heraclitan view that being what he was, Frank could not have acted otherwise. The pastoral is an enabling form in this and the other novels of the first stage; its very structure helps to achieve the integration in which "the design is the story and the story is the design," as she said of Jewett's stories. Both David Stouck and Hermione Lee recognize the complexity of Cather's use of the pastoral form; but in the context of the mystery religions, there is an additional level of meaning. The frequent use of the pastoral made by Theocritus and Virgil to introduce the mysteries transfers some of that meaning to the literature that follows the tradition. The nature of allegory is especially important to both mundane and mythic meanings of many passages in pastoral poetry. Cather uses the pastoral as she uses all her sources--just as far as it serves her purpose. So when Stouck and Slote discuss *O Pioneers!* in terms of the epic, there need be no dissent, even though Cather described the book to Sergeant as a two-part pastoral. Critics of antiquity faulted Virgil for writing eclogues that were not true pastorals.[16] Cather, like Virgil, needed a wider view than the pure form, if there is such a thing, could afford. Considering her experimental sense of design, it is best to approach her work as C. S. Lewis recommends we view all art: by asking how far it participates in the conventions of any form. Using the pastoral form with energy and skill, Cather was able to bring the Aphrodite and Adonis myth to contemporary awareness in much the same way as Theocritus had speculated in his third idyll on that myth and the mystery cult surrounding it, and at the same time she brings the story of a new beginning of a nation.

She provides a sign that more of the national story is to come. At the end of *O Pioneers!* a storm delays a telephone call until the thunder has stopped. That incident has no meaning in the story, until the realization that the Vichian epoch that begins a culture's rise is signalled by a thunderclap. The meaning becomes clearer when the next thunderclap appears in *Death Comes for the Archbishop, the novel of the ricorso*, or the second rise. With her history of a culture, its applicable myths, and appropriate forms, Cather has begun in *O Pioneers!* an interpretation of the story of the American West.

The Song of the Lark

The second novel of Cather's cycle, *The Song of the Lark*, explores further the story of the frontier past, placing it among her so-called "elegiac" works. The mythic background is chiefly Teutonic, echoing the early north tales of the Scandinavian and Germanic peoples. But the heroine's revelation comes only after a visit to the ruins of ancient Pueblo civilization and her resultant comprehension of the meaning of her musical gift. The Cliff-Dwellers, she finds, have "lengthened her past," and she knows that she has "older and higher obligations" to herself and to destiny than she had known (*SL*,276). The mystical experience that reveals this information to her is framed as a recapitulation of the Orphic mystery rites of Thrace and Greece. These seemingly diverse elements are pulled together to make a remarkably coherent whole. Just as Shakespeare could create a powerful drama by combining the events of a Scandinavian legend, the structure of Greek tragedy, and effects from the Spanish revenge play, Cather was able to control multiple meanings and literary devices in a single novel.

Written between *O Pioneers!* and *My Ántonia, The Song of the Lark* begins on the frontier in the same era and again has as protagonist a woman with greater-than-human powers. Her name, Thea, is the Greek word for *goddess*, but she is given a masculine nickname, "Thee," to parallel "Alex" Bergson and "Tony" Shimerda (and "Willie" Cather). All have names of conquerors in spite of the fact that Cather did not like feminine forms of masculine names. In Thea's case, because the mythic background of the story is Teutonic, we think of Theodoric, the great king of the Ostrogoths and a hero of the *Nibelungenlied*, and add his name to those of Anthony and Alexander in the list of heroes with whom these heroines of the frontier are linked. In her introduction to *The Kingdom of Art* Bernice Slote relates Thea's name to the daughter of Uranus and to Keats's poem in which Thea (or sometimes Theia) is identified as Hyperion's sister-wife and the most beautiful of the Titan children. According to Harrison, Thyia was mentioned by Pausanias as the mythical priestess who held orgies on the Delphian Plain in honor of Dionysus. Slote also connects Thea's surname--Kronborg--to Kronos. It is interesting to note that he was the Greek son of Ouranos (Uranus) and the husband-brother of Rhea, identified with a Great Mother figure from Asia. No doubt Cather knew all these connections; as H. L. Mencken said, "Her mind is plentifully stored."[17]

Thea's qualities are apparent only to those of special worth and are usually described as "unconscious powers"; she herself is aware from an early age of a second person lying deep within, and she recognizes that other people have second selves to which hers may speak. "How deep they lay, these second persons," she thinks, "and how little one knew about them, except to guard them fiercely. It was to music, more than to anything else, that these hidden things in people responded" (*SL*,197). The same kind of mystical power of the artist is described in the short story "The Sculptor's Funeral": "Whatever he touched, he revealed its holiest secret; liberated it from enchantment and restored it to its pristine loveliness" (*CSF*,180). As with the pioneer of Cather's earlier novel, much of the artist's power derives from the imagination. Thea's talent springs from two sources: "There's the voice itself, so beautiful and individual, and then there's something else; the thing in it which responds to every shade of thought and feeling, spontaneously, almost unconsciously" (*SL*,365). The magic that Thea possesses enables her to fill her music with a "legendary, supernatural thing." She understands the operatic role of the goddess because she, too, is a goddess of artistic wisdom and beauty. Cather presents many heroines with attributes of goddesses, who lead in the search for the goals that satisfy primal needs matching those of former civilizations.

Thea's guidance in artistic imagination begins with her first music teacher, who "came from God knows where." His name, Wunsch, in addition to being the Teutonic god Odin's ancient name, means *wish* or *desire* in Old German. It is Wunsch who teaches Thea that for the artist "nothing is far and nothing is near, if one desires. The world is little, people are little, human life is little. There is only one big thing--desire" (*SL*,69). His message becomes clear to Thea when she learns through her exploration of American Indian ruins that achievement in art "had come all the way; when men lived in caves, it was there. A vanished race; but along the trail, in the stream, under the spreading cactus, there still glittered in the sun the bits of their frail clay vessels, fragments of their desire" (*SL*,288). Desire becomes the key to spiritual quests in *My Mortal Enemy* as Myra decides that in religion, desire is fulfillment. The use of the word *desire* so often in *The Song of the Lark*, a novel about art, and *My Mortal Enemy*, a novel about religion, reveals the transference of the values from one to the other for Cather. In all her work, art, religion, and nature--her three major themes as well as the major subjects of myth--are identified with each other in an ineffable way. The connection in the mind of Tom Outland of *The Professor's House* is pointed out by E. K. Brown: "The mesa, which was at first a stimulus to adventure, assumed a beauty like that of sculpture, and finally aroused a religious emotion."[18]

The relation of the wild land to religion first appears in *O Pioneers!* where Crazy Ivar, choosing to live in a lonely section of the prairie, says that his Bible seems truer to him there. The author adds: "If one stood in the doorway of his cave, and looked off at the rough land, the smiling sky, the curly grass white in the hot sunlight; if one listened to the rapturous song of the lark, the drumming of the quail, the burr of the locust against that vast silence, one understood what Ivar meant" (*OP*,38). In *A Lost Lady* young Niel responds to a June dawn in much the same way, finding an almost religious purity in the new morning. A total identification of land with religion is made by a Navajo chief in *Death Comes for the Archbishop*:

> They asked nothing of the Government, he told Father Latour, but their religion, and their own land where they had lived from immemorial time. Their country, he explained, was a part of their religion; the two were inseparable. The Canyon de Chelly the Padre knew; in that canyon his people had lived when they were a small weak tribe; it had nourished and protected them; it was their mother. Moreover, their gods dwelt there--in those inaccessible white houses set in caverns up in the face of the cliffs, which were older than the white man's world, and which no white man had ever entered. The gods were there, just as the Padre's god was in his church (*DC*,294-95).

Cather's sense of the relation between religion and art is stated explicitly in her essay "Escapism," in which she says, "Religion and art spring from the same root and are close kin" (*OW*,27) and in *The Professor's House* where she has a professor of history say, "Art and religion (they are the same thing, in the end, of course) have given man the only happiness he has ever known" (*PH*,68). Her interrelating of nature, art, and religion is especially pertinent to a discussion of myth in her work, since myth itself is often a mingling of man's explanation for the meaning of his life, his interpretation of the cosmos, and the expression in language, painting, and music of those ideas.

In *The Song of the Lark* the three threads of nature, art, and religion are twined as Thea reaches her great artistic power with the help of nature and the religion of a dead people. The symbolic death and rebirth of the artist is the central motif of the book. The struggle that precedes the final crisis begins early in Thea's career as, hating her ignorance, she wishes she could die and begin anew. Her teacher assents gravely that every artist makes himself born. Like many significant passages in Cather's novels, this one includes language of the mystery religions. Thea's eventual rebirth occurs under two related influences--nature and the tradition of an ancient civilization.

Neither influence is new in Thea's life. She owes much of her strength to her childhood on the frontier, where many traditions were merged. Even the prehistoric existence of the plains where she lives as a child is mentioned: heifers standing there "were magnified to a preposterous height and looked like mammoths, prehistoric beasts standing solitary in the water that for many thousands of years actually washed over that desert; the mirage itself may be the ghost of that long-vanished sea" (*SL*,43). For Cather's characters, such links with the past are spiritually nourishing. Nature, too, confers spiritual benefits, as when Thea imagines that the spirit of human courage lives with the eagles on a nearby mountain. She shares the primitive attitude that the physical universe has anthropomorphic qualities that can be transmitted to humans. On a trip to the West, the sight of the land makes her think that "she had the sense of going back to a friendly soil, whose friendship was somehow going to strengthen her; a naïve, generous country that gave one its joyous force, its large-hearted, childlike power to love, just as it gave one its coarse, brilliant flowers" (*SL*,199). Most important is the quality that nature has imparted to her voice. It is, Wunsch thinks, a nature-voice, like the sound of the wind in the trees, or the murmur of water. Even the city-bred Fred Ottenburg understands the importance of her frontier background to Thea, the influence that Moonstone would always have on her artistic values.

Separated from nature during her study in Chicago, she experiences discouragement, restless misery, even torment. In her need for periodic renewal of her contact with the land she resembles Cather, who "had almost to dissolve into nature daily in order to be reborn to a task," according to Elizabeth Sergeant.[19] Thea finds her renewal in repeated rituals of isolation from society, which lead to new discovery and eventual rebirth, by undertaking a series of exiles with the start of a journey at the end of each chapter. The most painful of these occurs at the end of the second part of *The Song of the Lark*, as she leaves her family forever and "something pulled in her--and broke"; even then, however, she recognizes the personal growth that accompanies that wrench. The climax of this theme of exile and isolation comes in the chapter on "The Ancient People." There, total revitalization is possible because the canyon offers both natural beauties ("the earliest sources of gladness that she could remember") and an awareness of deeper roots than she has known before.

Hearing "a voice out of the past, not very loud, that went on saying a few simple things to the solitude eternally," Thea determines the direction her life must take. The ritualistic atmosphere of the canyon simplifies and defines life for her in terms of the realities of the rocks, the pine forest, and especially the sun. Her days on the rock ledges and in the Cliff-Dwellers' huts take on a religious significance, reflecting the wish of the Pueblo Indians to build their dwellings to represent both the basic harmony of man with his world and the hidden life of perfection. Thea discovers this harmony with the universe and something more-- that art has always been one of the necessities of life. Only when she understands the eternal reverberations of ancient myth, when she perceives the relations between the individual and a long tradition, can she emerge as a great artist. She is keeping the appointment to meet herself that has long been in her consciousness. Its beginnings are as early as her first piano lessons in Moonstone with Wunsch, who like Crazy Ivar of *O Pioneers!* is an archetypal figure of the wise old man. Like Ivar, he lives apart from the community and has his irrational moments, yet is a spiritual as well as a practical mentor. In his function as one voice from the collective conscious of the past, Wunsch begins the process that culminates in Thea's rebirth. Realizing her talent even before she is aware of it and knowing it will take her from him, he often plays an aria from Gluck's opera *Orpheus*, mourning the loss of the second Eurydice in his life. One significance of the Orpheus theme here lies in the Jungian interpretation, that of undeveloped intuitive or imaginative sensibility, the quality that underlies in Cather's work the compelling desire of the artist and the religious seeker.

The story of Orpheus in classical mythology is useful in understanding Thea's epiphany. First, of course, is the idea of his great musical talent, which has magical qualities to move plants and animals, even rocks. The marriage of Orpheus to Eurydice brings him in touch with chthonic myths because she, like Persephone, functions as a fertility goddess, disappearing below the earth for part of each year. Various versions of the story tell of the successful or unsuccessful attempt by Orpheus to rescue Eurydice, but all end with his death at the hands of the *Maenads*, although his head continued to sing after he had been torn to pieces. Thea, as musician, has a connection with Orpheus; she also is related to Eurydice, in that her impulse to greatness springs from the land, her inspiration comes in part from the obvious fertility symbol of the clay pots of the Indians, and her meeting with Fred in the canyon has a strong sexual context. Like Alexandra and Ántonia, the other heroines of this period of Cather's writing, Thea is a figure of completeness with strengths of both the god and goddess.

Beyond the well-known story of Orpheus and Eurydice in mythology, however, is the Orpheus of the mystery religions, who was a prophet accepted as a historical figure by many ancient writers, a founder of a mystery cult devoted to Dionysus, and a writer of the poetry--the Orphic hymns--upon which its rituals are based. Orphism was practiced in the ancient world from about the sixth century before Christ. In its concept of a series of incarnations to rid the soul of impure elements it is related to the idea of the death and rebirth of the chthonic deities, emphasizing the link between the living and the dead. In its dualism of body and soul, the Orphic mystery is often seen as the symbolic expression of the rebirth of a soul. The initiation, like that of the Eleusinian, Mithraic, and other mystery religions, was divided into four stages, beginning with a preliminary purification. Next came the communication of some mystical knowledge, followed by a revelation of holy objects. Finally, there was a garlanding of the initiates, often celebrated by a primitive dance of ecstasy. Although the name Orpheus may or may not be derived from the word for darkness, dark and light symbolism is important to his rituals. As in all the mysteries, these were rites kept secret from all except the initiated, but they are mentioned by Pindar, Euripides, and Plato among others.

One of the best sources of information about the Orphic mystery rites is the *Villa Item*, or Villa of the Mysteries, just outside Pompeii, where the pictures that lined the initiation hall are presumed to portray the stages of initiation into the later Dionysian mysteries. Willa Cather visited Pompeii with Isabelle McClung in 1908 but could not have seen the Villa itself; although excavation of Pompeii was begun in 1861, the Villa, located outside the city walls, was not discovered until 1910. At that time, however, its discovery was considered of enormous importance and was widely publicized in Europe and the United States. The ten panels of beautiful frescoes, now removed, are only one part of the information to be imparted by the Villa. The baths, the underground chamber with vulva-shaped entrance, and above all the taurobolium, still capable of communicating dread, tell of other activities.

The link with Dionysus prompts some accounts of sacrifice and cannibalism in the Orphic rites; other accounts say that the philosophy of Orpheus included a belief in transmigration and the sanctity of all life that would preclude such bloody practices. The Orphic gospel, however, emphasized the individual's divinity, a moral, even ascetic life, and the continual process of death and rebirth until the initiate hears the words "Happy and blessed one, you have become divine instead of mortal." The way that these ideas permeated the cults throughout the ancient world is briefly noted in the definition of Orphism in the American Heritage dictionary: "An ancient Greek mystery religion arising in the sixth century B.C. from a synthesis of pre-Hellenic beliefs . . . soon becoming mingled with the Eleusinian mysteries and the doctrines of Pythagoras, but continuing to influence later antiquity through the Orphic poems and kindred teachings incorporated by Neo-Platonic thought." Orphism was a complex, varied, and widespread doctrine, and modern scholars have revealed many of the more obscure philosophies and practices. Willa Cather, however, used only the more general ideas and rituals of the mysteries that were available in her time as background for *The Song of the Lark*, as for her other novels. Many of the known general ritual patterns in Orphism as well as some of the specific initiatory activities are repeated in "The Ancient People" chapter. Thea's removal to the canyon of the dead people in April, the time of the festival of Dionysus, recreates the descent of the initiate into the sacred spaces where the rites are performed. The very atmosphere of the canyon is described as ritualistic when she begins her preparations for the rites. She finds a pool at the bottom of the canyon where she feels a continuity with the life of an earlier people, and her bath--the preliminary purification that is the first step in initiation--comes to have a "ceremonial gravity."

The second stage, the communication of mystic knowledge, is in keeping with both the Orphic background and the Indian site where the ritual takes place. The revelations of Orphism, as of most mysteries, are not spoken, presumably because they are ineffable. Thea's own understanding comes directly out of the rocks, she believes--a very primitive conception of the conveying of knowledge. Thea knows only that

> a certain understanding of those old people came up to her out of the rock-shelf on which she lay; that certain feelings were transmitted to her, suggestions that were simple, insistent, and monotonous, like the beating of Indian drums. They were not expressible in words, but seemed rather to translate themselves into attitudes of body, into degrees of muscular tension or relaxation (*SL*,272).

Because of its close alliance with the Dionysian religion, Orphism was a sensuous rather than an intellectual address to the world. With her new mystical knowledge, Thea's thought turns to sensation: "She could become a mere receptacle for heat, or become a colour, like the bright lizards that darted about on the hot stones outside her door; or she could become a continuous repetition of sound, like the cicadas" (*SL*,270). After this awareness, even her music becomes more sensation, and less idea. Like the initiate in the ancient rites, she learns nothing that can be communicated, but undergoes a vital experience.

In the third stage of the initiation, the sacred drama, there are revealed, still silently, holy objects. These, for Thea, are chiefly the pieces of Indian pottery, so symbolic of both artistic accomplishment and female essence; but they also include the grinding-stones, drill, and needles pointed out by Old Biltmer. One important relic Thea finds is a shallow bowl with a serpent's head, a reference to the ability of Orpheus to charm snakes, and in the mysteries, a symbol of Dionysus himself. Having participated in these preliminary rituals, Thea waits for the moment of initiation, which takes place in a primal scene both crucial to the narrative and highly ceremonial in its structure. The fifth section of "The Ancient People" begins the initiation proper, setting it in a rare day reflecting the mood of the mysteries: "one of those cloudy days . . . when the life goes out of that country and it becomes a gray ghost, an empty, shivering uncertainty." From the shadows of a tower,

Old Biltmer sees Thea and Fred hurling rocks in the kind of game often played by the Greeks before a serious undertaking. The meaning here is greater than simply the recalling of Greek discus throwers; the images of the rocks sailing across the gulf represent the flight of the soul of the Orphic initiate. Fred's patient teaching and Thea's capacity to learn reinforce the idea of new accomplishment.

The sixth section of this chapter moves further, by means of nature images, toward Thea's development, from the dawn over the canyon in the first sentence to the flight of the eagle at the conclusion. The journey of Thea and Fred begins in the middle of the night, and they descend into the canyon by lantern light, in spite of a mysterious resistance by the very air. Thea watches the stars fade as she crouches against the wall and understands the courage necessary for the early races of man. The experience leaves her pale and grim. Then the sunrise brings a transformation scene: the pine trees flash with a "coppery fire"; a "golden light" hangs over the rim of the canyon, magnifying objects; streaks of light reach into the canyon; and the glow of the sun bursts, making the arch of the sky seem transparent. Fred takes on aspects of Dionysus as he lies beneath the pine tree, his shoulder against it-- signalling, as in *O Pioneers!*, the identification of the vegetation god with that tree. Thea thinks about his difference from other men and his preternatural energy; he says that being Apollo, that antithesis of Dionysus, would be tedious for him; that their visit to the canyon has an idea behind it. Thea's appearance on a cliff, larger than life, is a reminder to Fred that she, too, has superhuman "energy and audacity." The essence of initiation into all the mysteries was identification of the participant with the cultic god and the assimilation of his ennobling qualities. In the Dionysian mysteries those qualities have elements of frenzy, and Fred detects in Thea the spirit of the *Maenads*: "You are the sort that used to run wild in Germany, dressed in their hair and a piece of skin" (*SL*,287). But the grimmer message of the Orphic mysteries must have its ceremonies, as well. This is manifest in the seventh section, which starts with the threat of a storm, even while the sun is shining. Forced into a cave for protection, Thea and Fred find that their world has become a murky gray, and even their bodies are shrouded in a gray mist. The storm is terrifying, changing the aspect of all living things and obscuring the view of the world outside. The cold air sends Thea to the back wall of the cave, where she wraps herself in a blanket, repeating the practice in the Orphic rites of dressing in the skin of a kid. The parallel is made explicit by the language Cather chooses: "The wool of the Navajo sheep was soon kindled by the warmth of her body, and was impenetrable to dampness" (*SL*,290). In spite of the increasing darkness, they decide to return to the ranch, but not before two further rituals are echoed. The first is a ceremonial sip of brandy, and the second is a symbolic sacred marriage, or *hieros gamos*, which was the culmination of most mystery celebrations of the goddess. The exchange starts as Thea places her hands on Fred's shoulders, then kisses him for the first time without embarrassment. He whispers her name three times as he shakes her slightly. Even in midst of this most sexual of Cather scenes, the spiritual effect of this moment is apparent to Fred: "When she rose to meet him like that, he felt her flash into everything she had ever suggested to him as if she filled out her own shadow" (*SL*,292). The shadow sense of the ego of the protagonist appears with much the same meaning in *O Pioneers!* and *My Ántonia*. In the context of Orphism, this scene elicits the idea of the shadow of the soul after death, particularly in this chapter centering on the dead people of the canyon and the concept of rebirth.

Thea has been initiated into a new life through an ancient religion that taught of the divine spark in each human being. For her, the Orphic mystery of divine survival lies in art, whether it is the creation of a clay pot by an ancient people or the magic of a supreme voice. The emergence of her artistic imagination from the very rocks of the canyon, from the darkness of the primitive mind, and from rituals following an ancient pattern affirms Jung's claim that "Great art till now has always derived its fruitfulness from the myth, from the unconscious process of symbolization which continues through the ages and which, as the primordial manifestation of the human spirit, will continue to be the root of all creation in the future."[20]

The setting of the Orphic mystery rites in the Pueblo canyon is more than a convenience of geography for Cather; as in all nine novels of this cycle, she is revealing similarities of religious thought and practice throughout the world. Only a small amount of archaeological information was available at the time of her visits to the Indian canyon, but clearly she understood the possible similarities between the Orphic and American spiritual beliefs and religious practices, just as Vincent Scully discovered the same relationship when he later saw the pueblos. He knew immediately that his study of Greek religious architecture could be completed only in the pueblos, because the same ancient rituals are still performed in them. "The chorus of Dionysos," he said, "still dances there." The great Pueblo ceremonial system is still "an order of thought and action which is magical and scientific all at once."[21] Scully finds close analogies between Pueblo courtyards and their rituals and those of Minoan palaces. Cather may well have had some knowledge of the early dwellers: in 1893 Adolph Bandelier, one of the earliest visitors to the Pueblo canyons, wrote *The Gilded Man*, a novel reconstructing the lives of the prehistoric Indians, and his early report in the papers of the Archaeological Institute describes a story told by the Zunis in the region that resembles the Greek myth of Orpheus and Eurydice. He speculates that the story, like many others, may have originated independently in both places. Nearly a hundred years later an American scholar concluded that the Orphic story is nearly universal among American Indian tribes.[22] In the first volume of *A Journal of American Ethnology and Archaeology* in 1891, J. Walter Fewkes, anticipating Scully's conclusion, described the summer rituals at a Zuni pueblo that continued the ancient traditions: the ceremonies were similar to the ancient mystery rites, with a public portion of the ritual above the ground and secret rites held below in the kiva, where only the initiated were permitted.

Cather's use of the Indian background gave her an appropriate comparison of culture stages, as well as of religious practices. The stage of American civilization achieved on the frontier that had fostered Thea's growth was a time of sensual response to the natural world, the kind of direct intuitional relationship with the earth that could lead to her discovery of self. The clarity and simplicity of a people in the early part of the Vichian cycle of civilization was apparent, since the Pueblos had not evolved, even in eleven thousand years, beyond an agricultural stage. The same phrases describe the people and their land: "Their language is not a communicative one, and they never attempt an interchange of personality in speech. Over their forest there is the same inexorable reserve. Each tree has its exalted power to bear" (*SL*,265). Thea, with a new power of sustained sensation, responds to her subconscious in the environment of Moonstone or Panther Cañon, where a relationship to the earth is the primary experience. Implicitly Cather anticipates a judgment of J. B. Priestley that the final test of what Americans choose to do in art and politics should be a comparison with the ancient Pueblo culture; whatever is cheap and ephemeral would be revealed. For Cather, Moonstone provides the same kind of test.

One other source of myth as background for Thea's strength remains to be examined briefly. All of the strands of the book are held together by stories of Teutonic myth, both Scandinavian and Germanic. These myths are much closer to the surface of the story, just as the myths themselves were more openly acknowledged in their time than were the myths of the mystery religions. As a member of the Kronborg family, Thea has a Swedish heritage, with strong traces of Norwegian traits. An early intimation of the Scandinavian myth comes with the name of her younger brother Thor, a name chosen often by Swedish parents to place their children under the protection of that strong god. Thor's connection with the charioteer of the gods is explicit from the time we see him in his baby buggy (described as a chariot) to his eventual career. His very destiny lies in his name; he was born a chauffeur, Dr. Archie says, before there were cars to drive. The Teutonic tone is further established by such small notes as the description of Thea's handwriting as "Gothic," the maid who is called "the Hun," Thea's operatic roles--her debut as a daughter of the Rhine, her triumph as Fricka--and Fred's comparison of her with the wild females of prehistoric Germany.

Fred, Thea's lover and eventually her husband, plays his own role as a figure of myth. He is introduced as a "gleaming, florid" young man with a blond curly beard like Odin's and golden hair that resembles the god's golden helmet. The cape he wears when he first appears recalls the Grecian robes on famous statues of Odin, those by Fogelbert and Freund, for example. Even the first syllables of his surname, Ottenburg, suggest Odin. The name Fred, carefully chosen from Old High German (Frederick means rich and powerful), is a name related like Odin's to the Scandinavian goddess Freya, whose traits are often mingled with those of Fricka. His mother's name, Katarina Furst, provides the royal background so necessary to a hero-god, and twice he is referred to as a prince. The fact that he is a beer prince relates him again to Odin, who was skilled in art and poetry because he knew the secret of making the divine hydromel, the mead of the poets. (Cather may also have thought of the hymn to an early mystery god that praised him for having quenched the thirst of initiates. The principle of moisture figures prominently in all mystery religions.) Odin's role as god of nocturnal storms is apparent during the storm scene in the canon. And, finally, Thea's great operatic role as Fricka foreshadows her marriage to Fred as Odin.

The characterizations of Thea and Fred as gods are supported at the end of the book by the brief presence of Oliver Landry, who immediately evokes the memory of Wunsch. His appearance in Wunsch's native land, his help with Thea's study of music and German language, his remarkably ruddy face, and his fondness for anything alcoholic all bring echoes of Thea's first teacher. Such an interpretation supports Thea's (and Cather's) insistence that events in life all come full circle. In the context of Germanic myth his features suggest one of the small creatures so numerous in the stories of Teutonic gods:

> He was undersized and clumsily made, with a red, shiny face and sharp little nose that looked as if it had been whittled out of wood and was always in the air, on the scent of something. Yet it was this queer little beak, with his eyes, that made his countenance anything of a face at all. . . . His dress seemed an acknowledgement of his grotesqueness: a short coat, like a little boy's roundabout, and vest fantastically sprigged and dotted, over a lavender shirt (*SL*,372).

His collection of treasures reminds us that the dwarfs were guardians of precious stones and metals, and animal figures like his amber elephant. Like the dwarfs, Landry functions as a household spirit, stretching out before the fire, following Fred about, and assisting Thea with her work. Companion gods who surrounded the early goddess, Neumann tells us, always appeared in the form of dwarfs,[23] and here Thea joins Alexandra, who was "surrounded by little men." Landry does much for the spirit and pace of the last episodes of *The Song of the Lark*, affirming the observation of psychologist Rollo May that the life of modern man is impoverished because of the absence of elves and dwarfs who enriched the imagination of earlier ages.

The description of Landry matches in many details the selection from Charles Kingsley's *The Roman and the Teuton* printed as Appendix 3 in *The Kingdom of Art* as source material for some of Cather's work. But, as usual, Cather has more than one source: her characterization of Oliver Landry matches, almost point for point, a description of elves in Jacob Grimm's *Teutonic Mythology*.[24] In Grimm's list of traits of elves they are good-natured and helpful, provide services to men, have knowledge of plants and stones and food and drink, hate agriculture, have a fondness for music and dance which links them with goddesses, and are able to disappear quickly. Cather adds some of the appearance of the home-sprites that Grimm includes: Landry's red hair and his red face resulting from erysipelas mark him as a home-sprite. He also has qualities of Loki, the bisexual guardian of a home, who was sometimes a fire-god. His name must be connected with the Old Norse *alfr* or *alfar*, which Grimm says means *genius* or *good spirit*, and with Loki's mother, whose name was Landry. Incredibly, Cather managed to work all of these descriptions into the very few lines that this character occupies in the story.

Jacob Grimm may well have given Cather more than simply the description for Landry. He wrote in his study of Teutonic myths that he believed myth to be the common property of many lands, that he found it significant that the Greek and Asiatic myths correspond to the Norse and Teutonic views. Then he speaks of the Orphic poets who spread the myths. A student of Vico's work, Grimm traces the way in which, in the Norse tales, "mythic traits get mysteriously intergrown with historic." From all these points of view, it is easy to see how Thea can be an opera singer modeled after the real Olive Fremstad, and Fricka, a traditional Teutonic goddess, as well as a goddess of the Dionysian cult. Fred can play his roles as a tycoon, as Odin at a second level, and still display characteristics of Dionysus at a third. In Cather's language, in Grimm's theories of myth, and in the Orphic philosophy, all the levels of meaning are applicable. Grimm's more important contribution to *The Song of the Lark* may have been a theme very closely related to the Orphic message:

> The sum total of well-being and blessedness, the fulness of all graces, seems in our ancient language to have been expressed by a single word, whose meaning has since been narrowed down; it was named *wunsch* (wish). This word is probably derived from *wunja, wunnja,* our *wonne,* bliss; *winisc, wunsc,* perfection in whatever kind, what we should call the Ideal.

Poets, he says, personify *wunsch,* a relic of the pagan religions and so significant even as a mere name in Norse mythology.[25] In almost all of Cather's novels, the word, often translated into the English *desire* as Wunsch has done, stands for the highest aspirations of the artist, the pioneer, and the seeker after religious truth.

The myths on the surface of this novel are, then, principally Scandinavian, and Thea thrives and succeeds in part because of her heritage and those close to her who share it--her family, Wunsch, Fred Ottenburg, Old Henry Biltmer, Oliver Landry. But in addition to that group a remarkable number of men of various backgrounds and abilities contribute to her success. Dr. Archie protects her both early and late in her life. Ray Kennedy of the "open American face" is sacrificed for her career; his insurance, left to her after his railroad accident, enables her to study music in Chicago. Through his sacrifice comes Thea's early recognition of the Orphic truth that there can be no life without death. Kennedy becomes a part of Thea--her *animus*--as her image blends with his in a dream. His name, too, is carefully chosen: again a name of Old German origin, it means "wise protector." Added to those who help Thea are two other music teachers, the Hungarian Harsanyi and the New Englander Bower, as well as the rich Jewish Nathanmeyers, and to a lesser degree, the Swedish minister, Mr. Larsen. Such conglomerate help for her career and personal growth supports her mother's belief, expressed early in the book, that immigration from many nations was a benefit to all on the frontier.

Another man contributes by teaching her the old folk music that "binds the human race together," as Cather describes it. After a visit to the Southwest she told her friend Elizabeth Sergeant of finding "a young Antinous of a singer from Vera Cruz." She was reminded of an antique sculpture by "his golden skin, his ancient race, his eyes with their tragic gleam." Being with him, she said, was like living in a classic age.[26] In *The Song of the Lark* he becomes Spanish Johnny, whose music adds spirit to Thea's voice and whose behavior confirms for her the existence of a second self in those endowed with talent. Thea's introduction to the culture of the Mexican people is a small initiation into the sensual meanings of music and the intercommunication between people that a love of music affords. Thea, wearing white, walks through an evening glowing with colors of copper, rose, and gold. She listens to the soft music that she prefers to church music and watches as the usual trio of young maidens in their white dresses dance. The young men find Thea's fair beauty of religious significance: "*Blanco y oro, semejante la Pascua!*" At midnight, they put out the lights and follow an old woman in a procession to a yard where Thea sits on a velvet coat with two young boys, called "los acolitos," placed on either side of her. Thea sings under the bright moon, as the Mexicans respond, one boy falling on his back in adoration, "looking at the moon, under the impression that he was still looking at Thea" (*SL*,210). Thea's voice is transformed for her listeners into its counterparts in nature--a goldfish in the water and a butterfly in the air. Such initiations come frequently in Thea's life; their importance is underscored by Cather's use of ritualistic scenes to structure her story.

The Song of the Lark must be considered in terms of the pastoral form. Certainly, the novel could be called a *saga*, merely the Old Norse word for story or legend. Stouck's discussion of the book as a complex *künstlerroman* is full and apt, with its picture of the artist as a special being, the struggle to achieve mastery, and the initiation rites necessary for success.[27] But there are several conventions and themes of the pastoral here that cannot be ignored. The novel contrasts, as do all pastorals, the merits of country life with hardships of the city, not through a dialogue between two characters, but through the experiences of the heroine in a rural setting, then in the city, and again in the countryside. The first summer scene in Moonstone is so charming that it reminds Thea of her favorite fairy tale; in stark contrast, the first scene in Chicago finds her riding in a street-car through the depressing city; later, as she arrives in the Indian canyon she returns to "the earliest sources of gladness that she could remember" (*SL*,266). The pastoral qualities of *The Song of the Lark* also include, and not incidentally, the role that song plays in its development, as in all of pastoral poetry. The shepherds of Greece and Rome really did sing as they worked, and the *Eclogues*, especially, are structured by singing matches of shepherds using their natural mode of expression.

The Orphic theme of the novel, however, is the critical connection with the pastoral mode. The figure of Orpheus is the symbol of the inspired poet throughout Virgil's *Eclogues*; the story of Orpheus and Euridyce is the subject of the fourth book of the *Georgics*; and the Orphic mysteries occur in the twenty-seventh *Idyll* of Theocritus. The pastoral poem most closely related to *The Song of the Lark*, however, is the third *Eclogue*, in which Virgil expands the limits of the form to examine the nature of art and raise it to a level of the divine, as Cather does in this novel. Both works are structured on the cycles of the natural world, both use vessels as symbols for man's creations (Virgil uses cups with the likeness of Orpheus; Cather uses Indian pots), and both connect nature and song to love. The themes of the Orphic mystery cult--creativity, the search for truth and beauty, the transcendence of the individual, his relation to the cosmos, and the promise of immortality-- are effectively expressed in the timeless settings of the pastoral, and the Virgilian models for manipulating these themes on several levels through the pastoral conventions served Cather well in this first stage of her novel cycle.

My Ántonia

My Ántonia, Willa Cather's third book with a frontier theme, continues the primitive conceptions of the earth, expresses more strongly an ambivalent attitude toward human relationships, and develops more fully several themes only suggested in *O Pioneers!*. Written in 1918, *My Ántonia* is, like *O Pioneers!*, descriptive of life on the prairie thirty years before. Ántonia Shimerda, an immigrant girl, is the protagonist; but Jim Burden, the narrator, is at least as important to the development of the story, and his affairs usurp the central part of the book, as do Emil's in the first novel. The characters of Jim and Ántonia are drawn in a kind of counterpoint, effectively contrasting the consequences of their differences in social status, education, behavior, and gender. The denouement that brings them together after many years emphasizes the almost relentless use of irony that is evident in *O Pioneers!* and that touches nearly every human destiny in *My Ántonia*. Ántonia, who has had little education and many struggles, is a happy, fulfilled woman; Jim, who has had every advantage, is a disappointed, lonely man. The story, however, is not just about them and their families and friends, but about their relation to the new land that is the American frontier. Jim's situation is described by his colleague who introduces the story: "He loves with a personal passion the great country through which his railway runs and branches. His faith in it and his knowledge of it have played an important part in its development" (*MA*,2). Ántonia is, on an allegorical level, the representative of the qualities of the land that Jim loves so much, and together they carry forth the story of the cycle of civilization that began with *O Pioneers!*.

My Ántonia begins with reminders of the unsettled land of that earlier novel with the young Jim's arrival in the utter darkness of a Nebraska night. Only men with lanterns provide light to see by, as humans were the only points of light for each other in the darkness of neolithic times. No roads lead the way, Jim notes; not even creeks or fields provide landmarks; it is not yet a country. The theme of the new land is followed in the same paragraph by a statement, spelled out carefully, of the other theme of the book, the spiritual destiny of the individual. Jim feels that here at this moment even the spirits of his dead mother and father are not present, that he as a person has been erased, that prayer is useless in this fatalistic world.

Life on the frontier is centered around hard work, crude surroundings, and the dynamics of immigrant settlement. Hardships are overwhelming, especially for the members of Ántonia's family, who live at first in a dugout described as no better than a badger hole. The uncivilized ways of living bring primordial attitudes toward the world. Winter itself seems to come down savagely on the prairie town, leaving warmth and food as the preoccupations of the inhabitants. Human life, seen in vegetation images, is "spread out shrunken and pinched, frozen down to the bare stalk" (*MA*,116). Conversely, Jim remembers the conformation of the land as if it were a human face. This childlike primeval philosophy ascribing personal life to nature is necessary to mythological development, according to Edward Tylor.[28]

The frontier struggle renews many other primitive responses in the people. As Jim explores his new home he thinks, "The light air about me told me that the world ended here: only the ground and sun and sky were left, and if one went a little further there would be only sun and sky, and one would float off into them" (*MA*,13). When a great circle where the Indians once rode shows a remarkably distinct pattern beneath the winter's first snow, Jim is strongly stirred by the figure and inexplicably considers it a good omen. To the ideas of early Europeans and American Indians, Jim adds his interpretation of nature in the light of Judeo-Christian mythology: in the afternoon sun, "the whole prairie was like the bush that burned with fire and was not consumed. . . . It was a sudden transfiguration, a lifting-up of day" (*MA*,28). Finally, an aura of ritual and magic serves to ennoble the memory of Ántonia's father after his suicide; although Mr. Shimerda has been buried at the crossroads after all the churches deny him Christian burial, Jim believes that the released spirit will find its way back to its native land--a thought that brings much comfort to Ántonia. These superstitions and elementary ways of thinking serve several purposes in the novel. They locate this story in the early stage of the Vichian cycle of cultural growth; they are important links between Europe and America, showing the continuity of thought, emotion, and the essential nature of man from generation to generation and from place to place. The reverence for trees, especially lindens, that persists in Marie's communication with them in *O Pioneers!*, in the festivals held by the Germans in *The Song of the Lark*, and Ántonia's love for trees as if they were people, repeats the animistic religious feeling of early agricultural societies.

The recapturing of the Hellenistic-like melting pot that seems so supportive of Thea's development is more problematic in *My Ántonia*. Even in the small settlement of Black Hawk, each national group has its own living area and its own church. The Old World conflicts between the Bohemians and the Austrians continue here, and the distrust of the Central Europeans by the Anglo-Saxons emerges whenever a disagreement arises. People are seldom named without identifying their nationalities, and all the stereotypes apply. Lena, a Norwegian girl, thinks her troubling seductiveness can be traced to a grandmother from Lapland: "They say Lapp blood will out" (*MA*,154). Thea's family has the problem of a strain of Norwegian blood that troubles each generation in one way or another. As a result of the bewildering heterogeneity on the frontier, the pressures to conform are strong and often successful. Crazy Ivar, afraid of being exiled because he is different, introduces the subject in *O Pioneers!* as he repeats an observation made by Crèvecoeur, "The way here is for all to do alike" (*OP*,55). Thea in *The Song of the Lark*, thinking of her addle-pated but loyal and intuitive aunt who is a counterpart of Ivar, admires older countries where dress and opinions and manners are less standardized. Jim's grandmother and other powers in Black Hawk impose a "respect for respectability" that holds desire in line for the upper class in this rigid prairie society. The Vichian collectivity of social and cultural life operates in all of Cather's frontier novels, to be challenged only by the exceptional individual. The tensions among the social strata and ethnic groups add to the hardships of frontier life and to the uncertainties of Jim's relationships.

The hired girls from the country prove to be one cohesive element in the social structure in Black Hawk, with their knowing ways, their supple bodies, and their beauty. The three Bohemian Marys, with their scandalous sexual behavior, are another of Cather's trinities; Tiny Soderball, Lena Lingard, and Ántonia form yet another. Cather may have remembered well her visit to Arles, where a festival is still held in honor of the triple goddess. All of these frontier goddesses share the wildness of the *Maenads*, but Lena, with her yellow hair, violet eyes, and constant miraculous whiteness in spite of exposure to the sun, plays the special role of the "white goddess." It is Lena who drives men a little daft, at one point commanding simultaneously the attentions of a college boy, a middle-aged violinist, and an elderly wealthy man. One farmer chases her about the fields until his wife follows with a knife, threatening Lena with dismemberment. Lena makes dancing a "waltz of coming home to something, of inevitable, fated return" (*MA*,142), and comes to Jim in a recurring erotic dream which identifies her as a fertility goddess, "flushed like the dawn, with a kind of luminous rosiness all about her" (*MA*,147). Contrasted with her is Ántonia, with skin, eyes, and hair all the color of the earth, marking her as a goddess of the earth, a role that she increasingly fills as the novel progresses.

The *Maenad* attitude of the girls rises to a pitch with the arrival of the blind pianist d'Arnault to play at the hotel in Black Hawk. The

possessor of a happy face and master of the Dionysian art of music, he
has a vitality that causes restlessness in the young people long after they
have first heard his music. Like the real-life prototype whose
performance Cather reviewed for the *Nebraska State Journal*, he seemed
to have the soul of a Beethoven in the body of an idiot. He realizes a
music that is barbarous and true, transferring his excitement to his
listeners. His appearance is germane: "He looked like some glistening
African god of pleasure, full of strong savage blood" (*MA*,123). The
music of the black god and the dancing of the white goddesses make
the "Hired Girls" chapter a frontier rhapsody that recalls the Dionysian
rituals of another age.

A less joyous primitive idea, the need for human sacrifice, recurs
throughout the book. The first sacrifice must be, as it is in *O Pioneers!*,
that of the European father, in order to allow the female rule in this
agricultural society. His death in winter, again like John Bergson's of
the earlier novel, is related to that ritual in which a corn goddess
mourns for a dead loved one representing the vegetation. As Ántonia
thinks of her father's death, she sees a "red streak of dying light, over
the dark prairie," and then the "empty darkness" of a matriarchal world
returns. Another death, which is specified as a sacrifice by Cather, is
recounted by Peter and Pavel, the bachelor brothers. In their youth in
Russia, while driving a wedding party in a sleigh, they had been
overtaken by wolves and decided to throw out the bride to lighten their
load. Ever after they had been known as the two men who had fed the
bride to the wolves. Occurring as it does in Russia, the sacrifice of the
woman shows the contrast of her role in the Old World with the vital
role she plays in the New. The religious significance as well is apparent
afterwards, as the first thing either of them had noticed was the sound
of the monastery bell ringing for early prayers. One other sacrifice has
as its basis the ancient fertility rites. A tramp who throws himself into
a threshing machine on the hottest day of the summer is a substitute for
the human whose body is dismembered and scattered through the fields
to insure the next year's crop. He recalls the tramp in *The Song of the
Lark* who drowns himself in the Moonstone reservoir at the same time
of year. In a female-dominated world, the sacrifice is male. A glance at
the chapter on dying and reviving gods in *The Golden Bough* shows
how widespread this custom was in early civilizations.

Those mythic and ritualistic themes are a prelude to the final book of
My Ántonia, apparently simple in its actions and characterizations, but
in fact complex in its simultaneous presentation of daily existence on

the frontier and of one of the oldest fertility rituals known. "Cuzak's Boys" recreates in both meaning and structure the Eleusinian mysteries observed by the Greeks before the eighth century B.C., probably by the Mycenaeans before them, and by the Romans long after. Earlier scenes introduce Ántonia's representation of the earth mother. That she symbolizes allegorically the early Western frontier society is most clearly seen when Jim Burden thinks, "It is no wonder that her sons stood tall and straight. She was a rich mine of life, like the founders of early races." On the psychological level, her meaning is yet more explicit: "She lent herself to immemorial human attitudes which we recognize as universal and true" (*MA*,226). And further, she has religious import--the ability to reveal the meaning of everyday life. On all these levels, it is Ántonia's relation to the land that invests her with significance. The earth goddess motif builds to those rituals of the final chapter through parallels between Ántonia's story and Persephone's, beginning with the "marriage of death." Ántonia's abortive alliance with Larry Donovan, her reunion with her mother, the birth of her child, her later fecundity all connect her story with ancient myth. That story, recounted in the Homeric "Hymn to Demeter," assigned to the seventh century B.C., tells of the corn goddess who, having lost her daughter Persephone to the god of the underworld, wanders through the land carrying a torch in search of her. During the time of the search her gift of fertility is withheld from the earth, threatening famine. At Eleusis, disguised as an old woman, Demeter commands the people to build her a sanctuary where she can conduct the rites of her mysteries of fertility and immortality. The famine is dispelled as Persephone is allowed to spend part of the time on earth with her mother, part of the time in the underworld.

On this myth, or rather these several myths, were based the rites of the Eleusinian mysteries which were celebrated in the ancient world for perhaps two thousand years. What occurred precisely at Eleusis and the other sites of initiation may never be fully known; through the centuries the initiates of the cult seem to have taken seriously the proscription against revealing the secret meanings of the mysteries. But from many sources, ancient and modern, among them Plato's *Phaedrus*, Aristophanes' *The Frogs*, and works of Herodotus, Aristotle, Apuleius, and later the analyses of Harrison, Cumont, Murray, and others, scholars had reconstructed before 1912 a sequence of events that took place during the celebrations. The "Hymn to Demeter" is a useful source, not only for descriptions of the rituals, but also for the parallels with the

Iliad, the *Odyssey,* and the works of Hesiod in language, style, meter, and especially myths. Because the Eleusinian mysteries were the best known of all the rites, the descriptions of them are more complete than those of other mysteries, and although they vary, a basic pattern emerges in most studies. One of the earliest is Andrew Lang's account in his introduction to the 1899 translation of the *Homeric Hymns.* In his version the fertility goddess sits in her winter retreat below the earth where she is the "ruler of men outworn." The festival in her honor, according to Lang, includes many rites: a mystery play about the sacred legend, fastings, vigils, sacrifices, sacred objects displayed, sacred words uttered. This general outline finds agreement among nearly all authors who write about the ritual.

All agree that the Eleusinian mysteries were celebrated first on the Rarian plain near Athens in an agrarian festival honoring the goddess of fertility. That great ancient and beautiful space provides clues to the importance and meaning of the cultic rites to Greek society and other parts of the Hellenistic world. First in the sequence came the lesser mysteries at Agra in the spring to tell the story of Persephone's abduction and to celebrate her return from the underworld--preliminary instruction for the initiates in the knowledge to be imparted at the principal ritual in the fall. Such preparation is at the very core of the initiation; only those who have first been prepared by some rites of purification are admitted to the mysteries. Thus qualified, the initiates were ready to participate in the greater mysteries during the month of Boedromion, corresponding to our September and the beginning of October, the time of autumnal sowing in Greece. On the nineteenth the neophytes were led in a lengthy procession along the sacred way to Eleusis. There the first event after their arrival was the sacrifice of a pig, which was later buried in a subterranean chasm. The initiates then entered the *telestrion,* the sanctuary of Demeter, where in darkness and in complete silence they witnessed the sacred rites.

The ritual proper consisted of several parts, all mystical performances celebrating the "religion of nature," which to the early Greeks and Romans demonstrated the unity of man's life with the vegetative and animal world. One segment was the *legomena,* a kind of discourse whose chief purpose was to announce the birth of a divine child. Short liturgical utterances may have been included. Although it is not always possible to distinguish the second segment, the *dromena,* from the whole of the ritual, its function was dramatic--the presentation of a pageant depicting symbolically events in the story of Demeter and

Persephone. At the close of this part of the initiation, a door was opened to reveal the *anaktoron*, the smaller room with the *telestrion* where objects sacred to the goddesses were stored. This part of the ritual, called the *deikymena*, was conducted in total silence on the part of both the initiate and those representing the deities. Only when all these devotions had been observed could the initiate enter into the *epopteia*, the highest stage of initiation, again a revelation in silence--the reaping of an ear of corn in a blaze of light, according to Hippolytus, the writer of the early Christian era. Following this most sacred core of the ritual, the votaries emerged to complete the long celebration with song and dance, further torchlight processions, and a sacramental meal.

The meanings of this symbolism seem rather obscure even to those scholars willing to grope for them. Aside from a vague idea of the identity of the human soul with the natural cycle of the seasons, little of the significance of the Eleusinian mysteries has been explained. Erwin Rohde attempts some explanation in *Psyche: The Cult of Soul and Belief in Immortality among the Greeks:*

> In some way or other the *Mystae* must have had revealed to them the real meaning of the "nature-symbolism" hidden in the mystical performances. Witnessing these performances they are supposed to have learnt that the fate of the seed of corn, represented by Persephone, its disappearance beneath the earth and eventual rebirth, is an image of the fate of the human soul, which also disappears that it may live again. This, then, must be the real content of the holy Mystery.[29]

But even Rohde agrees that this is only the vaguest of generalities. Although the poets and artists may have revealed many of the events of the initiations and archaeologists may have reconstructed many of the rites in their physical surroundings, the core meanings of the mysteries at Eleusis seem to have been kept a secret indeed. And yet to recognize the epiphany undergone by Jim Burden in the final scenes of *My Ántonia* is to realize that this kind of religious experience cannot be articulated.

Of primary importance is the fact that these are matriarchal mysteries, and as such differ in purpose and structure from patriarchal mysteries more familiar to modern man. The primordial feminine mysteries are mysteries of birth and rebirth, chthonic in their nature, and relying more on the intuitive and less on the rational and communicable. This feminine symbolism signals the matriarchal mysteries, regardless of whether those initiated are men or women. Jim's final thought in *My Ántonia* reflects his experience: Whatever we had missed, we possessed together the precious, the incommunicable past." His initiation demonstrates to him that only through Ántonia and the symbols surrounding her can he understand an important part of his world, but just what he understands is too large to be precisely articulated. He can only say of Ántonia, "She still had that something which fires the imagination, could still stop one's breath for a moment by a look or gesture that somehow revealed the meaning of common things. She had only to stand in the orchard, to put her hand on a little crab tree and look up at the apples, to make you feel the goodness of planting and tending and harvesting at last" (*MA*,227). However penumbral this may be, it is undeniable that Jim experiences a spiritual transformation and that the mystical depth of his experience has great impact on many readers. Together Jim and the reader have been initiated into the mysteries of Eleusis.

Jim's initiation begins, properly enough, with instruction to prepare him for the principal ritual. Here, the "lesser mysteries" are imparted during his visit to the Widow Steavens where she tells him of Ántonia's "marriage of death." Even as he approaches Mrs. Steavens' farm, his observations are filled with images of fertility appropriate to the mysteries. The link with the classical era in which those mysteries were celebrated is provided by the reference to her massive head, so like a Roman senator's, and the ritualistic setting is sketched as she places a lamp in a corner of the room and turns it low, then sits formally in her rocking chair to deliver her information. The ritual implications are explicit here: "She crossed her hands in her lap and sat as if she were at a meeting of some kind." She tells Jim of Ántonia's departure on a cold, raw night from Black Hawk to be the bride of a railroad conductor, who later runs to "Old Mexico"--Ántonia refers to it as "down there"--when he and his fellow conductors are described as evil men. The allusions serve to identify Ántonia's would-be bridegroom with the underworld and hence with the drama of Persephone. Ántonia returns during a lovely warm May, wearing the veils that often distinguish statues of the earth goddess in classical sculpture. The strongest echo of the Demeter and Persephone myth, however, is Mrs. Steavens' strangely worded comments at the end of her story: "Jimmy, I sat right down on that bank beside her and made lament." At this point she is the ancient *mater dolorosa*, the mother mourning the abduction of her daughter, just as later Ántonia mourns the loss of her own daughter, even to a happy marriage: "I cried like I was putting her into her coffin." The cyclical pattern underlying the message of the mysteries is prominent in this episode, as in the whole of the novel.

Jim's preparation for the greater mysteries is completed when he visits Ántonia immediately after his conversation with Mrs. Steavens. The end of that meeting is marked by the kind of light symbolism mentioned by nearly everyone who has described the events at Eleusis: "In that singular light every little tree and shock of wheat, every sunflower stalk and clump of snow-on-the-mountain, drew itself up high and pointed; the very clods and furrows in the fields seemed to stand up sharply. I felt the old pull of the earth, the solemn magic that comes out of those fields at nightfall." As the sky darkens, Jim searches Ántonia's face, the "closest, realest face, under all the shadows of women's faces, at the very bottom of my memory." In those phrases can be discovered the two important meanings of the novel relating it to the Eleusinian mysteries--the supremacy of the female who is allied with nature and the depth of the racial memory.

The emphasis throughout the book is on Ántonia: as Cather told her friend Elizabeth Sergeant, she meant Ántonia to *be* the story. As in other early Cather novels, the woman remains rooted in her country, while the man travels; the woman is content with things of the earth, while the man seeks intellectual activity; the woman finds spiritual fulfillment, while the man fails spiritually. The male, then, must be taught the feminine secrets, just as we know he was initiated into the ancient Greek mysteries. "Happy is he among men upon earth who has seen these mysteries," the Homeric "Hymn to Demeter" tells us. Man's experience at Eleusis, Neumann says in *The Great Mother*, was predominantly emotional and unconscious as he "sought to identify himself with Demeter, i.e., with his own feminine aspect," or the *anima*, in Jungian terms.[30] In *My Ántonia* this identification actually takes place before the celebration of the mysteries, during the first of two visits Jim pays to Ántonia. He tells her: "I'd have liked to have you for a sweetheart, or a wife, or my mother or my sister--anything that a woman can be to a man. The idea of you is a part of my mind; you influence my likes and dislikes, all my tastes, hundreds of times when I don't realize it. You really are a part of me" (*MA*,206). And for Ántonia Jim is the masculine principle within--the *animus*. Even if he never returns, she tells him, he's there with her. During this exchange, nature herself blends male and female principles. Jim recalls:

> As we walked homeward across the fields, the sun dropped and lay like
> a great golden globe in the low west. While it hung there, the moon rose
> in the east, as big as a car-wheel, pale silver and streaked with rose colour,
> thin as a bubble or a ghost-moon. For five, perhaps ten minutes, the
> luminaries confronted each other across the level land, resting on opposite
> edges of the world (*MA*,206).

The awareness that each is irrefragably bound to the other is the most
significant development of the informal preparation for the rites to
follow.

   Jim's visit to Ántonia and her family twenty years later repeats rather
precisely the ceremony at Eleusis, as far as it is known. As he enters
the grounds, two of Ántonia's sons are examining their dead dog, the
equivalent of the animal sacrifice at Eleusis and a reminder that a
ceremony of resurrection must include a recognition of death. The boys
follow Jim's buggy solemnly to the house. After opening the gate for
him, another boy ties his team with a flourish and two girls welcome
him into the house. Ántonia's appearance on the scene overwhelms Jim:
"The miracle happened; one of those quiet moments that clutch the
heart, and take more courage than the noisy, excited passages in life."

   There follow in rapid succession the segments of the rituals at
Eleusis. First the *legomena*, or discourse, takes the form of an
introduction to Ántonia's children, especially to Leo, the favorite who
represents the divine child, a view he himself apparently shares. His
awareness of his "secret," his power of enjoyment, his intuitive
recognitions, and most of all his animal-like appearance all point to him
as one of those happy rural deities of the classical era. (Ántonia's
grandson, too, shares in her glory; although he is not divine, he is called
"a little prince.") In the *legomena*, the liturgical element is merely
suggested by Leo's well-rehearsed reply to his mother's question about
his age and by the girls' response of "mother" in unison as Ántonia
declares that she loves this child best. The second segment of the
ceremony, the *dromena*, or dramatic re-enactment, involves Leo, who,
beckoned by Ántonia, fearfully tells her softly in Bohemian about the
dead dog, while she soothes him. She later whispers to him a secret
promise which he in turn whispers to his sister.

   The next part of the ritual, the *deikymena*, or display of sacred
objects, becomes in the frontier version a descent to the fruit cave of the
farm. Each child very proudly shows some of the barrels and jars of
preserved food, maintaining the silence of the Eleusinian rites: "Nina

and Jan, and a little girl named Lucie, kept shyly pointing out to me the shelves of glass jars. They said nothing, but, glancing at me, traced on the glass with the fingertips the outline of the cherries and strawberries and crabapples within, trying by a blissful expression of countenance to give me some idea of the deliciousness." The blissful expressions lead us to reflect that on the Divide such secrets held almost religious import; on their mastery depended the very survival of that civilization. In the course of the ritual, Ántonia and Jim next ascend the stairs of the cave first, and here Jim's revelation, the *epopteia*, begins. The children follow them: "They all came running up the steps together, big and little, tow heads and gold heads, and brown, and flashing little naked legs; a veritable explosion of life out of the dark cave into the sunlight. It made me dizzy for a moment." The identification of Ántonia's children with the vegetative world, particularly the sacred ears of corn, is complete at this point. As Jim later reflects on this experience, he says, "That moment, when they all came tumbling out of the cave into the light, was a sight any man might have come far to see. Ántonia had always been one to leave images in the mind that did not fade--that grew stronger with time" (*MA*,218).

Even the transformation scene--that blaze of visible and intuitive light so prominent in the literature of the mysteries and the basis for the climax of the "Hymn to Demeter"--is included. In the hymn, before Demeter and her daughter vanish, the bare leafless expanse of the Eleusinian plain is suddenly turned, at the will of the goddess, into a vast sheet of ruddy corn. In the novel Ántonia takes Jim through the orchard, where "the afternoon sun poured down on us through the drying grape leaves. The orchard seemed full of sun, like a cup. . . ." Every tree, every fruit, even the ducks reflect this light. As Ántonia tells of her life on the frontier, she looks through the orchard, "where the sunlight was growing more and more golden." Jim's initiation into "that mystery of mysteries which it is meet to call the most blessed" is consummated as the skies shine their approval; there remains only the post-ceremonial merrymaking. At the feast, instead of the sacred cakes and *kykeon* of the Greeks, the celebrants dine on milk and *kolaches*, called "resurrection bread" still by Middle European bakers. All eyes are excitedly on Ántonia during the dinner, and carrying the lamp she leads the party in a re-enactment of the torchlight procession into the parlor where the children provide the musical entertainment. To the very last event, the rites on the Cuzak farm have paralleled the sequence of the Eleusinian mysteries.

In her vision of Nebraska Willa Cather has offered unsuspected meaning through those parallels between Eleusis and the frontier. Of even greater significance to the novel is the presentation of Ántonia as a goddess-woman--that female who is "no less a marvel than the universe itself," in Campbell's words. This stage of civilization is later than the early agricultural era of *O Pioneers!*, and so Ántonia's role is different from Alexandra's. Jane Ellen Harrison points out that "Demeter is not the Earth Mother, not the goddess of the earth in general, but the fruits of the civilized, cultured earth, the *tilth*; not the 'Lady of the Wild Things,' but 'She-who-bears-fruits.'"[31] Ántonia is a true fertility goddess.

Many critics have decided that Jim Burden's description of his own writing--the "thing about Ántonia"--applies to this novel as well: "I didn't take time to arrange it; I simply wrote down pretty much all that her name recalls to me. I suppose it hasn't any form" (*MA*,2). Other critics have found form; Stouck calls *My Ántonia* a "pastoral of innocence," and Randall traces its classical pastoral background; Slote and Robert Scholes relate it to the epic, particularly the *Odyssey*. Those are especially useful ways to analyze the novel, but the context of the mystery religions can provide additional vital meaning, as it did for the writers of the classical pastoral. Quite apparently *My Ántonia* encompasses the pastoral themes--the return to one's origins, the memory of childhood experiences, the contrasts between city and country life, deliberate and sophisticated simplicity, and a clarity of feeling brought by a view from a distance. Although the third book of Virgil's *Georgics* is mentioned several times by Jim in the chapter on Lena Lingard, it is the seventh *Idyll* of Theocritus that offers several points of comparison for Cather's novel. Some writers have found the major question of *My Ántonia* to be either the true nature or the precise role of Jim as the narrator, just as a major question of *Idyll* 7 is often the identity of Lycidas. The allegorical qualities of that idyll were long ignored, as have been those of this novel. The structure of *My Ántonia* can be explained by the pastoral form that goes beyond the superficial use of conventions to that level where the "pen was fitted to the matter as the plough is to the furrow" (*MA*,170). That Cather understood the subtleties of the pastoral form, especially as they carry a mythic message, can be shown by a comparison of *My Ántonia* with the seventh *Idyll*. Charles Segal reveals this pastoral poem as an extraordinary masterpiece that can be enjoyed for the beauty of its surface meaning as well as for its complex symbolism and structure. Theocritus, he says, "balances contemporary allusion and ancient myth, humor and erudition, sophistication and naïveté, city and country." His essay provides information for an analysis of *My Ántonia* which suggests not only that Cather drew much of her material for her novel from *Idyll* 7, but that she also created a work with many of the same qualities.

The idyll, like the novel, is an agricultural story reflecting a later stage of cultural development than do the more primitive pastorals. Theocritus, like Cather, shows us the bucolic world through the eyes of a sophisticated narrator, who is further removed because he is recollecting events in his past. In both works a frame introduces the story, forcing yet another step back in perspective. We are aware that we see not Ántonia, but only Jim's Ántonia, filtered through his consciousness, as the explanation of the title in the frame so clearly tells us. The *My* added by Jim to the *Ántonia* signifies a stage in the development of the masculine personality when a feminine, sisterly element can be added as "my beloved" or "my soul." Jim confesses that Ántonia has become a part of him, that the idea of her is a part of his mind, even before his final visit to her. His initiation into the mysteries follows some of the rites whose purpose included the transformation of the male initiate into the higher man. That same extension of the self outward by Simichidas, the city man, is an important part of the structure of the idyll.

At the very center of the poem, Segal says, is the tale of Comatas, a "divine" goatherd, an archetype behind the Lycidas agricultural figure, whose divinity is also suggested. Cather has changed these two male figures into female characters of Lena and Ántonia, but otherwise they have much in common with the characters of Theocritus. Lena's story occupies the third book of five in *My Ántonia*; she is divine as a goddess figure and at the same time a herdsman. Ántonia is a major goddess and a farmer. As Segal says of Comatas and Lycidas, both are associated with sweetness (Lena is "a sweet creature" and bees swarm above Ántonia); both recline (Lena is supine under an oak tree or propped up on a couch and Ántonia rests against an oak); and both have toiled (Lena describes in some detail her youthful labor and Ántonia is "worked down" at twenty-four). There are far too many correspondences to consider them casual similarities. Others include discussions of constellations, graves, and ways in which order is imposed on nature by the human hand.

The motif of the journey is important to both works, and operates on several levels in both the idyll and the novel. At the level of the author's own life, it represents, Segal says, an attempt to explore the nature and origins of his inspiration to write pastoral poetry. Then, it relates the encounter of the city dweller to the ancient myths of finding an unknown realm. The model for this journey in Theocritus is the *Odyssey*, to which the idyll specifically refers, and to which Cather's critics often compare *My Ántonia*. Finally, the journey of the city dweller to the country heightens the tone of irony, so important to the pastoral genre; here the uneducated rustic is the one who has the valuable information. The journey as symbol is emphasized in both the idyll and the novel by a connection between the beginning and the end. Jim Burden's cyclical progress begins with his arrival on the train and continues with his pursuit of Cleric and his cross-country train trips as a railroad lawyer. Segal calls the relation of the end of the novel to the beginning a "carefully contrived" one. Such contrivance explains the early attention to Jim's protector, a friendly conductor who is worldly and had been almost everywhere: his rings, pins, badges, and cuff-buttons, engraved with hieroglyphics recalling an Egyptian obelisk, can only be interpreted as symbols of secret societies such as the Freemasons, and prefiguring in the novel the mystery rites from which the societies borrowed their rituals.

Both the idyll and the novel can be read on many levels, the symbolism so complex and complete that they become allegorical. To say that is not to suggest a simple correspondence of a character with a single quality or idea, but rather to trace a broader meaning beyond the literal one--the difference that Segal makes between "static" and "dynamic" symbolism. Thus Theocritus makes the farmer Lycidas a god, an aspect of himself as poet, and a symbol of pastoral inspiration; Cather makes the farmer Ántonia a fertility goddess, a spiritual guide for Jim, and a symbol of the strength of the American frontier. The multiple levels of meaning are reinforced in *Idyll* 7 and in *My Ántonia* by references to Homer beyond those to the *Odyssey* as model, especially through Cather's use of Homeric pauses--legends that seem to interrupt the narrative, yet strongly reinforce the theme or emotion of the main story. Two versions of this technique are the stories of Blind d'Arnault's inspired music and the sacrifice of the bride to the wolves by the Russians Peter and Pavel.

At least one major allusion to Hesiod is important: both poem and novel are stories of initiation into the realm of the muses. As David Stouck has concluded, the dramatic turning point in the novel comes in Jim's successive interviews in his rooms with his professor Gaston

Cleric, and Lena Lingard.[32] Cather prepares us for the memorable scenes by describing Jim's study, with its map of ancient Rome and picture of the Tragic Theatre at Pompeii and a carefully chosen high-backed upholstered chair that both guests use as they instruct him about the meaning of his adult life. Cleric comes first to recall antique life and especially the sea temples at Paestum, where the two most impressive Doric temples housed the Great Goddess in days of Greek conquest--a scene that Cather may have known from her visit to Naples. Cleric then talks about poetry--Dante and his "sweet teacher" Virgil, the "divine flame" that had sparked later poetry, and Jim makes the connection between those things and the people and symbols about him, especially the image of the plough against the sun. That visit is followed by the appearance of Lena, who becomes in this chapter a "sweet creature," whose teaching rivals that of Virgil in Jim's young life. She sits in the same chair occupied by Cleric and, like the Nymphs who instruct in *Idyll* 7, through her mundane conversation she leads Jim to understand the relation between the hired girls and the poetry of Virgil: "If there were no girls like them in the world, there would be no poetry."

The immediate meaning of this revelation, as Jim calls it, seems to be that the young goddesses of desire are the muses of poetry, the immediate inspiration for the poet to write. The pastoral form as an exploration of the nature and inspiration of poetry, however, has more to offer as explanation. Certainly, for Jim the girls are not muses, since he says he will not become a poet, or even think like one. Here again, Segal's explication of the idyll illumines the novel: the poetry and mythology in the song of Lycidas place his love into a larger setting and thereby master his passion. The serenity of nature and the beauties of poetry can transfigure the world and "heal the passion-vexed soul"--a goal that poetry shares with the philosophy of the mystery religions. The revelation frees Jim to follow Cleric (and his own destiny) to Harvard.

In her borrowing from ancient pastorals, Cather used the symbols of the myths and mysteries--frequent journeys, hopeless love, sheltered gardens and groves, divine epiphanies, death and rebirth. Her allusions to the classical myths are interesting but perfunctory directional signals for her readers; it is in her use of the mysteries that she penetrates the realm of the true power of myth, in the tradition of the great ancient poets who were her teachers.

3

The Memory of Our Vanished Kingdom:
The Age of Heroes

Visiting France in 1920 to complete *One of Ours*, the novel that was to win her a Pulitzer Prize, Willa Cather refused to present any of her letters of introduction to her French contemporaries, and firmly announced that she wanted to live in the Middle Ages. Her interest in that historical period is abundantly apparent in *One of Ours* and *A Lost Lady*, her two novels that pattern the second stage of the Vichian cycle--the age of heroes. After her early agricultural novels with three goddess figures as protagonists, she now continues the cycle with a pair of leading characters, a male and then a female, to embody the ideas of the American West. In this second stage the two novels employ medieval backgrounds and allusions along with the other characteristics Vico describes as cultural developments in heroic ages. Government has evolved into aristocratic commonwealths; in place of interpretation by mystical wise men, the law follows literally and precisely what is set forth in the text; the nature of men makes them heroic creatures; their customary behavior is passionate and punctilious; language moves from hieroglyphics or sacred language to symbolic language and natural descriptions. Through the heroic figure of Claude Wheeler in *One of Ours* and Marian Forrester of *A Lost Lady* and the males surrounding her, Cather presents what E. M. W. Tillyard calls "faithful correlations of an historical epoch." The elegant essay on Cather in the eleventh edition of the *Encyclopaedia Britannica* recognizes her still incomplete cycle of civilization, calling it "Spenglerian." At this point in her work, the West had "passed through the creature stage of culture into the stage of reflection and material comfort." The future could be only decline.

"In Nebraska, as in so many other states," Cather wrote, "we must face the fact that the splendid story of the pioneers is finished, and that no new story worthy to take its place has yet begun."[1] In the second stage of her novels, her goddess-women of the first three novels are replaced by less powerful but still heroic figures who have some leadership ability, but who lack the magic to transform the people and landscape about them. The moral victory that Cather found in the attainment of prosperity was marred by its ugly side, materialism, which both Claude Wheeler of *One of Ours* and Marian Forrester of *A Lost Lady*, in spite of their admirable qualities, can do little to combat, as they display weaknesses and uncertainties not evident in Alexandra, Thea, and Ántonia, the protagonists of the novels of the early frontier.

One of Ours

The heroic age in the United States, corresponding to the comparable periods of Augustan Rome and of medieval Europe, in these two novels begins in Cather's cycle with the first World War in *One of Ours*. The marks of civilization that dominate this book are those usually connected with the male consciousness, including war itself. The actual conflict that began in 1914 brought great distress to Cather, as Elizabeth Sergeant reports, "soon tore her apart. . . . and loomed to her historic sense as the most important event since the French Revolution."[2] Cather had said that when a woman wrote a manly battle yarn she would begin to hope for something great from female writers (*W&P*,1:227). But instead of describing merely the bravery and honor of combat from the perspective of one side, as did many male writers in their typical war novels, she supplied a dialectic about the purpose or purposelessness of war, and--following Michelet's methods in his history of the French Revolution--allowed her characters to question its glory. This objective placed her in opposition to the contemporary popular support in the United States for the "war to end all wars." For those choosing an easy interpretation of a hero's idealized sacrifice, Cather's surface story accommodated their reading; but in fact a deft use of irony underlies and inverts the traditional story of the hero's triumph. Just as the wasteland theme must be placed alongside our stories of Camelot and knighthood, it balances--perhaps even controls--Cather's story of one of *our* heroes.

Claude Wheeler, brought up on a prosperous farm, questions and challenges commonly accepted events and attitudes in the masculine world of his time, particularly those derived from the materialism rampant in the country. The intrinsic value of the farmer's crop is contrasted with the shoddy goods for which it is exchanged, just as the strength and longevity of the farmer's horse is contrasted with the unreliable machine. Machinery causes even personal problems for Claude beyond the mere waste of resources when he is injured because a truck spooks his mules, and later when his wife Enid escapes the sexual intimacies of marriage by driving about the countryside in her automobile. An even stronger mechanistic image is that of the train on Claude's wedding night, with all its suggestions of sterility. More generally, prosperity in this novel fosters a sense of callousness toward the land and indifference toward individuality. Claude's older brother, the "narrow-gauge" Bayliss, is the ultimate salesman as the owner of a farm implement store; his younger brother, Ralph, is the ultimate consumer. Their conflicts reveal a kinship eroded by the accumulation and idolatry of wealth. Accompanying the materialism is a secularism apparent throughout the male segment of society and participated in by Claude himself. That the land has lost its hold on the mind and heart of the hero is revealed with Claude's dream in France of brown furrows of earth stretching to the horizon, which for him is a frightening prospect; the nearly identical dream of Jim Burden at the end of *My Ántonia* brings a sense of fulfillment. Perhaps as a result of the lack of spiritual goals, Claude is the first of Cather's protagonists to experience the alienation that pervades the novels of the second and third stages of her cycle. Lacking strong relationships with others through love or religion or common purpose, he is left to discover meaning through a search for self, an obviously painful, unproductive process through much of the book.

Cather further develops this second cyclical stage by many references to the correspondences between the medieval period and the emerging culture in the American West. The year of the publication of *One of Ours*, 1922, was the time when Cather stated that the world had broken in two, and, in fact, the dualism long associated with the Middle Ages pervades this novel and the three that follow. The polar opposites of good and evil, body and soul, life and death, faith and works control the thoughts of the characters. In one scene, as his mother reads from "Paradise Lost," Claude observes that Milton needed the wicked to make his books interesting, that even in the Bible only the sinners are interesting characters, and that from the Jewish point of view, even

Christ is a dangerous criminal. Claude's attention to evil gains intensity
when atrocities of the war make him realize that "something new, and
certainly evil, was at work among mankind" (*OO*,138). For his
intellectual training he must choose between two opposites--the dreary,
uninspiring "Temple" denominational college or the state university,
with its instruction in the arts and its enthusiasm for athletic recreation--
which parallel the rival medieval Universities of Bologna and Paris, or
even the competing theological and liberal arts faculties at the
University of Paris.[3] Claude's joyless brother Bayliss objects to athletics,
as did the clergy at the medieval universities; his mother has a medieval
attitude toward education in general: "The history of the human race, as
it lay behind one, was already explained; and so was its destiny, which
lay before. The mind should remain obediently within the theological
concept of history" (*OO*,23). Claude, however, dismissing Christian
theology as too full of evasion and sophistries, manages to enroll in a
course in European history at the state university, where he writes his
thesis on Joan of Arc, pointing to his rebellion against received ideas,
to his interest in France, and to the book's connection with the Middle
Ages. His most spirited response is to the idea that a character can be
born again in every generation, an idea that Cather may well have
borrowed from Michelet's beautiful *Jeanne d'Arc*, which revealed the
ten years he had spent reconstructing the tradition of the Middle Ages
and finding that period filled with the same restlessness and doubts that
Claude responds to. After describing his image of the Maiden, Claude
recalls Gibbon, to reinforce the underlying cyclical history and the idea
of the heroic age on the Western frontier.

The literary background of *One of Ours* is closely related to the
medieval epoch and the heroic mode. The shift is from the feminine
pastoral to the masculine epic, from the cyclical and mystical to the
linear and highly symbolic. There is a simultaneous change from the
feminine timelessness of the three early novels to a masculine
temporality. In this book, epic conventions are observed, oblique
references to earlier epics are frequent (Claude's transport ship, for
example, is named *Anchises*), names and events are freely borrowed
from classical epics (after an exceptionally bloody battle, Claude and his
troops, like Odysseus and his men, sit down to a satisfying meal).
Countless references to the epic, to heroes, to the heroic stage of
civilization--in Greece, Scandinavia, Western Europe--add to the heroic
milieu of *One of Ours*.

It was almost inevitable that Cather would cast her war novel into the form of epic, the secular literary form so popular in the Middle Ages, and one that reflected the political and historical realities of its time. Stouck labels this book a satirical novel, as of course it is; but as Tillyard points out, prose fiction had begun to be the best epic medium by the eighteenth century. Cather combines the suitable epic conventions with the novel form, as she had previously used elements of the pastoral. The Parsifal theme, especially, becomes more significant as the wasteland theme emerges in the novel, and more interesting as the Claude's story departs from the medieval and Wagnerian versions. He is clearly an epic hero: he "sleeps like the heroes of old"; he behaves like the hero of the *Odyssey*; his ideas are described as "Quixotic"; the references to the classical periods are reminders that this is an "ageless" story. Very early in the novel Claude is called a "mortal fool," identifying him with Parsifal; his realization that he is "tongue-tied" as he tries to participate in French discourse relates further to Parsifal's story. It is reasonable to consider the ideal of France as his holy grail and materialism as the mighty wound of his father, whom he fights to save along with his country. And small charming touches, such as the garden behind fortress walls where women provide important information, come directly from Wagner's "Parsifal." Some of the elements of the story are taken specifically from the *Perceval or Le Conte de Graal* of Chrétien de Troyes of the twelfth century. The male sun figure and the feminine moon figure, used several times in *One of Ours*, are his invention. A case can be made that the hero's relationship with his mother in *One of Ours* is a major part of the story, and that, as in the *Perceval*, the Grail is a feminine mother-symbol.[4] Claude's last word in his country is "Mother"; the dying soldier Tannhauser utters his last words, *"Mein arme mutter"*; the final scene in the book has Mahailey calling Mrs. Wheeler, "Mudder." Chrétien's work is especially strong in the attempt to examine the interior development of the hero. This, says Heer, is the literature of "wisdom": "danger, temptation, error, sinning, lack of purpose, and lack of achievement are all necessary if the inner core of a man's personality is to be truly and effectively unlocked."

But *One of Ours* departs from some of the main themes of the Parsifal story: Parsifal earns the love of a beautiful queen; Claude's marriage is part of his defeat rather than his victory; Parsifal survives his battle to become guardian of the Grail, and Claude perishes; Parsifal goes forth to save the wounded and impotent King Anfortas, and Claude struggles to save only his own soul. This last departure may be most indicative of the ironic twist to Cather's story, since Claude is the one wounded in what he considers a fateful, if mundane, accident, and the meaning of his name—"lame"—is like the meaning of Anfortas—"infirm." The ironies of the correspondences between the two stories show that more is meant than mere identification of a modern soldier with an earlier hero figure.

Typical of Cather's stories, this one has parallels with more than one source that are too compelling to ignore. *The Song of Roland*, a *chanson de geste* predating the medieval epic poem, yields many comparisons with *One of Ours*: the idealized French background; the indictment of German savagery and barbarism; the friendship of two knights, Roland and Oliver, so like that of Claude and David Gerhardt; and the heroes' deaths on the battlefield. The French landscape at times dominates the *chanson*; it also signifies in this novel, objectifying Claude's new sense of joy and power in the world even in the midst of the horrors of war: "Perfect bliss," he reflected. "To be so warm, so dry, so clean, so beloved!" (That the name *David* means "beloved" is notably relevant.)

> The journey down, reviewed from here, seemed beautiful. As soon as they had got out of the region of martyred trees, they found the land of France turning gold. . . . It all flashed back beside his pillow in the dark: this beautiful land, this beautiful people, this beautiful omelette; gold poplars, blue-green vineyards, wet, scarlet vine-leaves, rain dripping into the court, fragrant darkness . . . (*OO*,326).

Claude finds his youth in France, a sense of beginning over: "Life had after all turned out well for him, and everything had a noble significance" (*OO*,332). The belief in the cultural superiority of France also permeates *The Song of Roland*, which echoes the nationalism that arose in medieval France, fueled by the Roman Lucan's phrase of the first century, *furor teutonicus* to describe the enemy. At the same time a medieval attitude that found its voice for the first time in *The Song of Roland* is expressed here with the belief that the French cause is just and the enemy is morally wrong. The savagery of the Germans is manifest in stories of their killings and rapes of women.

The heroes of the *chanson* contribute as much to the novel as its historical and geographical background. Roland, who was dubbed the "Achilles of the West," like Parsifal was an innocent young man of open countenance and often called a fool. His competition with Oliver, like Claude's rivalry with David, shows that they are equal in their separate abilities. The rivalry of the *chanson* became a phrase, "a Roland for an Oliver," to show equality of prowess; the boast that "England all Olivers and Rolands bred" found its way into the first part of Shakespeare's *Henry VI*, another source that may have contributed something to *One of Ours*. Yet another similarity lies in the temperaments of the heroes of the *chanson* and the novel: Claude, like Roland, is intrepid and rash; David, like Oliver, is reflective and calm. In much the same way that Roland makes a decision which leads to Oliver's death, Claude makes a decision that causes despair when he realizes the danger in which he has placed David.[5]

Whether *One of Ours* has the standard love theme is a question that demands the application of a sense of irony and an acceptance of ambiguity, both of which pervade the novels of the second and third stage of this cycle. After the early *chansons*, the heroic epic moves away from historical and political comment to focus on the fantastic tales of chivalry. The later, more refined, Arthurian romances added the courtly traditions, which included courtly love scenes of a knight devoted to a high-born lady for whom he performs his gallant deeds and who reveals to him secrets to help him accomplish his goals. Claude has three trios of women who matter in his life: the three older women are his mother, Mahailey, and Mrs. Erlich, all of whom wear black, serve him, and are among his few admirers. Stouck's emphasis on their dignity helps both to contrast them to the younger women and to suggest that they may be outworn goddesses. The young women are the sensuous Peachy Millmore, Claude's frigid wife Enid, and Gladys Farmer, who may have been a suitable mate if she had not been busy manipulating his brother to impress the town. The Welsh name *Gladys*, probably derived from a feminine form of Claude in Latin, intimates that she shares many of Claude's problems. They have just one moment of intimacy, listening to the bubbling of the spring--the same sound heard as Marie and Emil of *O Pioneers!* find love (*OO*,127). Three Frenchwomen come closer to idealized women, but no one offers an experience of *Eros*. The middle-aged Mme. Joubert provides homely comfort, Mlle. de Courcy offers understanding, and Mme. Fleury, with her daughter, teaches a lesson about the religious role of the arts. These women and their houses represent what Campbell calls the three centers of medieval life--the cottage, the castle, and the cathedral.[6] But in *One of Ours* there is no instance of female to delight, inspire, obsess Claude as knight. His wife, Enid, whose only positive attribute that Mrs. Wheeler can think of is that she is a good Christian, nurses him to health as the Enid of the *Idylls of the King* nurses Geraint. But the contrast between the two stories is striking when we remember Tennyson's lines about Geraint after marriage to his Enid: he "rested in her fealty, til he crowned a happy life with a fair death." (There is some amusement in comparing Tennyson's Enid, who drives horses, with Cather's Enid, who drives her automobile everywhere.) If there is an inspiration for Claude, it is David Gerhardt, who is the embodiment of an ideal long held by Claude, who had been

> always hunting for some one whom he could admire without reservation; some one he could envy, emulate, wish to be. Now he believed that even then he must have had some faint image of a man like Gerhardt in his mind. It was only in war time that their paths would have been likely to cross; or that they would have had anything to do together . . . any of the common interests that make men friends (*OO*,332).

Any other feelings Claude might have for David are unacknowledged, as he is unable even to recognize overt signs that reveal a German soldier's homosexuality. David remains an ideal.

Idealism is the appropriate philosophical approach to arrive at Cather's meaning in the complexity of *One of Ours*. Besides the questions of materialism, the radical breakdown of culture, and a controlling dualism in thought, the epic--particularly the Parsifal quest of Wolfram von Eschenbach--brings to the forefront the need for the salvation of the individual.[7] The Middle Ages are a time of rapid development in the human consciousness, leading to a search for spiritual values in spite of, or perhaps because of, the reigning materialism. Epic is alive and prophetic, Elizabeth Sewell says in *The Orphic Voice*. "Its preoccupation with the structure of the universe and the place and course of man's life and death within it, its essential activity, its attachment to mythology" make it one of the greatest of postlogical disciplines. In the course of the spiritual development of the epic hero, the processes of the mind become the subject. These concerns of the epic link it firmly, both in the classical era and in the Middle Ages, to Neoplatonism, which addresses the questions that the epic milieu poses.

The leading Western thought of the Greco-Roman world from the third to the sixth century, Neoplatonism was revived as a powerful influence in the medieval period. It is a transcendental philosophy stressing idealism versus materialism, a dynamic pantheism, a separation of pure soul from the evil body, a series of tasks to ascend to the realm of deity which is known as the "One." Plotinus adapted Platonic ideas to the syncretistic religious cults of Alexandrian Rome, where they found acceptance by the best minds in that period of social and political unrest. The *Enneads* of Plotinus became the bridge to link Neoplatonist ideas to Christian theology through the writings of St. Augustine, who accepted the explanations of evil and of salvation that were to have a major impact on medieval Christian thought. Neoplatonism and Christianity, which had long vied for control of the minds of men, could be reconciled, as Augustine said, with only a few words changed. Thus, the epic form which expressed the spirit of the Middle Ages so well had a concomitant mode of thought in both the Christian and Neoplatonist schools.

There were differences of language and practices, however, which become important to the epic in general and to Cather's use of the genre in *One of Ours*. The Christian background of some versions of Parsifal and of the Arthurian cycles is part of our education in the Western world. Yet, scholars such as Herschel Baker and Joseph Campbell have noted the interesting relation of the Parsifal themes to Neoplatonist thought: some of the critical ideas of Neoplatonism--as they are used in *One of Ours*--were never incorporated, at least in the same mystical language, into Christian dogma, and remain identifiers of Neoplatonism. In several scenes Claude is quite adamant about his questioning of the Christian faith; the early conversation with his mother about evil is only the first of their religious differences, and although he knows that nothing "would give her so much pleasure as to see him reconciled to Christ," he did not wish to become like the young men who "leaned on their Saviour" (*OO*,43). Women ought to be religious, he thinks, and the more incredible the things they believed, the more lovely their faith. For him the story of "Paradise Lost" was as mythical as the "Odyssey." He rejects the denominational college, finds Preacher Weldon and his sister too stupid and silly to tolerate, and discovers that his wife's Christian goals are militantly negative. Even in his final hour Claude still does not reach toward his mother's Christian faith: "Soldiers, when they were in a tight place," he thought, "often made secret propositions to God; and now he found himself offering terms: If They would see to it that David came back, They could take the price out of him. He would pay. Did They understand?" (*OO*,363-64).

Claude, then, resists some of the ideas of Christianity; he develops the ideals of Neoplatonism to match the knightly role that he assumes.

The Neoplatonist theme starts early in the novel, builds slowly, and fills the final pages of the story. As Claude rises the "sun popped up over the edge of the prairie like a broad, smiling face"; the chapter in which he discovers his ideals is entitled "Sunrise on the Prairie"; and following his death the setting sun signals the presence of his spirit. After the extensive moon symbolism of the three goddess novels, the sun images not only indicate a male-dominated story, but in the light of later developments, begin to state the Neoplatonist symbol of the idea of Good as rays of light emanating from the sun. Much of the early part of the novel slowly and fully describes material and mechanical things that dominate the community, to begin the polarization of the material and the ideal. Claude, with "storms in his mind," imposes physical tests and penances on himself, an act that is knightly, but also fulfills the Neoplatonist requirement for an ascent to Good through a series of difficult and painful tasks. Life for him proves to be "mysteriously hard," with few rewards or interests until he begins to follow the events of the war. Then his thoughts begin to take on the vocabulary and ideas of Neoplatonism: the very name of Paris, for example, comes to have the purity of an abstract idea for him, as he reads about the war.

Neoplatonism appeared in the Roman Empire between the reign of paganism and the dominance of Christianity. Its idealism and individualism were strong appeals to both the Roman and the medieval worlds. The philosophy of Neoplatonism as defined by Plotinus became a mystical religion with three basic doctrines which remained the same over the centuries: the first was the doctrine of the One, the source of all good in the universe to which the human soul aspired; the second was the notion of the Self as a philosophical principle; and the third was the need for the purgation of the mind, with a double goal--one qualitative, a transposing of thought from a material to a spiritual plane, and the other quantitative, a progressive detachment from individuality.[8] Claude moves through a graduated series of virtues to achieve finally, in an ecstasy of mystical experience, the identity of his soul with its ultimate source. His salvation as an individual, without the gods as intermediaries, is the real story of *One of Ours*, with the war as a dramatic background.

Before Claude can begin his ascent, he must effect the purification necessary to separate himself from the lower world. First he acknowledges his shortcomings: "Claude knew, and everybody else knew, seemingly, that there was something wrong with him," and everyone has a favorite theory (*OO*,86). Even as he prepares to leave for France he believes that he has done nothing but blunder; yet he has begun his moral struggle by practicing those virtues that Plotinus finds necessary for purification. Claude's restlessness, guilt, standards of morality are typical of the tensions of heroic times. Overcoming his fear of death, so overwhelming in his college days, makes him courageous as he deals with the dying soldiers on the ship and with the necessity to face his own death in battle. "What else is courage," says Plotinus, "but being afraid of death, that mere parting of soul from body, an event no one can fear whose happiness lies in being his own unmingled self?"[9] Claude also espouses the Plotinian view of temperance, the rejection of the pleasures of the body. His wife, in her crusade for alcoholic "temperance," also enforces sexual abstinence on Claude. Part of the irony here is that he thinks of his marriage to Enid (whose name in Welsh means "soul") as the first dutiful thing he has ever done; "it would restore his soul" (*OO*,122). Although Enid's white clothing suggests a goddess or at least a healing angel, she is after all only a perennial virgin, who never drops into the "lower air" of human passion and who helps to keep Claude away from it as well. So the double irony is that the failure of his marriage helps to save his soul. Chastity, of course, is one of the virtues of the mythic knight as well as the Neoplatonist aspirant. But it is even more as an element of *One of Ours*; in the great epics, Rachel Bespaloff writes,

> chastity as a power is not sensuality's opposite but its most authentic manifestation. . . . A hint, a flicker will catch the slightest tremor of sensation and leave its purity unstained. Chastity is what gives this poetry its ability to describe the extreme with moderation and excess without excessiveness, to plunge into the vortex of war and soar up into the peace of the constellations.[10]

These scenes help Cather to tune the reader's responses to the "pregnant simplicities" that Tillyard finds necessary to the epic.

Claude's process of purification helps the development of his ego, that part of man that for the Neoplatonist is the individual soul seeking unity with the World Soul. He becomes more introspective, his power of vision turns inward, and he becomes as certain of the right thing to do as Alexandra is in *O Pioneers!*. The mystical language of Neoplatonism becomes explicit as he thinks that inside of living people "captives languished. Yes, inside of people who walked and worked in the broad sun, there were captives dwelling in darkness,--never seen from birth to death." In his mother he now understands that the imprisoned spirit, her soul, "was almost more present to people than her corporeal self" (*OO*,170). Later as he watches her hands they seem to "have nothing to do with sense, to be almost like the groping fingers of a spirit" (*OO*,209). The walls of Mahailey's prison are thick, but Claude perceives that she, like other "children of the moon"--the females with beautiful longings and futile dreams--are nobler than the men--"the children of the sun."

The sun and moon images, important to all the nature and mystery religions, are very specifically used in the Neoplatonist philosophy. Behind the seven planets there was a system of order, which could be transferred to human life. So much is made of Claude's innate love of order because in the Neoplatonist view, evil is lack of order; for the believer, the harmony between the heavenly bodies and the earth was a sign of the possible good to come with a relation to the One. Claude is sure that the stars "must have something to do with the fate of nations, and with the incomprehensible things that were happening in the world." His intuitive sense, begun on the steps of the Capitol in Denver--that youthful power is related to his country, which no longer had a West for young people, and to the "lonely splendour of nature" which symbolized the problem by the sky that was like a "lid shut down over the world"--now tells him that the choices he makes will be a matter of "life and death, predestination." In this decisive moment, with the inspiration of the stars he moves back to the question of order: "In the ordered universe there must be some mind that read the riddle of this one unhappy planet, that knew what was forming in the dark eclipse of this hour. The fate that he perceives, what was "hidden in the womb of time," now becomes clearer (*OO*,188). Claude's portion of the universal soul has begun to relate to the mind that knows--the One.

From that point, Claude moves closer to the One until he attains a mystical union--that ultimate goal of the Neoplatonist. First he must understand the lower world of the bodily prison and the world as a dream, or as a lie, in the words of Enid's father. His descent into the hold of the troopship, where many men die without ever knowing themselves, helps him, because he is prepared, to understand the ship as Fate and himself as a leader: "He awoke every morning with that sense of freedom and going forward, as if the world were growing bigger each day and he were growing with it" (*OO*,252). The miracle happens--his feeling of fateful purpose. He grieves not at all for the dead soldiers, who were "merely waste in a great enterprise, thrown overboard like rotten ropes" (*OO*,258). They were noble only in the mass, as their youth flows together to create a noble aura. Everything seems to have happened for the personal salvation of one soul, that of Claude Wheeler. He is, as he says, "over."

His experiences in France heighten his sense of destiny, as the light in this part of the world shines more golden, the women are more beautiful and understanding, the language improves the spirit, and even everyday things are more attractive because of his new state of mind. His friendship with the musician David Gerhardt makes him recognize what he might have been as a finished product if someone had known how to bring about that result. The war scenes serve to bring to mind the connections between the present and earlier periods through the emphasis on romanesque architecture and Captain Owens' obsession with Julius Caesar's roads. The grimmer facts of war, in the scenes with the bloated, gaseous corpses which refuse to remain buried, recall the young Claude's fears of the putrefaction and decay of death. He has been transformed through an awareness of something larger than himself: "Life was so short that it meant nothing at all unless it were continually reinforced by something that endured; unless the shadows of individual existence came and went against a background that held together" (*OO*,328). As he dies his only thought is that he commanded wonderful men; "they were mortal, but they were unconquerable" (*OO*,366).

There is throughout a dialectic on the meaning of their sacrifice. Claude has achieved the goal of his journey, first in the separation of body from its torments in Lovely Creek, and second in the separation of his soul from its bodily prison. History, he thinks, has condescended to him to bring this "whole brilliant adventure," but others are dying merely "because death was in the air" (*OO*,251-52). It is David who defines the question. A fatalist after his violin and his career are ruined, he doesn't believe that the war will accomplish its putative goals. Asked why he was there, he replies:

Because in 1917 I was twenty-four years old, and able to bear arms. The war was put up to our generation. I don't know what for; the sins of our fathers, probably. Certainly not to make the world safe for Democracy, or any rhetoric of that sort. . . . I've sometimes wondered whether the young men of our time had to die to bring a new idea into the world . . . something Olympian (*OO*,331).

He then confesses he has come to believe in immortality, and Claude, like a typical Neoplatonist, says he has never been able to make up his mind about the matter. The whole question, like several others in the novel, is left in the air. That Cather means to do this is supported by an interview in which she describes David Hochstein, the musician after whom David Gerhardt is modeled, as someone who can understand both sides of an argument and deal with competing ethical values. His attitudes, as Cather related them, pervade the book beyond the character of Gerhardt:

> "I got the impression that Hochstein himself had given a good deal of time to the study of philosophy. He knew too much about history to draw rash and comforting conclusions. He didn't believe that any war could end war; he didn't believe that this one was going to make the world safe for democracy, or that it had much to do with democracy whatever. He couldn't see any Utopia ahead. He didn't believe that the war was going to get the world anywhere, no matter how it came out."[11]

Gerhardt, the musician, the lover of beauty, and the philosopher, represents all three of the types of men to whom Plotinus would impart training in the dialectic, in his words, the art of reasoning that "enables us to say what each thing is, in what it differs from other things, in what it resembles them. . . what is good and what is not. . . .It allows the soul, as Plato says, to feed in the 'meadows of truth'." It alternates between synthesis and analysis until it has arrived at principle; only after it has arrived at unity, it stops to contemplate.[12] Cather, who had studied with James T. Lees, a Platonist professor at the University of Nebraska, uses the concepts of the dialectic--the dominant mode of thought in the heroic ages--to characterize David, to instruct Claude in his quest, and to make several important observations in the story.

In spite of his brief appearance in the novel, Gerhardt, far from being the pale figure in *One of Ours* that Sergeant considers him, provides the book's intellectual core and one of the most illuminating examples of Cather's "negative capability" in dealing with complex issues. In adapting Keats's view of the writer's posture of "being in uncertainties, mysteries, doubts, without any irritable reaching after fact and reason," she manages an imaginative insight that can suspend judgment between two philosophical positions.[13] She allows Claude his glory in war and his recognition that "ideals were not archaic things, beautiful and impotent; they were the real sources of power among men" (*OO*,339).

At the same time she allows the sacrifice of men who will never achieve even Claude's victory, and she includes, in an ironic epic return to the beginning of things, the greatest hope of Claude's loyal aide--to run a garage and look at the "logical and beautiful inwards of automobiles for the rest of his life" (*OO*,369). Her historical sense of periodic repetitions informed her that the Hun had invaded Europe in the time of the Roman Empire, the France of Roland in the medieval period, and the France of the early twentieth century; the Hun would again descend to threaten Western civilization before the end of Cather's lifetime.

Other dialectics concern religion even in small ways, as when Mrs. Wheeler believes that the prayers of the French will save Paris, and Claude observes that the Germans are also praying and are even more pious. In a larger dimension there is a continuing undercurrent about the relation of Christianity to Neoplatonism, after Claude has rejected the religion of his mother and his wife. This question is addressed through the examination of both the similarities and the differences between the two systems of belief. The final scene of the novel shows Mrs. Wheeler believing that the war that Claude found so glorious is only evil, but understanding that God has saved him from a disillusionment that he could not have borne had he survived. Mahailey, whose meekness is related to the Christian Gospels, helps to maintain the image of Claude near because her simple virtue removes the distances between her and the ultimate good. All religions are pretty much the same, as Dr. Archie tells Thea in *The Song of the Lark*; for Cather, faith can provide the necessary spiritual support, whatever the chosen path may be.

Neoplatonism is closely related not only to medieval Christianity, it also has intimate connections with the mystery cults of the first three novels of Cather's cycle.[14] Although usually considered a philosophy, Neoplatonism flourished in the Roman Empire during the years of rampant syncretism among all systems of belief. Plotinus in his writings often invoked the rituals of the mysteries as helpful to the purification process necessary for the union with the One; in fact, the need of the individual to unite with a god or gods is part of every mystery religion. After Plotinus, Porphyry and Iamblicus further adapted some of the rituals of the early cults into the Neoplatonist practice, producing a theurgy in place of intellectual philosophy. To appeal to the populace of Hellenistic Rome that rejected the rationalistic approach in favor of the mystical, the later Neoplatonists incorporated the language and rites of the mysteries. Since there is a continuity of spirit and development

between the pagan past and the Middle Ages, according to Joseph
Campbell, the later period perpetuated the rituals in religion and
poetry.[15] That background explains the power of some of the ritualistic
scenes in *One of Ours*. Claude's retreat to an ash grove that he "would
have died defending" allows him to "let his imagination play with life"
(*OO*,174). Here is where he meets his "second self," so much a part of
the spiritual seeking of Cather's characters, and where he digs an
exceptionally deep cellar in this "most beautiful spot in the world"
(*OO*,144). Another sacred spot is the Royce mill with its connections
to the grain, a mysterious place of contrasts of sun and shade, sound
and silence. The dark cave where the water-wheel rests is the first of his
cave experiences. Later in France, his significant conversation with
David occurs in a forest that is like an amphitheater, with underground
chambers at one end, looking like the sites of mystery rites. The
presence of the barefoot girl, her concern with the pigs sacred to the
goddess, and the two young men whose heads resemble suns, amber
and reddish bronze, and who are indistinguishable from the woods--all
bring to mind the nature cults that were, in fact, part of the philosophy
that dominates this novel.

Neoplatonism retained much of the mystery religions' wonder of
nature that Christianity dispelled in its dogma, and some of the most
lyrical of passages in *One of Ours* are those that directly reflect the
sense of dynamic nature that Plotinus included in his treatises. During
a snowstorm, "millions of snowflakes hurried like armies, an unceasing
progression. . . . There was a solemnity about a storm of such
magnitude; it gave one a feeling of infinity. The myriads of white
particles that crossed the rays of lamplight seemed to have a quiet
purpose, to be hurrying toward a definite end" (*OO*,80). At times, it
seems to him that "Nature not only smiled, but broadly laughed at him"
(*OO*,173). And the sun, whose morning rays signalled the beginning of
Claude's story, tells the end of him as only a thought held by his mother
and Mahailey: "always there, beyond everything else, at the farthest
edge of consciousness, like the evening sun on the horizon" (*OO*,331).

This appropriate Neoplatonist destiny permits the use of an epic
convention--making the end of the story the same as the beginning, now
renewed by the quest of the hero. Nature as a sentient force related to
the destiny of man is relevant also to the role of the mystery religions
in the Neoplatonist philosophy. The same connection is found in
Wagner's "Parsifal": the legend as he uses it, says one critic, has the
usual accompaniment of paganism and magic that is part of the

medieval tradition; even further, "it reminds one of those great religious dramas, scenic and musical, which were given at night at Eleusis, near Athens, in the temple of the Mysteries."[16] Cather, long a Wagner fan, wrote the introduction to the 1925 edition of Gertrude Hall's *The Wagnerian Romances*, and was especially impressed by the first chapter on "Parsifal," which she read during her memorable stay in the Southwest.[17] Wagner, who read the Greek tragic writers each day before he began to compose, had an intense interest in the meaning of mythology. "It is the function of art to preserve the inner kernel of religion"; he wrote, "and the way it does this is to take the mythical symbols which religion insists on having men believe, in their literal sense; to conceive them in their emblematic sense; and by ideal representation, to call attention to the deep truth which is concealed within them."[18] Cather's work, certainly in *The Song of the Lark* and *One of Ours*, her novels with Wagnerian themes, concerns itself with religious truths.

During the period of great interest in the Parsifal legend in the first decade of the twentieth century, Jessie L. Weston wrote her two-volume study, *The Legend of Sir Perceval*, which argues that the story had originally nothing to do with the grail, but instead was a vegetation myth, related to the mystery cults and later given Christian overtones. Weston's later book *From Ritual to Romance* was a source for T. S. Eliot's *The Waste Land*, which, as Stouck demonstrates especially well, has many resemblances to Cather's wasteland novel published in the same year. Just as Cumont emphasizes the use of the Attis-Adonis story by the Neoplatonists, Weston connects the quest of Parsifal to the lesser and greater initiations of the mystery cults. The fifth book of *One of Ours* presents those initiation rites: the first, the mysteries of the physical life denied to him at home, are disclosed to Claude in France through the joys of nature, music, food, and love. The higher, divine mysteries, in which man is united with his god, the *One* in Neoplatonist terms, are revealed to Claude as his idealism succeeds in finding what it has been seeking--the release of his soul from the material world. His quest ends in the attainment of his spiritual goal and of eternal life, through his image retained by those who love him.

Cather gathered together these themes of the Neoplatonist philosophy, the mystery religions, and the Parsifal legend, and related them to the second, heroic stage of national development. Using the related medieval conventions of the epic and *chanson de geste*, she worked the whole into her modern novel.[19] Other writers related these elements historically, or philosophically, or poetically, but she created connections among them all to make a dazzling whole. Contemporary critics of *One of Ours* may have missed some of its complexities in hurried assessments, but the Pulitzer Prize committee must have recognized the literary skill, the historical scope, and the ironic argument that composed a significant work.

A Lost Lady

In many ways the emerging society of the midwestern United States paralleled the world of medieval Europe. As the quite feudal social structure formed, it consisted of two classes, the first composed of a few strong wealthy men, the other composed of settlers who never rose above peasant rank. Each settlement had its great house, set apart from the town, where the man of substance and authority attempted an elegant, almost courtly life with others of his station. The rigid social system was one manifestation of the struggle toward order and away from a formless, lawless past. But the same kind of change that occurred in the late Middle Ages broke the pattern in the United States in the nineteenth century. Those changes catalogued in *A Lost Lady* begin with the investment of money by bankers and gentlemen ranchers to "develop our great West," as Cather phrases it. Some of the ambivalence she felt was expressed in an article written the same year this novel was published, admitting a certain moral victory in the attainment of prosperity under difficult conditions, and at the same time condemning the materialistic attitudes soon established. The wild speculation accompanying the new commercialism led to financial catastrophe, as it does in the novel and as it had in the banking houses of Italy and Germany in the Middle Ages. Another inevitable accompaniment was the rise of a middle class unable to comprehend its place in the social structure or to appreciate the mode of the upper class. The threat of the new bourgeoisie was not less in the social and economic scheme of the West than it had been in Europe five hundred years before. There is still another characteristic change that can be understood here only in relation to Cather's earlier novels, in which worship of the land is the chief function of the religious impulse. The desecration of Western land, not to be understood by Americans until generations later, is begun in *A Lost Lady* by the villain who drains a beautiful if apparently useless marshland.

The man who can behave in this manner and then prevail points to a crisis of the time--the loss of heroic leaders, or at least the loss of the illusion that there were such heroes. Cather laments:

> The Old West had been settled by dreamers, great-hearted adventurers who were unpractical to the point of magnificence; a courteous brotherhood, strong in attack but weak in defence, who could conquer but could not hold. Now all the vast territory they had won was to be at the mercy of men like Ivy Peters, who had never dared anything, never risked anything. (*LL*,89-90).

Her strongest regret is for the demise of a class of men whose chivalric behavior had briefly provided a noble perception of human beings in the world. With the vanquishing of those men went the political, cultural, and moral ideals they espoused. Even in the early novels Cather was aware that the age she was eulogizing was past--"elegiac" is the word that many critics apply to her writing. Like the historian Turner she recognized that the frontier had been a formative influence on American life, a tremendous force while it had lasted; like him she knew that it had ended before she began her study. "Our present is ruined," she repeated often, "but we had a beautiful past."[20] But then she also knew, as the "Old Beauty" in a later Cather short story says, "Nobody ever recognizes a period until it has gone by." *A Lost Lady*, her poetic acknowledgement that the vital strength of the pioneer was no more, was begun in 1922, that year in which she said the world broke in two. One of the consequences of her idealization of the early frontier had been to make nearly impossible for her the confrontation with the later industrial and commercial West. As a result, both *One of Ours* and *A Lost Lady* look toward South America as the next frontier.

In other ways the novels resemble each other. From the opening page of *A Lost Lady* medieval references begin to strike the reader. Much is made of the two-fold social strata in the prairie states: there exist only the aristocracy and the lower class of homesteaders and handworkers. Adolph Blum, a young member of this latter group, understands with his feudal mind that a privileged class was fact in the social order and keeps secret his knowledge of aristocratic indiscretions because he dimly perceives that these people are different. While they lead elegant lives, not much happens to the Adolph Blums of the world but weather. The two-dimensional world of the novel further divides into good and evil, as Niel Herbert and Ivy Peters recognize each other from childhood as the "natural enemies" developed earlier by Cather in several stories. On the surface the moral dimensions are as immediately identifiable as any captured in a medieval morality play.

In its setting *A Lost Lady* seems almost a medieval tapestry, with a castle, the poplars, even a moat. To approach Captain Forrester's property, one crossed a wide creek by footbridge or ford and entered his land, bordered by poplars. A second stream curving through the meadows below the hill where the house was built completes the composition of the landscape. The plume-like shadows cast by the trees, the sharp sloping roof of the house, the inlay on the heavy walnut furniture, the Captain's narrow iron bed and even his comment, "A man's home is his castle," all further establish the medieval mood. Captain Forrester himself offers one of the strongest suggestions of medieval times by his resemblance to King Arthur. A massive man, with dun-colored mustache, a "grave courtesy," and a rigid code of behavior, he seems an anachronism even in the Western community he had helped to build. But there are many more specific references to identify him with the most famous of fisher kings. His illness, like Arthur's, begins with a fall from his horse, and his death, like Arthur's, occurs in December. The dependency of the land on the strength of its leader is a direct, almost primitive relationship; one paragraph describes the Captain's failing health; the very next paragraph describes the changing fortunes of the town of Sweet Water, including the crop failures which break the farmers' spirits. To further relate the Captain to the medieval warrior, there is a great deal of witty sword symbolism, such as his deftness with the carving knife at the table, his use of the garden shears, and later in his illness, the brandishing of two canes. But for all his posturing (the chivalric mode was indeed a series of stances), the important fact about the Captain is that he is ultimately powerless to prevent the disintegration about him--nature's decay, society's corruption, even his own wife's faithlessness.

Perhaps of all the secular medieval virtues, loyalty must be deemed pre-eminent. The loyalties of the "lords and barons of his realm" (in this novel they metamorphose into the railroad barons) are consummately feudal; the men themselves are "great-hearted adventurers," "a courteous brotherhood" in Cather's words. As a result of her admiration for the exceptional person, she was able to see the builders of the railroads as figures of nobility at a time when it was popular to consider them robber barons. She talks in the past tense of the visions they had seen and followed, and yet the idea that pervades the novel accepts the king's observation in *Morte d'Arthur* that "the old order changeth, yielding place to new," which might be a motto of heroic epochs. A comparison of two dinner parties, one with the aristocrats at the beginning and the other with the crude youths of the town at the end of the book, serves as immediate symbol of that fact. One man who figures prominently in the story as a part of the aristocratic group is Frank Ellinger, called "a prince of a fellow." This second cliché in the work of a writer notably free of clichés calls attention to the reference. Ellinger's costume, manner, and "well-visored countenance" present him as a chivalric character. If the men are knights, the railroad is amusingly pictured as a dragon when the townspeople say that it is drawing in its horns as the Captain's town declines.

Although Marian Forrester, the long-lost lady, still retains a connection with the fertility goddesses of the earlier novels, she is, within the context of the courtly romance, an elegant, polished noblewoman, the embodiment of the chivalric ideal. Her personality can be equated with the frequent descriptions of medieval society as elegant but static. She proves incapable of the kind of leadership exerted by Cather's earlier, simpler heroines, demonstrating the decline of usefulness of woman's intuitive powers in a male-oriented, conscious society. The story of Marian is a series of episodes revealing, through her relationships with men of all stations, the possibilities of love. As Captain Forrester's wife, she plays the role of beautiful queen and gracious hostess. Her husband, who understands her best even in her perfidy, can still appreciate her more than can lesser men. As object of the courtly worship of young Niel, she, as principle of the female, retains her mysterious power over him even after her physical charms have faded and her moral weakness is manifest. To him she is many things, from mother as he is injured to flirtatious woman to whom he does not respond because of his innocence. As the lover of Frank Ellinger, she is a sexual female with heightened beauty and sensibilities, but subject to the unattractive qualities that come with the jealousy and vulnerability to rejection attendant on her illicit love. Interestingly, she becomes real, casting off her mask and mocking manner only at the moment her love is physically realized. As object of Ivy Peters' attentions, she loses her dignity, her authority, her reputation, and gains only material advantage from her association with him. Finally, as symbol of a privileged life, she elicits from the young males of the village at first admiration, but eventually indifference as she ages, they mature, and the class structure changes. Marian Forrester's strength in her encounters with men steadily deteriorate in the course of *A Lost Lady*. Her fall from grace, as in most myths of the Fall, is accompanied by sexual awareness and guilt.

Only vaguely aware of her plight, Marian plays her role as lady superbly, with her long black hair to her shoulders, the velvet dress with its train, the silver-buckled slippers. Her name, of course, links her to the supreme female inspiration for medieval heroes, although ironically her power is ephemeral. (The Captain's nickname for her--"Maidy"--carries a more secular sense of the name for a virgin.) Her rise and fall are neatly symbolized in scenes involving the rose, the sign of the Virgin. Niel first encounters her as she arranges a bunch of old-fashioned blush roses; his disillusionment begins as he carries to her an armful of wild roses, which he discards in a mud hole after a glimpse of the tawdry side of his lady. The lily, another symbol of Mary, is used ironically in connection with Marian, as Niel comments that lilies that fester smell far worse than weeds. If she allegorically represents the West in men's ideals, the tone of despair in the book becomes evident in the final chapters as her beauty and power fade. She, however, still hopes. Exercising her aging charms, she explains that she wanted to see whether she had anything worth saving. Her vehemence in declaring that she has retained her powers belies her words; she, like the author, knows that her charms will never again really matter, because there are no more Captain Forresters to be attracted.

The brief hope in the era of the empire builders was soon dispelled by the men who followed, epitomized in *A Lost Lady* by Ivy Peters, whose profession--law--characterizes a conscious, masculine civilization and whose unblinking, lashless eyes identify him with evil. The scene introducing him as a youth shows him blinding a woodpecker, an act usually interpreted as mere senseless cruelty, but one that has greater significance in the context of the novel. The woodpecker, according to Jungian theory, is a symbol of the feminine, and much is made of the femaleness of this particular bird in *A Lost Lady*.[21] Often connected with the mysteries--Robert Graves in *The White Goddess* recounts stories of Triptolemus at Eleusis and Dryope in the Phrygian mysteries--the woodpecker is an instrument of prophecy. Thus, the cruelty foreshadows Ivy's later subjugation and ill treatment of Marian, just as Niel's inability to rescue the injured woodpecker foreshadows his later powerlessness to save his lady. Birds sacred to the goddess, as the wild duck in *O Pioneers!* and the eagle in *The Song of the Lark*, are also symbols of transcendence for Cather.

This theme of destruction is carried even further as Ivy's disregard for the spiritual, the unconscious, the *anima* of man's nature culminates in his draining of the swamp on the Forrester property, in spite of the Captain's attempt to preserve that section until his death. The significance of the swamp is made clear in a passage invested with symbolic description of Niel's worship, loyalty, and submerged erotic feeling for Marian. As he is drawn to the swamp by his devotion and sense of guardianship,

> The sky was burning with the soft pink and silver of a cloudless summer dawn. The heavy, bowed grasses splashed him to the knees. All over the marsh, snow-on-the-mountain, gloved with dew, cool sheets of silver, and the swamp milk-weed spread its flat, raspberry-coloured clusters. There was an almost religious purity about the fresh morning air, the tender sky, the grass and flowers with the sheen of early dew upon them. . . . Niel wondered why he did not often come over like this, to see the day before men and their activities had spoiled it, while the morning was still unsullied, like a gift handed down from the heroic ages. (*LL*,70).

Not understanding the worth of beauty for its own sake, Ivy drains the swamp for the profit he can make, signaling the end of both the natural beauty of the West and the power of the men who could appreciate it. And because the swamp stage of civilization, as Neumann says, represents the early matriarchate,[22] its drying up is a symbol not only of the human dominance of nature but also of the male drive for knowledge that succeeds the female acquiescence to nature. What follows in the American context is the evolution of the West from an agricultural to a commercial and industrial society and the emergence of an urban middle class dominated by such men as Ivy and his friends, who lack all aristocratic grace.

The hope for the younger generation resides with the character of Niel, whose very name--at least in its more traditional spelling--means *champion* and whose role is precisely that of the worshipping feudal attendant of royalty. His willingness to make any sacrifice necessary for the lady he adores proves him a knight in the most romantic vein. Combining the qualities of the scholar with those of the knight, he begins his studies in law, but later chooses architecture as a profession, where he can participate in the kind of creative life that for Cather was the only escape from an undesirable world. Even this he gives up for a time to care for the Captain and Marian, a chivalric decision. His feats include a more dramatic rescue of his lady. That occurs when Marian Forrester, after drinking too much brandy, telephones her recently married lover. As her conversation changes to a tirade, Niel cuts the wire with his large shears, saving her in her distress from a loss of dignity.

At this point she becomes absolutely unconscious. The lady who once had the strength of tempered steel, who was like a "blade that could fence with anyone and never break," is, without the Captain, as useless as Excalibur without Arthur. Or, to change the simile, without him she is like a ship without ballast. The glory of the era she represents ends not with a triumph but with Ivy Peters' grasping hand on her breast. Observing the incident, Niel thinks, that it was nothing, yet it was everything. It was the Captain, he decides, who had been the reality. Like the world view of the Middle Ages, Cather's concept of civilization held that an ideal order was the true reality. Her frontier age, like the age of chivalry, had fastened onto an ideal that could not survive the disappearance of heroes who briefly signaled the attainment of the power of consciousness. And while they prevailed they were inspired by the lady who symbolized the female principles so necessary for either a fully developed individual or a successful society. The eventual failure of the lost lady allegorizes what Tennyson discovered as the condition of civilization in Arthur's time and in his own--"sense at war with soul."

Given her theme (the passing of the heroic era) and her historical sense (the awareness of the similarities between the Western United States of the nineteenth century and medieval Western Europe), it was no accident that Cather chose to structure her novel as a *roman courtois*. Her previous "medieval" novel, *One of Ours*, as an epic or *chanson de geste* in which war is the subject, is now followed by *A Lost Lady* as an Arthurian romance in which courtly love is the subject. If the first reflects the crude power of romanesque art, the second carries the complexity and refinement of later Gothic art. The romance was an ideal, and traditional, vehicle for the expression of the attitudes of a society comprised of many conflicting forces. The original romance literature, Heer says, was nourished on the awareness of the crisis in the conscience and instincts of twelfth-century man.[23] Cather's use of the genre of courtly romance seems naturally to follow in view of her acute sense of the moral crisis of her time.

In addition to the theme of weakness in men and institutions, *A Lost Lady* displays all of the other prominent elements of the *roman courtois*.

The plot is the classic one: a young knightly protagonist dedicates himself to the service of his lady, the wife of his king who eventually falls. Through a series of adventures, including journeys, battles (sometimes psychological), adulterous encounters (perceived rather than participated in), and many defeats, the knight undergoes his initiation into awareness of the world about him. Further, as Heer defines the *roman* ". . . a woman is always at hand to transform and ennoble a man. Through his relationship with the woman the man gains access to his own soul, the deeper layers of his 'heart'; his sorrowing quest for his 'queen' makes him wiser, more sensitive, more scrupulous as a person."[24] Based on this pattern, *A Lost Lady* becomes part of the tradition of such famous romances as Gottfried von Strassburg's *Tristan*, the works of Chrétien de Troyes and Malory, and Tennyson's *Morte d'Arthur*. She gives her readers a clue with the attention given by Niel to Ovid's *Heroides*, which along with his *Amores* and *Ars Amatoria*, were well known in the Medieval period and influenced the literature of courtly love. His critique of the *Heroides* might well describe *A Lost Lady*: "living creatures, caught in the very behavior of living,--surprised behind the misleading severity of form and phrase" (*LL*,67). The Roman world had what some would call romances and others would call novels, the most famous of which is the *Satyricon* of Petronius, whose extant fragments tell of a declining world of materialistic values, vices, and excesses of the imperial society.[25] The dinner party scene bears resemblance to *A Lost Lady* in allowing the parvenus to indict themselves by their own language and behavior. The sociological and historical comment, focusing on the figure of a rich man's wife, while a much broader and more vicious attack, is a similar exposé of the debasement of manners and art in a greedy society of a new middle class. Reading the satire of Petronius with its relentless piling up of detail makes the gentle irony and spare prose of *A Lost Lady* seem even more a work of art. It is the artful and adroit passages of Ovid that are the link from the Augustan Age to the Middle Ages and then to the time of Cather. The *Heroides* was particularly useful in his analyses of the relationships between men and women, and even the *Metamorphoses* became a vehicle for the morals of medieval allegory, often in Christian terms.

The medieval writer of most interest here is probably Chrétien de Troyes, who was well versed in the works of Ovid and whose psychological insight, especially into the emotions of women, is notable. His are the earliest Arthurian romances that we know: *Erec et Enide*,

Cligés, *Lancelot*, *Yvain*, and *Perceval*, written in the late twelfth century
and translated into English by W. W. Comfort in 1913 for the
Everyman's Library. There was renewed interest in chivalric tales in the
period just preceding Cather's *Lost Lady*. Cather uses chiefly the broad
conventions of Chrétien's stories, but a few specific parallels are likely.
The ironic components of the novel especially relate to the *Yvain*,
considered Chrétien's masterpiece. Crucial to the story of Yvain is the
perron, a base for a monument, which appears in Cather's tale as the
pillar from the Garden of the Gods brought for the Captain's sundial.
The *perron* of the romance became central to the rites of challenge, and
the passes that Ivy makes before it without even looking at Captain
Forrester show his disdain for aristocratic authority. The importance of
the sandstone base to the story is clear when it becomes the Captain's
gravestone. Further similarities, some amusing, exist: like Yvain, Ivy
woos a king's widow; the gun he carries on the Forrester property
recalls the medieval lance; the name *Ivy*, usually female, probably is a
connection with *Yvain*, as well as with the climbing plant and its
poisonous form so carefully explained in the story. The connections of
Niel's narrative with the Gawaine motif, often paired with Yvain's story,
are apparent: it tells of a *rite de passage* of the narrator, who is being
initiated into an understanding of himself, of the values of his life, and
of the true meaning of the king and his court.

One of the advantages of the genre of courtly romance for Cather is
that it provides opportunity for more complete manipulation of allegory.
Chrétien's stories have been interpreted at many levels. "It is, in fact,"
says Heer, the veil of form and symbol that gives the *roman courtois*
its power, for this veiling at once reveals and conceals the varied
parentage of the figures and emblems of good and evil met with along
the way."[26] Although Cather's novels from *O Pioneers!* on have
allegorical qualities in their implications for historical interpretation of
the West, *A Lost Lady* is allegorical in the medieval manner, where
characters are both historical and figurative; they are not only
themselves but also representatives of something else and signs of their
own spiritual condition. Allegory and symbolism convey to this story
a power immediately felt if not comprehended. The dual view of the
world and even the modes of thought lead easily to at least two
meanings for characters and action. Even one more attraction of the
romance for Cather might have been its possibilities for experimentation
in a style that was new for her, that allowed her, in working through the
genres in a historical pattern, to achieve an elegance that is quite

different from her earlier novels, and even from *One of Ours*, in spite of the common heroic period that is the background for both.

The setting of Sweet Water in the American West at the same time depicts the two earlier comparable heroic stages of civilization--the Empire of Rome and the medieval period in Europe. All follow what had been considered the age of gods in literary terms; all have many of the same political, historical, and religious conditions; all are in a *corso* that will lead to further decline of the respective nations. Cather focuses on the medieval period here, but she gives enough clues to keep the reader's mind on the three eras at once; the study of any one of the eras illuminates the others. The feminine traits of Marian Forrester as the protagonist of the story balance the male traits of Claude Wheeler in the preceding story set in the same era. She is at once the lady of the manor, a goddess figure, and a personification of the trend of her civilization. The people about her serve to fill in the allegory on all levels.

Captain Forrester's role contributes substantially to an understanding of the religious background of the novel. In the Augustan age there developed a strong cult of the emperor, who was saluted as "Benefactor" and "Saviour." The practice had been encouraged by Alexander and given impetus when Julius Caesar was hailed as "God manifest and Saviour universal of the human race," and later Augustus became "Ancestral God and Saviour of the whole human race."[27] Virgil celebrated the divinity of the emperor in the *Aeneid*, and Ovid did the same in the *Metamorphoses* and in the *fasti*, the calendars that scheduled the festivals of the gods. The rulers participated in varying degrees, from merely allowing worship of the "genius" of the sovereign in Rome, to erecting temples where they installed statues of themselves beside the gods. In the provinces the consecration of the emperor as a messiah was a force in the political and social life of the people. The Imperial cults had their altars for sacrifice, their priests, their hymners. The Caesars declared themselves "Sol Invictus" to associate themselves with the sun, and in their palaces burned eternal flames that were carried before them during ceremonies. The scene in *A Lost Lady* showing the Captain in his garden with a sundial takes on significance in the context of the association of the ruler with the sun.

In a world filled with religions borrowing beliefs and rites from each other, the Imperial cult took its place among the mystery religions. Octavian, whose title was Augustus, perhaps had the most complete trappings. He was an initiate of the Eleusinian mysteries, he supported existing Roman cults and linked himself to them. His coins carried the legend "Apollo of Actium"; his name was coupled with that of the gods in hymns; his statue is placed above those of Mars, Venus, and the deified Caesar in the temple of the Forum of Augustus. To make his identification with the sun god as close as possible, he built a temple for Apollo on the site of his house, and transferred the Sybilline Books, the chief oracle for Rome, to that temple. He was worshipped often jointly with Roma, the feminine personification of his capital. His symbolism was successful: according to one historian, "Augustan literature and religious rites, such as the Secular festival, emphasize both the Sibylline Books and the cult of Apollo, in part as a chthonic spirit destroying evil, but also as the sun, the patron of the arts; poetry and art often identify Augustus with Apollo."[28] The Imperial cults would have their correlations in the Middle Ages, as that era repeated the heroic stage of civilization. The barons of France and England, holding on to whatever divine rights they could, scheduled their feast-days to coincide with the festivals of the church. Their claim of "God and my right" established both law and economic power. In a further continuance of the Imperial cults, the medieval knighthood that served Charlemagne, Arthur, and other kings became the subjects of the great *chansons* and epics.

The idea of the Imperial cult illuminates *One of Ours* in several ways. (As usual, Cather provides clues to her meaning: the fact that Mr. Ogden wears "an imperial" is repeated at the beginning and end of the story; Marian's manner is "imperious.") Niel's devotion to the two main figures in his world relates directly to the double worship of the Captain as regal symbol and Marian as the accompanying goddess who is a culture symbol as well. The citizen of the Roman Empire could choose to pay homage to one or both, and Niel's recognition of the Captain as the reality makes his final choice inescapable. The amount of significance given to the relation between the Captain and the sun dial is more understandable in the context of the Roman cults, and Marian's role as waning female deity is clearer in many passages, such as, "she was an excitement that came and went with summer" (*LL*,23), and "her eyes . . . seemed to promise a wild delight" (*LL*,147).

The mature Niel understands her as aging beauty, as fertility goddess, and as emblem of his world in decay. His resentment that "she was not willing to immolate herself . . . and die with the pioneer period to which she belonged" is at the very last overcome, as he is "very glad that he had known her and that she had a hand in breaking him in to life." (*LL*,145-47). His final ambivalence is a statement of Cather's view of her country as she knew first its golden age of "ever-blooming, ever-burning, ever-piercing joy," and then came to realize that in the succeeding age of the American West as of other civilizations, the fall was inevitable.

4

In Media Vita: **The Age of Men**

Marian Forrester of *A Lost Lady*, as the symbol of the declining West in a heroic age, still has some beauty and a wistful and haunting charm. Cather, in her next two novels, *The Professor's House* and *My Mortal Enemy*, represents the Vichian "age of mortals" by protagonists who fully capture the despair of the degeneration of a culture. The eras she chooses to provide the parallel to the first decades of modern America are the beginning of the Renaissance period in Europe and the last years of the Roman Empire in the earlier cycle. According to Vico, in this historical age the discipline, respect for law, and social solidarity of the patrician orders give way to a decline of public spirit, an easy tolerance, and eventually license. Birth is displaced by wealth as a sign of fitness to rule, and political power is extended to those who cannot exercise it wisely. The decay of society follows inevitably.

Although Cather is not following a precise outline, many of these conditions of the Renaissance period are clear in this third phase of her cycle. Depending on the respective views of the historians, the Renaissance began in the fourteenth, the fifteenth, or the sixteenth century. Like most historical periods, this had no sharp break with the previous one, and the countless references to the Middle Ages establish the flow of ideas and customs as one age evolved into the other. The author of a recent book on Cather who finds much that is medieval in *The Professor's House* is well supported in her position.[1] Moreover, traces of the Middle Ages remain in our own era; Jung suggested in 1934 that from the future we will be able to see that we are still stuck in medievalism up to the ears.[2]

A survey of the culture of the early Renaissance by Frederick Artz matches Vico's pattern for the third stage of civilization and at the same

time summarizes the background for this part of Cather's cycle, and
particularly for *The Professor's House*, the first novel of this transitional
period:

> The genesis of the styles of the Early Renaissance in part is to be found
> first in a more secular attitude toward life and then in the discovery of
> new meanings in the art and letters of the classical world. The growth of
> towns and of the middle class which began in Italy as early as the tenth
> century, had, by the twelfth century, become a very marked feature of the
> society of northern Italy. The accumulation of wealth in the Italian cities
> and their very active civil life helped to bring a more worldly view of life.
> An old society that was agricultural, feudal, and ecclesiastical now had
> growing within it a new society that was urban, national, and secular in
> outlook. A new society, centered less on nobles and priests and more on
> bourgeois men of affairs, was coming into being.[3]

A time of prosperity, a rational approach by man to his environment, an
understanding of scientific principles, an emancipation of humanism, are
all for Vico signs of the beginning of the "disintegration of the social
texture." And in the Renaissance, social problems assumed a personal
and psychological rather than collective and practical character, leading
to a more problematic relationship to God, society, and self.

In the Renaissance world, a struggle for clarity and order in religion
and the arts gave way to a struggle in the next centuries that would see
schism in nearly every area of life. The movement to mercantile
capitalism brought social revolts, and rich merchants sought political
control; state and church quarreled over rights of emperors and popes;
the church battled reformers and critics within. A corresponding period
in every culture can be expected to display similar attitudes; those of the
earlier Greco-Roman world are catalogued by Gilbert Murray, a
classical scholar whose books Cather read. There is a change in the
whole relation of the writer to the world about him in the third stage,
he says:

> The new quality is not specifically Christian: it is just as marked in the
> Gnostics and Mithras-worshippers as in the Gospels and the Apocalypse,
> in Julian and Plotinus, as in Gregory and Jerome. It is hard to describe. It
> is a rise of asceticism, of mysticism, in a sense, of pessimism; a loss of
> self-confidence, of hope in this life and of faith in normal human effort;
> a despair of patient inquiry, a cry for infallible revelation; an indifference
> to the welfare of the state, a conversion of the soul to God. . . . There is

an intensifying of certain spiritual emotions, an increase of sensitiveness, a failure of nerve.[4]

The Professor's House

The Professor's House is a significant study of a phase comparable to this time of failure of nerve in American culture, as some interesting analyses affirm. David Stouck sees the pervasive concern with material possessions and power as the focus of a satire; Paul Comeau carefully explicates the use of Anatole France's *Le Mannequin d'Osier*, with its discussions of the Dreyfus Affair, for plot and meaning; E. K. Brown's emphasis on the house as structural principle and psychological symbol is one of several insightful approaches to that topic.[5] More recently, A. S. Byatt says that the novel "is certainly, in a very deliberately patterned way, concerned with the history of Western, and American, culture."[6] But there seems more to explore here in the context of Cather's historical cycle and her use of the mystery religions as spiritual background.

Cather's references to the era of the late Middle Ages and early Renaissance are frequent and, as usual, eclectic. She uses a miscellany of ideas and structures, as well as specific allusions, all related to the period. The art forms that she acknowledged using to structure her novel were directly out of the Renaissance: the first is the device of inserting the *nouvelle* into the *roman*; the second, somewhat vague, but resembling the loosely structured sonata, is the Dutch picture that so often includes a square window opening from an interior (*OW*,30-31). Although Cather counts only to two in the letter that explains her plan, she has incorporated into *The Professor's House*, it seems, techniques from three arts--literature, music, and painting. Wherever techniques interpenetrate this way, says Sypher, "they cause ambiguous 'transformations' of style. . . . Renaissance art and literature are filled with intersecting techniques, which is one reason for the mannerist 'disintegration'--or transformation, if you will."[7] For Cather, that disintegration comes in her next novel, *My Mortal Enemy*; such manipulations of structure moved some distance from the "two-part pastoral" of *O Pioneers!* or the memoir that "hasn't any form" of *My Ántonia*.

With the Medieval and Renaissance background, E. K. Brown's suggestion of links with the techniques of Cervantes and Smollett (who both translated and borrowed from *Don Quixote*), must be included in any list of sources. It is also impossible to dismiss the correlations of *The Professor's House* with *The Divine Comedy*.[8] Certainly the solitary middle-aged man's search for his soul parallels Dante's theme, and the three-part structure of *The Professor's House* follows the Platonic stages successively, with the family representing the world of matter; Tom, the world of becoming; and St. Peter, the world of being. The same progression fits the appetitive, emotional, and rational states, as well as the three levels of love of gain, development of ambition, and pursuit of truth which are in the background of Dante's poem. The recurrent emphasis on the number three is apparent in Cather's story: three men and three women in the St. Peter family; three men on the mesa; the three books of the novel. (Neither Cather nor Dante invented the idea of the number three as magic; both pagan and Christian religions used it, and Vico was obsessed with it.) Hell is the allusion as St. Peter speaks of his "perilous journey down" through the human house very early in the novel; Heaven is glimpsed once he has reached a sort of state of grace in the final scene, and he knows that he is "outward bound" with a "world full of Augustas" (*PH*,257). Through the "secrets" that have been disclosed to the young Tom in his journey through the seven stages St. Peter can purge his own soul of guilt and, as at the end of the *Purgatorio*, find once more his unfallen childhood. Cather is touching lightly on *The Divine Comedy*, but the suggestions are there. *The Professor's House* must be considered a comedy in the sense that it is an ironic struggle of man with his society, even though St. Peter's solution to his problems, although inevitable, is a less than joyful reconciliation with his world. This, according to Cather, is her first deliberately ironic novel, a mode that Vico says is appropriate to the third stage of men when they no longer have the simplicity and truthfulness of earlier ages.[9]

As a newly invigorated arm of literature, history was developed by the humanists of the Renaissance to an art form. The return to the classical sources for information, the removal of divine plans from historical accounts, and sometimes the reintroduction of the cyclical idea of history from the ancient authors helped to change history into a modern enterprise. The Renaissance historian, like Cather's Godfrey St. Peter, contested the scientist for the attention of the university students. The historical allusions are most often drawn from the Renaissance period, but include the eleventh-century Bayeux Tapestry, because it allows St. Peter to compare his work on his chronicles amidst his domestic life with Queen Mathilde's tapestry depicting battles of knights along with pictures of birds and animals. The careful design of the weaving that incorporates so many aspects of life is part of Cather's theme in this story. Another historical reference, this time to the crusades of the twelfth century, is the historian's "little joke" in his tableau posing Louie as the Saladin and Scott as Richard Plantagenet. Richard I is standing, handsome and arrogant, while the Saladin sits patiently, in an attitude of reason. The "joke," of course, is that, like the Saladin, Louie (whose name means "famous warrior") has conquered and established new commercial ventures, and Scott's haughtiness in defeat is as futile as Plantagenet's. In the context of the three decadent eras of late Roman Empire, the Renaissance, and twentieth-century America, the role of the Jew in those societies is consistent. In contrast to Cather's earlier portraits of cultured Jewish families like the Erlichs, or Jewish benefactors like the Nathanmeyers, Louie Marsellus (the last two syllables of his name are a little joke, too) is a practical, not a creative, figure, successful in accumulating the wealth that is his chief goal. Although James Schroeter finds both psychological and cultural sources for what he sees as an anti-semitic portrait of Marsellus, it seems more likely, in light of Cather's whole canon, her ambitious intent to portray the condition of a country, and her discipline in controlling her art, that Louie is not primarily a means to objectify her personal feelings, but is a stereotype in her social satire.[10] Indeed, he is not the only one in *The Professor's House.*

Some of Cather's ideas are revealed in this narrative by the professional attitudes and pronouncements of Godfrey St. Peter, who defends a philosophy threatened by the scientific and materialist attitudes of the time. His lecture in the first book helps to unify the novel, as David Daiches points out: "The professor and Tom are linked to each other by a sensitivity to history--not academic history, but history of past adventures whose implications reverberate excitingly into the present."[11]

Sources of the character of St. Peter and his ideas about history are interesting, as sources always are in Cather's work. Parallels have been drawn between St. Peter and Adolph Bandelier, who wrote four papers about the Spanish explorers in the Southwest and projected four more. His explorations of the Pueblo ruins and his friendship with Archbishop Lamy, who became the prototype of Father Latour in *Death Comes for the Archbishop*, would have been of interest to Cather. As it is so often, however, her work is indebted to more than one source.

Another likely source for the portrayal of the professor is Francis

Parkman, whose seven-volume history, *France and England in North America*, was completed in 1893. Parkman wrote that "each work is designed to be a unit in itself, independently of the rest; but the whole, taken as a series, will form a connected history of France in the New World." Beyond the similarities of the multi-volume works and their names--St. Peter's is called *Spanish Adventurers in North America*--are the parallels of Parkman's philosophy of history with that of the fictional professor. Parkman believed, says C. Vann Woodward, that history demanded imaginative and literary art, and the historian's subject "had to be large enough to accommodate vast events--the conquest of continents, the clash of cultures or struggles of mighty consequence between future and past or progress and reaction, perhaps even between right and wrong."[12] Parkman and Cather had comparable and intense interests in France and that nation's affinity for ancient Rome; his subject "seized, possessed, and obsessed" him; he uses Cather's language of being "haunted" with wilderness images day and night. His works, like hers, are filled with stereotypes of national character, humor, and ambiguity. His use of light symbolism is as striking as hers. But most important to the connection between Cather and Parkman is his Vichian sense of history. John Fiske, the intellectual historian popular in the latter years of the nineteenth century, ranked Parkman's work with that of Herodotus, Thucydides, and Gibbon. He stressed the scope of Parkman's history when he wrote: "The book which depicts at once the social life of the Stone Age and the victory of the English political ideal which France inherited from imperial Rome, is a book for all mankind and for all time."[13] Here is the equivalent of Vico's placing of Cicero beside Boccaccio, Virgil beside Dante, and Horace beside Petrarch. Parkman's method, one historian says, may be summarized as "an attempt to bring back the past just as it was." His work recalls to many the remark of Michelet that history is not narration nor analysis, but "resurrection."[14] When Edith Lewis says that Cather found Parkman the most interesting of American historians, she reveals much about the novelist's philosophy of history and her approach to the evolution of the American West.

Jules Michelet, already seen as an influence in Cather's literary development, must be considered one of the models for her historian in *The Professor's House*. Michelet, whose academic career encountered even greater political obstacles than St. Peter's, was a man of solitude, working late into the night and lecturing passionately to his students. He, like the professor, was suspect among his colleagues for his popularization of history, in Michelet's instance, the story of Joan of Arc. His accomplishments, like St. Peter's (and Cather's), were personally costly: he complained that he was "never at one with himself." His seventeen-volume *History of France*, like the professor's *Spanish Adventurers*, was a new departure, with a bold emotional context, mingling history and philosophy. Michelet says, "I am trying to twist those threads which have never been woven together in science. . . . This double thread is twisted of the arts and religion."[15] Denying any great contribution of science, St. Peter agrees with Michelet when he says that art and religion are the same thing.

Vico, Michelet's master, must be included with the historians who provide Cather with inspiration for the character of St. Peter. As a Renaissance writer who virtually invented the discipline of the "philosophy of history," he advocated humanism as the tradition that would best help men understand the world in which they live. In the Renaissance era where science reigned, Vico expressed the same rejection of science and embraced the same intuitive responses as did St. Peter. Although Vico thought the physical sciences might help the advancement of medicine, he said they "could contribute nothing to the philosophy of man"; further, the "language was so barbarous."[16] For the study of man, he demanded a doctrine of the human soul and its relationships. Cather's debt to Vico clearly goes beyond the character of her historian to encompass many of the ideas of *The Professor's House* and indeed of the whole of the nine-novel cycle. But Vico is also a part of her impressive conglomeration of real historians who contribute to the creation of St. Peter as a credible and complex professional figure.

One of the tasks of the professor is to teach the reader Cather's intention in writing her novels. To this point, the author's clues have been brief, often elliptical, references to a myth she wants the reader to have in mind, to an era or a place that will illuminate a story or broaden its context. *The Professor's House* has many such small nudges to prod ways of thinking. Allusions to patterns occur three times in an exchange with Augusta; her patterns and St. Peter's manuscripts are "interpenetrated." The word *pattern* is again emphasized in the reference to the Bayeux tapestry. It is impossible not to notice that Cather is talking about her own art in the passages describing the professor's work. His multi-volume project is the focus of his life, an original contribution to scholarship, even though "nobody saw that he was trying to do something quite different" (*PH*,22). The inspiration for his opus came to him in a great natural setting as hers had come--hers in a vast canyon and his in sight of a mountain range where "everything seemed to feed the plan of the work that was forming" in his mind: "The design of his book unfolded in the air above him, just as definitely as the mountain ranges themselves. And the design was sound. He had accepted it as inevitable, had never meddled with it, and it had seen him through" (*PH*,89). St. Peter's last volumes are simpler and inevitable after Tom brings to him the secrets of the great dazzling country. Cather's essays on literature confirm that her own sense of submitting to her material developed and expanded as her own plan became increasingly clear. This discussion of the generation of her design within a work of fiction is typical of the Renaissance self-conscious literary style that uses itself as a referent; it is also a technique much used in the 1920s, the years of Cather's mature novels.

The United States of Willa Cather's middle years was a nation of a machine-made materialism, producing, in Henry Seidel Canby's words, "a generation which seemed to be losing the spiritual force and virility of its ancestors." Only the male writers of her time responded to the larger questions of a troubled society, he said; she is "almost antiquarian, content with much space in little room--feminine in this. . . . She knew evil, and suffered from the grossness of materialism and the smugness of cheap success, but preferred to celebrate the vitality of the good."[17] She did not experiment, he added, except within the limits of her purpose. For his review of *The Professor's House* twenty years before, however, it appeared that he had read the novel carefully as he talked of the "new technique," and of her belief, the strongest since Hawthorne, in the profundity of American life. Canby was interested in this book, he said, because, "the soul, after all, is the greatest subject for art."[18] In his later essay, he adds that Cather's art is essentially a representation of the reaction between the soul of man and its environment.

Even though some of his critical judgment seems shallow and sexist today, his framework of the soul and the environment provides an understanding of her direction in her novel cycle. The bird symbol for the soul remains constant throughout her novels--the wild duck related to the goddess for Alexandra in the first book, the eagle's nest related to the male cults of the sun for Tom and indirectly for St. Peter in *The Professor's House*. Some symbols of the environment, however, differ dramatically: in *O Pioneers!* it is the Genius of the Divide bending low to assist Alexandra; in *The Professor's House* it is the one thing the country has contributed to civilization--indoor plumbing. The conflicts in the professor's middle-aged life, sometimes so darkly comic, are always trivial in the context of the larger schemes of the earlier novels-- the settling of a country or the winning of its wars--but meaningful in the era of individualism.

Both the beginning and ending of the novel find St. Peter alone: the opening paragraph is crowded with words that describe at the same time the professor's house and "The Family," as the first book is titled: *over, done, ugly, sagging, empty, echoing, cramped, awkward, bumptious,* among others. Most of the novel is given to St. Peter's relationships with his family and a few colleagues. St. Peter, whose given name, Godfrey--popular in the twelfth and thirteenth centuries--means "God is my judge," is, in fact, a severe judge of everyone else. Although he seeks isolation in his study in an old house apart from his family's new ostentatious one, his unavoidable contacts are filled with discord. His wife and older daughter are acquisitive, and his younger daughter is jealous and self-pitying; his sons-in-law are opposites: Louie Marsellus is a Jewish engineer whose only interest is wealth, and Scott MacGregor, as Anglo-Saxon as his name suggests, is a writer who squanders his talent because he needs money. St. Peter is equally judgmental of his colleagues, who include a historian who does not teach but merely entertains his students and a physicist who is narrow-minded and unattractive. The distasteful plea of the physicist's wife for money is a reminder of Vico's analysis of the law in the age of men and his insistence that there is a justice beyond man's laws, as she both threatens to sue and tries to manipulate legal argument to her own advantage: "There are some things the law don't cover," she says mysteriously (*PH*,120). Of the people St. Peter encounters, only the sewing woman, Augusta, receives his tolerance, however condescending.

St. Peter's strongest criticism is reserved for himself, particularly in the brief third book, "The Professor," although the language of his thoughts about his own life is diffuse and mystical in contrast to the rapier thrusts of the early book. Convinced that he is nearing the end of his life, he comes to the realization that he loves his solitude and would, in fact, welcome it as an eternal condition, since he has fallen out of love with his wife, his family, the whole human race. It is Augusta who saves him when he makes no move to escape asphyxiation in his study, and it is Augusta who helps him face the reality of life to come. Her image tells him of its joylessness: she is bloomless, grave, "like the taste of bitter herbs," and, most important, she understands the inevitability of death. St. Peter is moving into Jung's final stage of life--

"submersion in unconscious psychic happenings." He has reached this point after an inner struggle that makes him aware of the Jungian idea that "the art of life is the most distinguished and rarest of all the arts. . . . So for many people all too much unlived life remains over-- sometimes potentialities which they could never have lived with the best of wills, so that they approach the threshold of old age with unsatisfied demands which inevitably turn their glances backwards."[19]

St. Peter's glance backwards is the link between his alienation in the first book and his resignation to his fate in the last. In "Tom Outland's Story," the middle book of *The Professor's House*, the young man tells of his adventure in the canyons of the Southwest, where he discovers the Indian pueblos abandoned long ago. Tom represents the "second self" that so many of Cather's protagonists search for; the name Thomas means "twin." His story begins with a string of accidents, in the same way as the professor's story talks of the important events of his life being determined by chance. Tom, too, is involved with people whose lives are ruled by money, from his partner Rodney, whose name in English dialect is defined as "a shirk, an idler, a vagabond, anything worthless," to the Washington bureaucrats whose attention can be bought for the price of a good lunch. By chance Tom finds the ruins of the extinct civilization of Cliff City.

Several of the events of the second book of this novel expand the themes and characters of the first part. There is, for example a pervading question of retribution for one's actions. After Tom has broken his ties with Rodney, he says, "Anyone who requites faith and friendship as I did, will have to pay for it. I'm not very sanguine about good fortune for myself. I'll be called to account when I least expect it" (*PH*,229). Earlier, as St. Peter regrets that he must have Sunday breakfast with his wife, he says to himself, "There was no way out; they would meet at compt" (*PH*,35). The phrase is puzzling until it is traced to *Othello*, where Othello addresses the dead Desdemona:

When we shall meet at compt,
This look of thine will hurl my soul from heaven,
And fiends will snatch at it (5.2.273-75).

And as he expects, Lillian makes Godfrey account for his behavior of the preceding evening. His atonement is trivial and humorous in contrast to Tom's serious question of guilt. Tom's discovery of Indian artifacts provides a contrast with another earlier scene: the beauty of the clay pots, he understands, comes in part because they are useful and shared by the entire community; the gold necklace that Louie has set with emeralds for Rosamond is meant for him alone to enjoy. Later, as St. Peter recognizes Augusta's value, it is because she, too, is useful to the community at large.

As she so often does, Cather reserves the last segment of this second book of the novel for the re-enactment of the mystery rites. The first part of Tom's story is a standard hero story: in the broader interpretation of the hero myth, Tom repeats the pattern of separation from the world; a journey into a region of "supernatural wonder" where he has a mysterious adventure; and a return with powers to bestow a boon. The story also incorporates many of the conventions that apply in American Indian stories, as well as in Western literature: Tom is an orphan who finds a second set of parents, does not know his age, becomes half of "twin" heroes, accomplishes a great task, and dies young before the world can corrupt him. (All he has accomplished, says the insensitive Louie, is death and glory.) The surface story supplies all the conventions of the hero myth; the hidden myths in the Tom Outland story, however, belong to the mysteries of Mithra. The seven chapters of the brief central section equate to the seven levels of initiation of the Mithraic cult.[20] Plutarch tells some of the history of Mithraism: by the first century A.D. it had passed from the Persians to the Phrygians and from them to the Romans. By the third century it had spread throughout the Roman world, and the fourth century found Mithraism and Christianity vying for official recognition from the emperor. Constantine's decision in favor of Christianity determined the course of religion in Western civilization, but a relic of Mithraism continued in the custom of releasing an eagle at the funeral of an emperor to signify the flight of his soul to heaven. Willa Cather may have learned of the cult from the Latin sources--Lucian, Plutarch, or Christian scholars Jerome or Tertullian, among others; but Cumont's work was available to her, as well. His writing on the Oriental cults in Rome included *The Mysteries of Mithra*, published in the United States in 1903, the more general *Oriental Religions in Roman Paganism* of 1911, and *Astrology and Religion among the Greeks and Romans* of 1912. There was intense interest and much archeological activity surrounding the mysteries and their sites during the early years of the century, and in 1912 the largest known Mithraeum, the chapel of the god, was discovered at the baths of the emperor Caracalla. With these sources the Mithraic cult and its practices can be described.

The mysteries of Mithra imported Persian dualism into the West, bringing both its powerful metaphysical concept and a system of ethics.[21] The cult shared with other mysteries the basic ideas of death and rebirth, identification with one's god, and the duality of soul and body, but was unique among the cults in dividing the world into equal powers of good and evil. While recognizing the powers of darkness, at the same time the Mithraist struggle against them demanded a new sense of truth, of loyalty and fidelity, of chastity and honor. "No religion on earth has ever been so completely dominated by an ideal of purification," one historian of religion claims.[22] In a period of anarchy and confusion, the Mithraic cult gave a sense of brotherhood and a new meaning to life.

Astrology, important to most religions of the time, was especially prominent in the Mithraic rituals. The twelve signs of the zodiac were displayed in the Mithraeums, each planet was assigned its special virtues, and the number seven, for the known planets, became a sacred number. The seven grades, or degrees, of Mithraic initiation, corresponding to the seven planets, were called *Raven, Occult* (or *Man of the Secret*), *Soldier, Lion, Persian, Runner of the Sun*, and *Father*; interesting masks that correspond to these categories have been found in the caves. Cumont surmises some of the meanings of these degrees, but the important concern of the initiate was to rise through them to acquire wisdom and purity. Ladders in their temples symbolized the ascent of the soul through the seven planetary spheres to the abode of the blessed, shedding the appetites and passions acquired on the descent to earth. The soul, man's divine essence, survived the body after death to receive merited punishment and reward.

The masculine cult worshipped the sun and the sky, rather than the moon and earth revered by the goddess mysteries. Popular with military men, Mithraism joined several emperors in homage to *Sol Invictus*, and Mithra was commonly called by that name. Although in this age of syncretism Mithra's chapels were built near temples of the goddess, and some priests of Mithra served also in the Eleusinian rites, women were always excluded from the Mithraic mysteries. Ceremonies took place in mountain caves or in forest shrines designed as caves that were images of the cosmos, with their heaven-like vaults and special apertures in the walls for penetration by the sun. Initiates were subject to terrifying ordeals, such as passing through flame blindfolded, jumping down a precipice, or swimming rivers. They were purified with water, and were branded on their foreheads; they shared a ceremonial meal of bread and water or wine. Sacrifices of birds and animals were made in the shrines, and in some Mithraeums actual or symbolic human sacrifice took place.[23] At least in the Eastern chapels, a perpetual sacred fire burned, and a spring was always found in the vicinity; both were accorded superstitious respect. The great festival of the Mithraic cult was December 25; the sixteenth of each month was Mithra's holy day.

The sun god Mithra (or Mithras in some texts), often identified by a conical Phrygian cap, was an incarnated deity born from a rock whose role was as a mediator between the highest levels of the divine spirit and the human being seeking both a better life and a preparation for death. Those goals were common to the mystery religions, but the presence of mediator was new in the rituals of initiation. The task of Mithra is to find the cosmic bull and sacrifice it for the fertility of the earth, before he himself ascends to the heavens, borne by the sun. Again, the cattle-herding or cattle-stealing god is not new in Hellenistic religion, as pictures of Heracles and Hermes prove, and the *taurobolium* for the sacrifice of a bull or a substitute animal for the "washing in the blood" was common in the mystery shrines. The interpretation of the myth according to the best scientific principles of the ancient world appealed to many educated men of the time; yet the myth in terms of slaying the animal in man, of allegiance to the truth and one's fellow men, and of continuous death and rebirth appealed to all social classes.

A reading of the central book of *The Professor's House* in the context of the mysteries of Mithra solves some problems of meaning and adds depth to Tom Outland's story and to the attitudes of Godfrey St. Peter. In spite of Lillian's urging, for example, Tom firmly keeps his secret of the mesa from her, and only reveals it as he initiates St. Peter into his "secrets." Tom's loyalty to Rodney Blake, teaching the little girls about his "remarkable friend" and interpreting his behavior as "always noble" in spite of Blake's betrayal, can be explained by the strong vows of fidelity taken by the Mithraists. St. Peter's thoughts in the first book about Tom's behavior describe the attitudes of the Mithraic brotherhood:

> In personal relations he was apt to be exaggerated and quixotic. He idealized the people he loved and paid his devoir to the ideal rather than to the individual, so that his behaviour was sometimes a little too exalted for the circumstances. . . . One of his sentimental superstitions was that he must never on any account owe any material advantage to his friends, that he must keep affection and advancement far apart (*PH*151).

St. Peter engages in a sentimental idea of his own: there is, he is persuaded, a dream of self-sacrificing friendship and disinterested love among men of the working classes (*PH*,151). As Lillian becomes less cordial to Tom, he and the professor meet in an alcove at the university, suggesting Mithraic meeting shrines. The red casquettes that St. Peter wears to swim are made much of in both the first and last books. They are identified as looking like the helmets of warriors on the Parthenon frieze, but their softness would make them even more resemble the Phrygian cap of Mithra. St. Peter's strong associations with France, where his caps are made, make the possibilities more interesting; as Campbell tells us, the Phrygian cap was adopted as a symbol by the followers of the Enlightenment during the French Revolution.[24]

Mithraism has much to say to the dualities of *The Professor's House*: St. Peter, we learn early, lives two lives; part of his problem is having two houses; the whole country, Scott says, is split in two socially. Even the polarities of personality in his daughters and their husbands impose a problem for the professor. His final assessment of his life is that he had known two romances: one of the heart and a second of the mind. By struggling against the "evil" side of his dualities, he hopes that he can overcome them and establish order with the elements of good. Thus Lillian and Rosamond will no longer matter with their snake-like hate; he will discard the part of his personality that has been grafted onto the original; he will give his loyalty to the memory of the young dead soldier. He will reject his second house and enjoy his removal from family and society to his vault-like attic and his reborn self. Mithraic ideas help to explain some of the obscure language of these ideas and, further, to solve some of the small puzzles of the novel: a phrase like "the descent through the humanity of the house" (the means of gathering unwanted passions in the Mithraic dogma, as well as Dante's descent), or the otherwise meaningless repetition of the fact that his family would sail for home on the sixteenth of the month (Mithra's sacred day),[25] or the symbolism of the "seven motionless pines" as they drink up the sun, and of the "stars with the same immobility" (astrological signs of the cult), or the description of his existence after marriage as a "catching at handholds" (the way up or down from the heavenly spheres).

The seven chapters of Tom Outland's story use much of the information found in Cumont's accounts of the Mithraic solar cult. It sets the scene, with Rodney and Tom becoming herders of cattle, in the same way that Mithra is represented, and then the two establishing a fraternal bond. Tom describes Rodney in much the same terms as those the professor had used for such men: "He was the sort of fellow who can do anything for somebody else, and nothing for himself. There are lots like that among working-men. They aren't trained by success to a sort of systematic selfishness" (*PH*,164). Tom reads aloud to Roddy a hundred lines of Caesar each day, as the Mithraist soldiers read their liturgy. Their winter cabin is located in a grove by a hill, as the shrines often were. The river at the foot of the mesa is a site of danger and challenge. One of the chief symbols of the Mithraic mysteries, very visible in most friezes of the god, was the panther. Cather uses a simile to introduce that animal into the story: black thunder-storms pounce like a panther without warning. Tom says: "I've never heard thunder so loud as it was there. The cliffs threw it back at us, and we thought the mesa itself, though it seemed so solid, must be full of deep canyons and caverns, to account for the prolonged growl and rumble that followed every crash of thunder" (*PH*,172). Thunderbolts as symbols of the power of the sovereign sky god can be traced to the Persian sources of Mithraism.[26] Lightning, which in addition to being a symbol of the power of the sky god is a sign in the mysteries and in psychoanalysis of male transformation, accompanies the thunder. And for Vico, thunder and lightning are primitive communications of the gods. Immediately following the blackness, the thunder and lightning, horizontal rays of the sun appear, recreating the Mithraic ritual in which total darkness, often filled with threatening sounds, was pierced by blinding light. A revelation followed in the Mithraic mysteries; in the canyon there is revealed to Tom the first evidence of the Pueblo past.

The third chapter celebrates Christmas, the day of divine services at the time of the winter solstice for the sun god as well as for the Christ. (It is interesting that a celebration of or preparation for Christmas is mentioned in every one of Cather's twelve novels.) The holiday brings Henry Atkins to complete the trio that often represents the Mithraic cult. Henry has no faults, apparently, except a fondness for drink; his later death--or sacrifice--involves the snake that is part of the cult symbolism and the branding on the forehead. In a conversation about his family Henry leaves Tom and Roddy wondering as he counts his siblings: "Eighteen we was in all, when we sat down at table. . . . Mother and father, and ten living, and four dead, and two still-born" (*PH*,184). He is, as a natural Mithraist, counting souls, not bodies, that exist in the family. On Christmas eve Tom makes the dangerous crossing of the river and finds a golden land where he experiences a sense of exaltation at the sight of a great cavern and the "little city of stone." His response

is appropriately religious: "Such silence and stillness and repose--
immortal repose. The village sat looking down into the canyon with the
calmness of eternity" (*PH*,180).

The exploration of Cliff City in May discloses some elements
common to both the pueblo culture and the mystery cult: the large
cavern with the sloping roof, the sacred spring, a ladder, and even a
corpse of a young woman. Father Duchene, who knows enough ancient
civilization to identify the design of the Pueblo pottery as identical to
that of Crete, surmises that the woman, "Mother Eve," was an unfaithful
wife murdered by her husband. For some reason, he makes this
judgment "slyly"; in primitive societies this punishment is permissible,
he says. With his study, he would have known of the sacrifices in
primitive worship, as well. Mother Eve is found apart from the city in
a structure in a high arch, possibly a kiva for religious ceremonies, and
the fact that she was placed on a yucca mat and covered after her death
suggests something other than revenge. Her look of terrible agony
matches the expression of the "tauctoronous," or bull-slaying, Mithra--
the most frequent form of his statuary, and one used in his mystery
rites. The Mithraic sacrifice, according to Campbell, is a new, or
perhaps resurgent, interpretation of that mythic symbol: "The world is
to be not improved, but affirmed, even in what to the rationalizing
moralist appears to be its most horrible, ungodlike sinfulness: for
precisely in that resides its creative force, since out of death, decay,
violence, and pain comes life."[27] This mystical interpretation states the
essence of St. Peter's submissiveness to his new condition in the final
book of *The Professor's House*.

Father Duchene's further speculations are focused on the religious life
of the Anasazi, or "Ancient Ones," as the later tribes named the Indians
of these pueblos: "I see them here, isolated, cut off from other tribes,
working out their destiny . . . purifying life by religious ceremonies and
observances. . . . Like you, I feel a reverence for this place. Wherever
humanity has made that hardest of all starts and lifted itself out of mere
brutality, is a sacred spot" (*PH*,199). His hypotheses, coinciding with
archeological theories of Cather's time, serve to relate the Indian
practices to the whole of man's religious impulse. Cather's interesting
use of a priest in this setting intensifies the idea that this chapter
conveys the kind of sacred knowledge transmitted in Mithraic rites.

Tom's visit to Washington serves to contrast the lives of the
bureaucrats--slaves, he considers them--with those of the Pueblo people
and to allow for Rodney's betrayal by the sale of the artifacts. The brief

final chapter is an approximation of the rituals of the mysteries of Mithra. Because the cults were small groups of about twenty men, there were so many of them spread over the vast Roman Empire, and very little written liturgy remains, the rites revealed by the physical evidence of the cave shrines, the statues of Mithra, and the numerous friezes extant are the primary sources of information. Nevertheless, using what is known, it is apparent that Cather again uses the very last part of her story for the moments of transformation--the rebirth into another condition that is the goal of the initiate.

It is, says Tom, a night he will never forget. Crossing the river, he finds the sun and moon both in the sky--an astronomical moment that Cather had used before in both *My Ántonia* and *One of Ours*. He lies on a solitary rock, connoting Mithra's origin, and watches the sunset, which, like the sunrise, signals an important scene whenever it appears in the book. His state of mind alters, bringing a new awareness and happiness:

> "I remember these things, because, in a sense, that was the first night I was ever really on the mesa at all--the first night all of me was there. This was the first time I ever saw it as a whole. . . . Something had happened in me that made it possible for me to co-ordinate and simplify, and that process, going on in my mind, brought with it great happiness. It was possession. . . . For me the mesa was no longer an adventure, but a religious emotion" (*PH*,226).

His mystical monologue takes us back to Rome, with the idea of filial piety, so important to the Mithraists, and his reading of the *Aeneid*. His euphoria continues as he wakens when "the sun's rays hit the mesa top," and, like the sun god, he feels that he assimilates the solar energy in some direct way. He is consumed by the sun, until he can bear no more. He understands, as the professor will later, that instead of losing everything he has found everything. Finally, he tells the professor, "I landed here and walked into your garden," as if he had moved down through the ether. As in Cather's other use of the mysteries, the language is just elaborate enough and the allusions to the rituals are just pointed and frequent enough to suggest the mysteries without impeding the story.

The end of St. Peter's narrative plays out as the middle-aged professor remembers and assimilates the secrets told to the young Tom by the old trails and stones and water-courses. What St. Peter has learned affirms that it is a mistake to be middle-aged, that Tom Outland, like Claude Wheeler of *One of Ours*, has been fortunate in escaping the drudgery and disillusionment of the adult world to become "Our Tom," in Kathleen's words and a "glittering idea" in Scott's words. Tom, by remaining eternally young and close to nature, has taught St. Peter to recover that state in his own development. The professor knows that "adolescence grafted a new creature into the original one. . . . What he had not known was that, at a given time, that first nature could return to a man, unchanged by all the pursuits and passions and experiences of life" (*PH*,242). In his near-death experience, he has been reborn: he has lost allegiance to family, especially to his wife, and has become as one with Tom, who represents Mithra--"eternally young and vigorous," in Cumont's description, pursuing the powers of darkness without mercy, and assuring salvation both in this world and in that to come.[28]

The overlap of the Mithraic and the Anasazi Indian cultures is substantial. First, there is the important fact of the architecture of both--built to reflect a similar sense of man's place in the cosmos. The cave of the ritual where the Mithraic initiates met represented the cosmos contained by the vault of heaven and governed by the planets, as ancient authors wrote.[29] Like the pueblos, the caves or shrines have only small slits to allow passage of the sunlight at certain hours. In reflecting the world and its order, the structure takes on a sacred aspect. The location in the forest, where the human can become a part of nature, allows for the frequent rituals of purification. Another similarity is the sudden disappearance of both groups from their customary habitats, only to emerge in different organizations later--the Anasazi reappeared in Pueblo, Hopi, and other tribes; the Mithraists returned first as Manichaeans and later as a variety of "brotherhoods." Scholars are still debating the origins and fates of both groups. Of the Pueblo Indians, however, Cather could have known little besides their cities and the artifacts left behind in the thirteenth century; of the Mithraic cult she could have known the Roman writers as well as the numerous scholars researching the mysteries in the early the twentieth century. As Orphism is a philosophical and religious background for the events in the canyons of the Southwest in *The Song of the Lark*, Mithraism provides a doctrine useful for the articulation of Tom Outland's experience and the professor's rebirth as a result of the revelation of that experience.

The similarities between the Mithraism represented by Tom and the Christianity represented by Augusta are also striking. Because Christianity was developing in the Roman world as Mithraism spread, their culture in common assured a connection with many contemporary mystery religions. Ultimately, both are the products of the rampant syncretism of the time. Both religions revere incarnated young gods born on December 25 who are mediators in the human search for redemption and salvation, both celebrate a communion after a sacrifice, and in both initiates anticipate eventual resurrection, after which they will be judged. In *The Professor's House* Cather continues her comparisons of religions, finding the many correspondences of essential dogma as well as of symbolism in these two "sister-religions," as Jung calls them.[30]

From the beginning of the novel St. Peter resists conversion "back to the religion of my fathers." He is reminded of holy days only when he talks to the pious Augusta. She rescues him when his life is threatened, but she saves only the body to which he is indifferent; his soul is transformed by those secrets shared by Tom Outland after his mesa experience. Significantly, those secrets are revealed only in the results they have on St. Peter's life; like all mysteries, they are ineffable. St. Peter's lecture in the first book of the novel expresses admiration for the mystery of the services in the early Christian cathedrals, the biblical literature produced by the theologians, and the great art that followed. However, the lecture concludes abruptly with a sentence pregnant with meaning: "But I think the hour is up" (*PH*,56). The professor's Christian environment is indicated by the names of his wife, Lillian, and her "second self," their older daughter, Rosamond. Their names are derived from the flowers that are symbols of the Virgin Mary, and the name Kathleen is derived from one that means "pure"; together they must relate to the professor's questions about the Magnificat and the "Mystical Rose, Lily of Zion, Tower of Ivory" in the Catholic liturgy. Yet, in spite of the religious connotations given to the women in the family, they all have a dark side of cruelty or hate or jealousy. Another, rather oblique, allusion to St. Peter's Christian background is his preparation of lamb *saignant* (literally "bleeding") for his ceremonial meals with Tom. This suggestion of Christian sacrifice would be less noteworthy if it were not for Tom's comparable meals on the mesa with Rodney. They cannot shoot the sheep because it has a priestly look, but instead kill a cow--an act more in keeping with the Mithraic sacrificial practices.

These symbolic sacrifices are critical to the meaning of the professor's story. As hero, Tom Outland has been sacrificed in the service of France, to save a country. But St. Peter also submits to what Jung calls a fatal compulsion that draws the hero towards sacrifice and suffering. The danger to the hero is "isolation in himself" because he differentiates himself from others. Neumann elaborates on Jung's analysis: "Whereas the average individual has no soul of his own, because the group and its canon of values tell him what he may or may not be psychically, the hero is one who can call his soul his own because he has fought for it and won it."[31] Sacrifice is necessary--of an earlier part of life, of normal living, of part of the self--in order to save one's soul. The professor has won his struggle to return to himself as a young boy--a primitive, a part of the lake and the clouds and the seven pine trees turning red in the declining sun. What he must do to achieve that state is to deny the years between the time of his boyhood and the present, which had been "accidental and ordered from the outside" (*PH*,264). Like the Mithraists, he will exclude women from his life, escape the house that is a symbol of the female world, and retreat to those spaces that promise isolation-- his attic with the desk that was a "hole one could creep into," his walled-in garden, his sand-spit by the lake. His "women," his "ladies," that are only dressmaker forms who make no human demands will stay, along with Augusta, who reminds him of the realities of life and the inevitability of death.

Death and rebirth are more dramatically achieved in the two books of this period--*The Professor's House* and *My Mortal Enemy*--than in the earlier Cather novels. The protagonists are middle-aged and concerned with physical death, as well as spiritual rebirth. The periods of national development represented by the figures of the stories, are those of full maturity, just before decline. Godfrey St. Peter and Myra Henshawe reveal much about us all.

My Mortal Enemy

For those scholars who write biographical criticism, both *The Professor's House* and *My Mortal Enemy* reflect strikingly the attitude of their author toward the world after 1922. Edith Lewis wrote of Willa Cather in her early years in New York: "I think that, unperceived by most of the people who knew her, there was in her also a deep strain of melancholy."[32] The desolate, ill, unlovable protagonist of the second half of *My Mortal Enemy* sees the world as the middle-aged Cather must have seen it in an unhappy period, when she asked Elizabeth Sergeant, who had begun analysis with one of Jung's students, whether psychoanalysis might help her. Jung's view in "The Stages of Life" that we often falsely assume that our truths and ideals will serve us as we move past the afternoon of life is applicable: "For what was great in morning will be little at evening, and what in the morning was true will at evening become a lie. . . . An inexorable inner process enforces the contraction of life."[33] In Vico's analysis of cultures, the same process takes place; and when the age of the author and the corresponding stage of development of his nation occur at the same time, the effect intensifies. Goethe explained his own creative exuberance in those terms: "When I was eighteen, Germany was eighteen"; Cather and her country arrived at their declining years at the same time. "There is a time in a writer's development," she said in the 1922 preface to *Alexander's Bridge*, "when his 'life line' and the line of his personal endeavor meet. This may come early or late, but after it occurs his work is never quite the same."

Cather's attention to her own stages of life are undeniable in this brief story, as characters remembered or realized are presented during Myra Henshawe's last days. There is little Billy (a nickname for Willa as a child and again at the university), "the most truthful, noble-hearted little fellow," whom Myra hasn't seen since he was sixteen, and who killed himself at twenty-three--the age at which Cather left Nebraska for the East. (*MME*,71). Next come the nameless young journalist, whose short hair, rather heavy face, and clear, honest eyes are descriptive of Cather after her college years, and Nellie as a young woman wasting her talents in a dead-end teaching job, yet learning about great literature and the paradoxes of life. Together the two younger women represent Cather in her early years as journalist and teacher. Cather's life, in the form of the deaths and rebirths which she understood as constituting all existence, flashes before our eyes as Myra Henshawe lies dying.

Myra, in her mature years, reveals additional personalities: she is the imperious woman of the New York artistic set in the first book, and later is the pathetic invalid without resources or friends. Nellie remembers her as the Druid goddess of *Norma*, and at times she takes the role of a lower-class Irishwoman in her behavior and speech. She is Mrs. Henshawe or Mrs. Myra to Nellie, but is forever the fascinating Molly Driscoll to her husband, who is the only one who can, through eyes of love, see her whole. Like the name Billy, Molly comes from Cather's own past: it was Isabelle McClung's private name for Willa.[34] If *My Mortal Enemy* is read even in part as biographical, the question of the multiple personality must be addressed. Many writers cite 1922, the year she said the world had broken in two, as the beginning of her attention to dual manifestation of character, but in a letter to Sarah Orne Jewett in 1908 Cather confesses that she has been in a deep perplexity for the past few years because of her habits of mind, and asks about the new disease called split personality.[35] There is, moreover, greater meaning to the duality of Cather's view than the habits of her own mind. Her books, from *O Pioneers!* to *My Mortal Enemy* increasingly employ the double meaning, the second self, the pairs of opposites, until in this novel there is little that is not split in two.

Through the commanding figure of Myra, Cather presents a vivid portrait of an alienated woman in a deteriorating world, a literary contribution that she had hoped Henry James might make. In a Lincoln *Courier* article of 1895 she had written, "I wish James would write about modern society, about 'degeneracy' and the new woman and all the rest of it," although she doubted that he would throw much light on the subject. (*WP*,1:275). In *My Mortal Enemy* she brought together the themes, illuminating the pervading darkness that she saw. The light falls ruthlessly on the figure of Myra Henshawe, focusing on the worldly woman in her own sophisticated milieu in the first half of the novel and in shabby circumstances ten years later. She is presented first in Parthia, Illinois, where Nellie Birdseye, a young Midwesterner, is introduced as the narrator; the events of the novel, however, occur in New York City in the early years of the twentieth century and on the West Coast ten years later. The pace and style of New York during the Christmas holidays furnish the sense of the modern world. Much movement, from the train to the ferry to the crosstown street car, introduces Nellie to the big city. Non-fictional persons, as well, sharply bring the specific time and place to mind. Helen Modjeska, the guest of honor at the Henshawes' New Year's Eve party, and Jefferson de Angelais, another actor, help to provide the dramatic final scene of the first book. The conversation in that scene centers on current performances of two other artists--Sarah Bernhardt in her role as Hamlet and Jean de Reszke in his return to the Metropolitan Opera stage. The introduction of real people into a work of fiction, a device that seemed remarkable to critics when it was used by novelists--Capote and Doctorow are two--some fifty years later, here lends a sense of immediacy and reality.

Two parallel historical eras unfold, to reveal the similarities between the modern period and the Renaissance of the sixteenth and seventeenth centuries. Myra's intense interest in the arts, for example, points to the Renaissance stage, from the moment she is first seen in Parthia strumming a guitar. The emphasis on the arts--opera and tragedy, sculpture and architecture--summons the spirit of the awakening of the Western world to its power. The Renaissance respect for the arts became awe and even a belief in the artist as a divine creator.[36] This idea is dramatized in *My Mortal Enemy* during a scene in which Modjeska, formally seated as on a throne in the moonlight, is surrounded and adored by other artists as the *"Casta Diva"* aria from *Norma* is sung. One of several responses evoked by the music is the vision of Norma, the Druid high priestess of Bellini's opera. In this scene, Modjeska is the divinity for Myra and her friends, although Nellie's memories of the aria make Myra *her* divine figure. The atmosphere of a sacred ritual is stronger than anywhere in Cather's novels to this point. Her belief in the identity of art with religion, so frequently expressed in her fiction and criticism, has gathered such power that she can create this memorable moment in fewer than ten sentences.

The background of late Renaissance attitudes can explain some of the puzzling passages of *My Mortal Enemy*. Myra knows two classes of people--artists and the "moneyed" people. The materialism of Oswald's rich German business friends from the North irritate Myra and their solemnity is too much for her sense of humour. Their wives excite her envy, exposing her when she is least attractive. Southerners, however, fare no better in Myra's esteem. She criticizes the southern family living in the apartment above, finding fault with their speech, appearance, and behavior. Myra's prejudices help to increase her alienation, but ironically the prevailing Renaissance idea of her own Irish nationality was of a wild race "without knowledge of God or good manners."[37] That Myra's own coarseness is just beneath the surface is demonstrated in a rude outburst against Nellie: her manner and language are those of an unlettered Irishwoman, as she dismisses her young friend after a quarrel: "It's owing to me infirmities, dear Mrs. Casey, that I'll not be able to go as far as me door wid ye." The lower-class Irish strain is more lightly noted earlier by the "Irish Washerwoman" tune played on the penny whistle in New York as she passes and her reference to herself as "Biddy." Her jealousy of women better placed than she in society reinforces the images that Myra has of herself as an outsider.[38]

These strong prejudices suggest a general insecurity and unrest of the kind that developed in Western Europe in the sixteenth and seventeenth centuries, resulting in what Wylie Sypher calls a "tremor of malaise and distrust."[39] He describes the period as one marked by "disproportion, disturbed balance, ambiguity, clashing impulses."[40] Myra and the world she inhabits exhibit all these frightening qualities. Her own extremes of values, the instability of her relationships, and the ambiguities of her life reflect Cather's view of twentieth-century America and its parallels in the late Renaissance in Europe and in the days of the waning Roman Empire.

For Myra, as for the intellectuals of the sixteenth and seventeenth centuries, the response to lost hope in depressing circumstances was withdrawal from society and intense soul-searching. The resulting "crisis of faith and conscience" in Sypher's words and "failure of confidence," in Clark's words (echoing Gilbert Murray's "failure of nerve" of the classical period), which characterized both eras, is the dominant theme of the second half of *My Mortal Enemy*. Confusion and a sense of lost control fragment the three chief characters in the novel: Myra's illness invades vital organs, Oswald loses his position and income, and Nellie is trapped in an unsuitable profession, without direction or purpose. All participate in a collective despair that dominates Cather's view of the age.

In the seventeenth century the oppositions that had long been held in balance broke into their polarities, signalled by the philosophy of the split between body and mind, mind and feelings, body and soul. It is this fundamental perception that illuminates many facets of this *My Mortal Enemy*, including its two-part structure, the many images of opposites, and especially the mystery religion that underlies the meaning of *My Mortal Enemy*. Much that is puzzling about the structure, the symbols, and the characterizations of Cather's fiction comes to a solution if seen in the light of Gnostic philosophy and ritual.

Gnosticism generated in the early years of Christianity, out of the Persian and Syrian notions of good and evil. Its mystical forces swept the Oriental cults of the Near East, then moved westward to Egypt, Alexandria, and Rome. During the first centuries of the Christian era the Gnostic world view competed with the beliefs of other major religious philosophies. Like the many other syncretistic sects of the time, Gnosticism developed its philosophy from ancient and contemporary sources and found expression in many diverse forms. Elaine Pagels in *The Gnostic Gospels* offers an explanation of the origins of Gnostic thought: it was a "reaction to the shattering if traditional religious views" after the fall of Jerusalem; a "potentially universal experience of the self projected into religious mythology"; a mystical experience.[41] Cather, of course, could not have known the scholarly conclusions that have been made since the discovery of the Nag Hammadi texts in 1945. But most of what was known earlier came from the writings of Gnostics such as Valentinus and Basilides or their Christian enemies such as Clement of Alexandria, Ireneus, Tertullian, and, of course, St. Augustine, all of whom Cather undoubtedly was familiar with as a student and teacher of classical literature. The work of many later writers whom she admired, among them Chrétien de Troyes, Anatole France, and Goethe, reflected their interest in Gnosticism.

Although the beginning of Gnosticism was contemporary with Christianity in Rome, the systems resurfaced in the Middle Ages and had a resurgence again in the Reformation of the seventeenth century, when a militant mysticism made popular such writers as Jacob Boehme and George Fox. Gnostic thought, along with Neoplatonism, was again fashionable in Europe and would rise again with the corresponding cultural patterns in the twentieth century. In modern times, Gnostic beliefs have become so strong that Jung said in "The Spiritual Problem of Modern Man" of 1931: "The world has seen nothing like it since the end of the seventeenth century. We can compare it only to the flowering of Gnostic thought in the first and second centuries after Christ. The spiritual currents of our time have, in fact, a deep affinity with Gnosticism."[42] In *The American Religion*, Harold Bloom concludes that obsessed Americans are practicing a "religion of the self," which is a throwback to Gnosticism in the emphasis on individuality, self-deification by identifying with a god, and religious solitude. Cather's *My Mortal Enemy* and Jung's "Spiritual Problems of Modern Man" make parallel suggestions that Gnosticism lurks in the background of the human social consciousness, constantly ready to reappear when a civilization begins to fray. The philosophy began as a strong force and remains one. The characteristics of Gnostic thought were the boldest expression of many of the general ideas in religious development at the beginning of the Christian era. Hans Jonas, in *The Gnostic Religion*, summarizes Gnosticism as "dualistic transcendent religion of salvation"; that is, its nature is religious, it concerns itself primarily with salvation, it exhibits a transcendent conception of God, and it maintains a radical view of the dualism of all existence.[43] That dualism, especially the polarization between good and evil, is the strongest identifying feature of Gnosticism. The struggle between good and evil, spirit and matter, soul and body, was the primary concern of the initiate, whose goal was to escape the iniquities of life, called the "mortal house" in the Gnostic literature.

In the syncretistic age of the rise of the Gnostic religion, many cults developed out of the Oriental mysticism and philosophy of the pre-Christian era. One important cult was Hermeticism, itself an "eclectic conglomerate." Its rites included the initiation, the divine revelation, and the experience of rebirth common to the mystery religions. So similar were their practices to those of the mystery religions that Valentinus, an early Christian Gnostic, was accused of following the Eleusinian mysteries in his initiation rites. More than most mysteries, however, Hermeticism imposed an ascetic self-discipline, as its scriptures stress: "There are two sorts of things, the corporeal and incorporeal; that which is mortal is of one sort, and that which is divine is the other sort; and he who wills to make his choice is left free to choose the one or the other." The seven specific steps to rebirth, as they are formulated by Hermeticism, are relevant to an understanding of *My Mortal Enemy*. They are: a call to repentance, intimate instruction in Gnosis from a "father," the initiate's self-preparation for the choice between the temporal and the eternal, silent meditation, an ecstatic vision of light, an interpretation of the mystical experience, and a final regeneration.[44] The initiate, as in all mystery religions, was not free to communicate any of this experience to others.

The most powerful of the systems of Gnosticism and the one considered among the great religions of the world was founded by Mani (sometimes spelled Manes), a third-century Parthian, who blended the Gnostic, Christian, and mystery religions with Zoroastrian philosophy to suit the spiritual needs of the time. As Mithraism was disappearing from the Roman world, Manichaeism became its successor. During the period of intense interest in the mystery religions at the beginning of the twentieth century, the knowledge of Manichaeism was made available when the hymn cycles were translated from Parthian, the language of Mani, and began to be published in 1904. A translator summarizes one cycle, which begins with a soul in distress, "for whom the hour of life is ended. Fire and fog daunt it, and hideous demons, and it beseeches its Saviour for redemption. Life ebbs from its body, and its distress deepens; it no longer invokes the Saviour confidently, but asks in despair 'who shall save me?'. . . . In the last extant verses from the eighth canto the soul tells how, rescued from all sins and clothed in a garment of Light it has looked upon the dark prison of the body it has abandoned."[45]

A strict dualism of good and evil, symbolized by light and dark, was the chief characteristic of Manichaeism. The world was one of evil, not because of sins of individuals, but because it was created that way; the material body, part of the evil world, must be denied in order to purify the soul, which will survive it. The religion offered a strict morality, revelation, redemption, and immortality. The worship was simple, with prayers, hymns, special feasts, and the equivalents of baptism and the Lord's Supper. In contrast to the Mithraic cult, women were welcomed, and some female figures were worshipped. Although many followers concealed their allegiance to Manichaeism while openly ascribing to another creed, the very nature of the doctrine that found evil in marriage and friendships, and good in withdrawal from the world made concealment possible. As in all Gnosticism, the Manichaean message to awaken came when death was imminent. The demand for the real rigor of the process was limited to those of the "elect," who were to lead an ascetic life with rules for giving of alms, frequent fasting, a vegetarian diet, and the prohibition of preparing food, drinking wine, and owning property. On a second level of believers were "soldiers," who followed a less rigorous regimen, but whose service accommodated the sanctified life led by the elect, often women and members of the upper classes. While the elect were freed into the world of Light upon release from the prison of the body, the soldiers must return to the world of darkness and wander far until they achieve the status of the elect. A third group, the "sinners," were doomed to Hell.

The philosophy and practices of the Manichaeans help in many instances to solve the enigma of Myra. Cather helps by very pointed clues crowded into her spare story, starting with the mention of Parthia eight times in the first twelve pages, combined with Lydia's name, Oswald's oriental half-moon eyes, and the comparison of Myra's hair to that of a Persian goat. The geographic directions lead to Asia Minor, the source of this final pagan mystery religion. The dualities of the entire book are so numerous that they become almost awkward--the number two, the mention of pairs, and especially the sygyzies, or pairs of opposites. A few examples: Myra's sarcasm leaves Nellie not knowing whether she has been burned or chilled; Madison Square Garden has a double personality, social and commercial; there is something both hard and soft in Oswald's eyes; Myra remarks that people can be lovers and enemies at the same time; Oswald concludes that Myra's life has been both hard and glorious. Even St. Gaudens' statue of Diana, appearing twice (once on Nellie's way to church), is a reminder of the dual light and dark aspects of that pagan goddess, who is both the mother of all living things and the destroyer. Myra is presented as both the dove

("When she was peaceful, she was like a dove with its wings folded") (*MME*,29), and like a serpent ("She was smiling, but her mouth curled like a little snake, as I had seen it do long ago") (*MME*,72-73). Although many of these pairs of opposites might refer to any dualistic system (or any writer obsessed with dualisms), the dove and serpent are the chief syzygies of Gnostic thought. When these dualities are combined with the many other symbols and allusions, so dense in this brief story, they fit, in the aggregate, the Manichaean philosophy.

The symbolism of the moon relates here to that philosophy as well. Slote notes that the moon-myth is one of the most complex of Cather's symbols and that its meaning is of "some high, illimitable beauty; the sign of yearning and desire; the radiant or mysterious illumination of darkness; and the sign also of the voyage perilous" (*KA*,97-98). Slote connects the moon-myth with Diana, but that goddess (sometimes as Artemis, her Greek name) is simply the one known best in traditional mythology of the Western world. Cather uses the Diana myth prettily as Nellie's first view of the beautiful Saint Gaudens statue reinforces her sense of New York as a wonderland. Even winter was tamed, like a polar bear led on a leash by a beautiful lady. We are not told, but Cather is using the Roman ideas that the statue of Diana never suffered rain or snow and that she is the master of wild beasts. As so often in Cather's fiction, the presence of divine spirit is symbolized by the murmur of water: "I lingered long by the intermittent fountain. Its rhythmical splash was like the voice of the place. It rose and fell like something taking deep, happy breaths; and the sound was musical, seemed to come from the throat of spring" (*MME*,21-22). Nellie is "moon-struck," too, part of the ritual, as messenger boys dodge about her carrying plants and wreaths and a young man pipes a tune. As so often in Cather's novels, the classical moon myth is on the surface of the story, and as the meanings move deeper, the myths become buried in the story and are more profound.

The dozens of goddesses in the mystery religions were always identified with the moon, and their rituals were timed to coincide with its appropriate phases. The moonlit scene on New Year's Eve in the first part of *My Mortal Enemy* is clearly an adoration of Modjeska as goddess with a ritual arrangement of figures around her. In that numinous setting, the singing of the "*Casta Diva*" from Bellini's *Norma* reinforces Nellie's sense of the mysterious power of Myra and begins an extensive metaphor for the development of her character. All of Cather's heroines are related to the moon; they are what Claude Wheeler calls "children of the moon." In the second part of the book, with Myra confined to her sickroom most of the time, the moon is mentioned only as a memory of that New Year's Eve scene, and the sun appears only as it is making "his final plunge into Pacific." Myra expresses the cosmic view of the Manichaeans as she says, "I'd love to see this place at dawn. . . . That is always such a forgiving time. When that first, cold, bright streak comes over the water, it's as if all our sins were pardoned; as if the sky leaned over the earth and kissed it and gave it absolution" (*MME*,61). The Manichaeans consider the light of both the sun and the moon as agents of salvation; Oswald and Nellie are comforted by their reasonable assurance that Myra had seen the dawn before her death.

The religious theme envelops the beginning of the story with Myra's youthful rejection of her uncle's Catholicism, and her dying acceptance of that faith provides the resolution of the novel. Cather recreates the religious ferment of the Renaissance: the general confusion of beliefs and the split from the church by the leaders of the Reformation are mirrored by that bitter estrangement of Myra and John Driscoll because of her choice of a Protestant husband. At the same time the scene is a re-creation of the first step of the Manichaean soul's descent into the world of darkness. There are multiple sojourns in the world, called "houses" or "mortal houses." Myra's journeys take her from a dwelling that is "like Sleeping Beauty's palace" to a New York brownstone and finally to a miserable apartment on the West Coast, where she is near death and ready to undergo the suffering and rituals that will purify her soul for its ascent to the Light. The world itself, in the Gnostic scheme, is the underworld, or hell, and escape is the goal. Even Nellie thinks perhaps John Driscoll, whose Catholic funeral was a great pageant, now seems a more romantic figure than Myra: "Was it not better to get out of the world with such pomp and dramatic splendour than to linger on in it, having to take account of shirts and railway trains, and getting a double chin into the bargain?" (*MME*,16). The first part of *My Mortal Enemy* shows Myra as a focus for the attentions of young men, receiving their homage and fostering their love affairs. She is generous to her friends, envious of the rich and powerful to the point of "insane ambition," and, in the young Nellie's eyes, the possessor of a mysterious presence. But with a quarrel between Myra and Oswald come both the revelation of Myra's duplicity and Nellie's comprehension of evil:

And now everything was in ruins. . . . What I felt was fear; I was afraid to look or speak or move. Everything about me seemed evil. When kindness has left people, even for a few minutes, we become afraid of them, as if their reason had left them. When it has left a place where we have always found it, it is like shipwreck; we drop from security into something malevolent and bottomless (*MME*,42).

The last clause could be borrowed from the Manichaean descriptions of the human soul's entrance into mortal life.

This scene highlights the sense of uncertainty that dominates the themes of the novel. Cather works to maintain the ambiguities, as the question of Oswald's fidelity to Myra shows. The reader is given no proof that Oswald's story of the topaz cuff-links is not true or that he has any but a friendly interest in either the young journalist or Nellie or anyone else. Yet Aunt Lydia assumes an affair, and Nellie is of two minds: she thinks him properly served as he anticipates Myra's accusations, but often after that she wonders at his gentle heart. When Oswald has an opportunity to set Nellie (and the reader) straight, his qualifiers confound the question, no matter where previous sympathies may lie: "Of course she was absolutely unreasonable when she was jealous. Her suspicions were sometimes--almost fantastic" (*MME*,84).

The second part of *My Mortal Enemy* is the story of Myra's preparation for her death, after the loss of her friends, her status, her glamorous surroundings, and her health and beauty. She is a Gnostic figure in the dualities of her person: "She sat crippled but powerful in her brilliant wrappings. She looked strong and broken, generous and tyrannical, a witty and rather wicked old woman, who hated life for its defeats, and loved it for its absurdities." She reveals her philosophy as she greets shock or sorrow with a laugh that seems to say: "Ah-ha, I have one more piece of evidence, one more, against the hideous injustice God permits in this world!" (*MME*,55). This evidence of the power of evil in the world that she is gathering is part of her revelation, her *gnosis*, that leads to her salvation.

Some of the more cryptic scenes in this second half of the book are illuminated by the Gnostic imagery embedded in Cather's pauciloquent prose.The problem of the southern women who live in the apartment above the Henshawes' seems at first glance to be somewhat humorous, with its most telling point an uncovering of Myra's ill temper and the blame assigned to Oswald. In fact, the "noise of the world" is a major symbol in the Gnostic view of the seduction of the human being by the conspirators who would claim the soul. "Come let us make him hear a great upheaval, that he may forget the heavenly voices," ask the evil forces in a Gnostic poem.[46] The women, although just back from church, are called by Myra "animals," "cattle," "pigs," "hens." The intensity of Myra's objections seems out of proportion as she says, "I"ve two fatal maladies, but it's those coarse creatures I shall die of," and Cather seems to spend excessive space on this conflict. In the Manichaean realm of light, peace and harmony prevailed; in the realm of earthly darkness, "the inhabitants of the world of matter jostled and drove one another hither and thither, chasing about frenziedly," says a scholar of Gnosticism. An interesting part of that myth is that "the realm of light was unbounded on three sides--to the north, to the east, and to the west. But to the south, it came up against darkness."[47] Nellie's request to the women for silence brings the comment that this was an "old story," repeating the phrase used earlier by Ewan Gray in a context more flattering to Myra.

Further allusions are found in the descriptions of Oswald as a sentinel at one time, and at another dressed in a suit with frogs and military collar to serve Myra's breakfast. His first appearance in the second book--looking like a servant, with downcast eyes, carrying a black tin tray--presents him as the Manichaean "soldier" who serves the member of the "elect" forbidden to prepare food. Nellie's analyses of him at the end of each part of the novel tell all: "I wondered . . . at the contradiction in his face: the strong bones, and the curiously shaped eyes without any fire in them. I felt that his life had not suited him; that he possessed some kind of courage and force which slept, which in another sort of world might have asserted themselves brilliantly. I thought he ought to have been a soldier or an explorer" (*MME*,52). The "force which slept," another of the major Gnostic images, describes the soul while it is condemned to earthly existence, which can be for many lifetimes until purification is complete. Sleeping or numbness is the state that in other religious systems would be suffered by the dead in the underworld. The explorer image matches the Gnostic command to wander in this world, a requirement fulfilled by Oswald rather amusingly in his professional connections with both railroad and steamship companies, and finally as he moves to Alaska. He, like Myra, will eventually find himself in "another sort of world," a phrase that says more than Nellie knows.

Other passages help to make *My Mortal Enemy* a coherent whole when they are placed in the context of the Gnostic journey. The recurring emphasis on gates and doors can be explained by the heightened importance of those images in the Gnostic doctrine. In many mystery cults the door is a gate to the seven zones of paradise. From the moment that Myra comes through the gate from her uncle's estate to the frequent knocking at the door in the second part of the book, the metaphor of moving to another realm is maintained. The Gnostic images of opposites--light and dark, noise and silence, cold and heat--are brought together in one passage at the seaside: "Light and silence: they heal all one's wounds--all but one, and that is healed by dark and silence. I find I don't miss clever talk, the kind I always used to have about me, when I can have silence. It's like cold water poured over fever" (*MME*,60-61). The dispelling of heat, often in the form of fever, was one of the frequent images used by Mani.[48] Some of Myra's odd behavior can be explained by comparing it to the practices of the Gnostics. Fasting is important for Manichaeans, for example, and mandatory on Sunday. At one point when Myra locks both Nellie and Oswald out her room from Saturday until Monday, Oswald confides to Nellie that she often secluded herself for even longer periods, times when she would have no source of nourishment. In further parallels to Gnostic rituals Myra makes a confession of the sins of her life to Nellie, and then they read from what is for Myra sacred literature: "How the great poets do shine on, Nellie! Into all the dark corners of the world. They have no night" (*MME*,68). The money Myra keeps "for unearthly purposes" satisfies the demand that followers of Mani contribute money for alms and other charitable purposes. The assurance Myra gives to her driver that a friend would meet her derives from the Manichaean belief that angels would meet the liberated soul on its ascent to the light.

Even seemingly insignificant matters can be threads in the Gnostic pattern of the novel: the jewels that appear throughout the book augment the meanings of the events to take on the kind of importance given to gems in the Gnostic systems, where each of the seven planets was associated with a stone with corresponding qualities. The opal, a symbol of bad luck, plays a part in Ewan Gray's courting of Esther, which brings Myra's dire prophecy. The topazes of Oswald's cufflinks, so prominent in the story, symbolize fidelity. And Myra's necklace of amethysts is, in the Gnostic system, a symbol of knowledge and awareness. The name *amethyst* is from the Greek *amethystos*, a remedy for drunkenness. Along with sleep and numbness, intoxication is a Gnostic metaphor for unconsciousness, a feature of existence in the mundane world.[49] Nellie's fear at the end of the book of the amethysts she has inherited from Myra is an indication of the power of full knowledge of the self. The gem of greatest significance, however, is the pearl. Myra disposes of the question of the topazes in a statement that it is disgusting for Oswald "to lie about personal decorations. A woman might do it now, . . . for pearls!" Coming at the end of a major division of a book, where Cather's emphasis is always important, this is unlikely to mean simply that women value personal decoration more than do men, or that pearls are better than topazes, or both. What then? The meaning is found in one of the major symbols of Gnosticism, where the pearl is used to represent the lost soul which must be recovered. Here Myra is foreshadowing the meanings of the second half of the novel.

To heighten meanings Cather also meticulously chooses the names of her characters, indicating national origin or personal characteristics. Oswald, from the Anglo-Saxon, means "divine power" or "chief appointed by the gods." Nellie is a diminutive of Helen ("light"), one of the four female figures in the Manichaean literature. Myra is a variant of Mary, another of the Manichaean females, whose role is much like that of the Christian Virgin. Oswald's nickname for her-- Molly, a derivative of Mary--confirms the connection, (and recalls that Molly was Isabelle McClung's pet name for Cather). The name Myrrha must be considered--the goddess who loved her father, even though the older man here is an uncle instead.[50] Especially in this very terse work, every word carries its share of the meaning of the whole. Even Esther, the name of a woman who is merely mentioned in the story, is from the Persian and means "star."

The central myth of Manichaeism is that of marriage--with the dualistic and inverted meanings that pervade the religion. The first statement that Nellie makes in the book reveals that Myra's marriage has always been the theme of the interesting stories told at holidays-- that time when myths central to a group are told. When Myra predicts in the light of the moon that Ewan and Esther will love "and very likely hell will come of it," she is not referring to marital spats, but to a religious punishment for desire, which is the beginning of evil, according to Mani. Myra's confession of guilt at having part in the romance is a serious judgment against herself. The mistrust of love and pleasure is a widespread theme in Gnostic philosophy, so much so that the Neoplatonism, which assimilated a great deal of Gnostic doctrine, treated Epicureanism as its "mortal enemy." But Mani went further to claim that "the main weapon of the world in its great seduction is love."[51] Because Myra's need is to destroy her love for Oswald so that she can purify her body and save her soul, she revises the story of her marriage to emphasize her unhappiness, while Oswald remembers their joy. Her jealousy springs from a love still strong, and it grieves her to accept service from the man she has loved so well. "Perhaps I can't forgive him for the harm I did him. Perhaps that's it," she says, in an intriguing bit of self-analysis. "People can be lovers and enemies at the same time, you know," she tells Nellie, reaffirming the co-existence of opposites in the Gnostic world.

These insights into love and its consequences help to solve the riddle of Myra's dying utterance. The Gnostic soul talking, asks, "Why must I die like this, alone with my mortal enemy?" Knowing Myra's love for Oswald, and understanding the Gnostic view that love is the greatest force of darkness, elevating the passions of the body and dimming the sacred fire of the soul, we might conclude that Oswald is her mortal enemy; that is, he is her enemy because she has loved him so intensely, and he is mortal because he is still subject to death. But he is only a manifestation of her distress. He does not react to her question, dreadful as it seems on the surface, because he has no reason for guilt. He is aware of her unconventional path to salvation, as his explanations of her behavior clearly show. And of course he understands her Gnostic world.

Myra's question is repeated twice in the book, once as she first asks it, and at the end as Nellie remembers it. Both times, it is immediately preceded by a discussion of love for others: Myra says, "I could bear to suffer . . . so many have suffered. But why must it be like this? I have not deserved it. I have been true in friendship; I have faithfully nursed others in sickness" (*MME*,78). The passage may seem to say that Myra does not deserve excessive suffering because she has been so faithful to friends. The reading depends on an ambiguity of referents for pronouns, not customary in Cather's writing, and undoubtedly intentional. Myra seems quite resigned to physical suffering, and she is courageous in her illness, as Oswald tells Nellie; so her problem lies elsewhere. Her question concerns the destiny of her soul. In her answer, the first *it* is her spiritual struggle that we are witnessing; *this* is the difficulty of her struggle; the second *it* is the release of her soul. To her own question, which is "Why must my spiritual struggle be so difficult?" she answers, "Because I have not deserved the release of my soul from the world. I have been a true friend, spending so much of myself on mortal love." This seeming virtue is the love for the world and others in it that the Gnostic doctrine denied by placing primary importance on the salvation of the soul. "I gain strength faster if I haven't people on my mind," Myra tells Nellie when they first meet again after ten years (*MME*,52), and Oswald thinks that Myra has used up the part of herself that fostered generous friendships. The final repetition of Myra's question is introduced by Nellie's description of the kind of love that must have once belonged to Myra and Oswald: "a common feeling exalted into beauty by imagination, generosity, and the flaming courage of youth." Ever after, Nellie's recognition of such beginning love brings remembrance of a dying woman and the "confession of the soul" that damns the material world and its assault on the soul's desire for salvation.

There can be no doubt that in the Gnostic system the body and the soul are constantly at war, and that the interpretation of Myra's last words must include some recognition that the body is the mortal enemy of the soul that is speaking, as many of the ancient religions insisted. Both times the question is repeated: "Why must I die like this, alone with my mortal enemy?" Nellie insists that we understand that this is a confession of the soul. Myra as the whole person is not, of course, her own mortal enemy in this moment before death, and she is not alone with Oswald; Nellie is there. Myra's soul, however, faces only one last enemy in this moment--her body. But in this dark, profound story, the single interpretation of the body as enemy of the soul is too simple-- almost simplistic. In keeping with the dense dualisms of the book, there are two interpretations, both of them useful. Oswald is the major representative of the enemy that is passion, but Anne Aylward, Ewan Gray, and Madame Modjeska also share in their demands on Myra's love.[52] Nellie begins to understand that violent natures like Myra's "sometimes turn against themselves . . . against themselves and all their idolatries" (*MME*,78). Myra's excessive love has been directed toward Oswald and her friends. To her dying day, she is unable to divest herself of that mortal feeling. Appropriately enough in a Gnostic novel, a dual interpretation of meaning is the most satisfactory.

The same kind of dual answer applies to the question of Myra's religious status at her death. She has made a full circle, leaving her devout Roman Catholic uncle to marry a protestant free-thinker and give up her religion, only to request the attentions of a priest and the sacrament as she dies. But there remain some ambiguities as she seems to return to the faith of her childhood. She argues with the priest, even when he is not present: "Ah, Father Fay, that isn't the reason! Religion is different from everything else; *because in religion seeking is finding.*" Nellie hears this and explains that Myra is saying that desire is fulfillment, the seeking is rewarded (*MME*,77). This paraphrase of Cather's often-repeated "*Le but n'est rien, le chemin, c'est tout*" is an inversion of the Christian belief that the goal is what matters. Myra's concern includes the question of faith as the way to salvation, in contrast with the Gnostic belief in knowledge through revelation. The name of her priest, Father Fay, reminds us of the doctrinal question: *fay* is an Old French word for faith, that after the medieval period came into the English language and was used nearly as frequently as the original word. Spenser, for example, uses *fay* in both *The Shepherd's Calendar* and the *Fairy Queen*. Myra's insistence on seeking and desire as the cornerstones of her religion is hardly orthodox Roman Catholic doctrine. Neither is her wish, carried out by Oswald, to be cremated and have her ashes scattered at sea.[53] Her choice to die on the ground is another Manichaean custom. As Myra sends money for a celebration of a mass for Modjeska, she says that in spite of breaking with the church she believes in holy words and holy rites, without naming specific rites or words (*MME*,70). She is continuing the idea set forth in *The Song of the Lark* that all religions are much the same in what they seek to do. But instead of choosing one faith to die by, she is of two minds, subscribes to two creeds, follows two roads to heaven.

In these seemingly contradictory beliefs Myra is following the same path taken by St. Augustine as he studied and accepted the creeds of Manichaeism, Neoplatonism, and finally Christianity. The nine years that Augustine spent as a Manichee helped to explain to him the source of evil, the problem that Myra deals with as she seems to be collecting evidence for the injustice that God permits. That comparison accounts for Father Fay's interest in Myra: "I wonder whether some of the saints of the early Church weren't a good deal like her. She's not at all modern in her make-up, is she?" Myra's incorporation of faith with gnosis would not have been surprising to the early Christians. In the syncretistic world of the mystery religions and early Christianity, Christ was included as a messiah who brought revelation to man, and some Manichaeans found the "mystery of light" through Christ.[54] Much of what we know as Christian creed today has been traced to Gnostic thought. Cather has brought her exposition of the mystery religions to the point at which Christianity will signal the *recorso* of her cycle and become the subject as well as the underlying mystery of her next two novels.

Like the whole of the Gnostic world, *My Mortal Enemy* is structured by pairs of opposites. The novel is divided into two approximately equal books; the six chapters of the first part focus on the arts; religious images pervade the seven chapters of the second part. The divisions are not arbitrary; just as the seven chapters of the central book of *The Professor's House* reflect the seven steps in the Mithraic philosophy, the seven books in the religious second part of *My Mortal Enemy* correspond to the realms of and the seven parts of the canon of Mani's writings. The number thirteen--the total--says Campbell, "represents a creative transcendence of the boundary . . . an achieved life beyond death."[55] In the first half the New York scenes are those of action and many stimuli for the senses, in contrast to the later tedium of a physically inert life of illness and meditation. Myra's transition from an outward to an inward world suggests the direction taken by the followers of the Gnostic religion and at the same time draws our attention to similar changes in the arts at the time of the late Renaissance. We have only to look at the work of the mannerist painters of the time, who, seeing shifting planes of reality all about them, "by inverting perspective, transformed aesthetic to introspective space," in Sypher's words.[56] In their move from the object to the subject, from the external to the interior, they were expressing in their paintings the Gnostic planes of reality, the inversion of many perceptions, the examination of the soul.

The mannerist style, Sypher affirms, is a constant principle in the arts, a "reaction against the norms of classicism, in whatever period, ancient, medieval, or modern."[57] The characteristics of that style include malaise, double vision, and tormented sensibility along with the dualistic forms that permeate mannerist works of art, whether painting, drama, literature, or architecture. To read Sypher's description of mannerist art and literature in *Four Stages of Renaissance Style* is to recognize the special devices of *My Mortal Enemy*. For example, John Donne's "shock tactics" at the beginning of a lyric ("Batter my heart, three personed God," or "Go and catch a falling star/Get with child a mandrake root") can be matched with Myra's aggressive first words which so hurt Nellie, followed by an impulsive embrace. Myra's treatment of Nellie from that first meeting follows a pattern of extremes. We can substitute the personality of Myra in Sypher's analysis of the double personality of Donne (or Hamlet), which "operates within a moral framework of extreme values: pure and impure, vicious and virtuous, profane and saintly."[58] Other typical mannerist formulas that are strong elements in *My Mortal Enemy* include emotional overreaction, incongruous images, and much paradox. The doubleness of vision, the pairs of extreme values, the violent emotional address to life, and the lack of balance all evoke the Gnostic response to a world similarly out of kilter.

The literary genre of *My Mortal Enemy* is the Italian *novella* or the *nouvelle*, as the German form is known. Developed in the Renaissance, notably by Boccaccio in his *Decameron*, the *novella* was from the time of its invention a short prose narrative, most often about women and priests. Sometimes moral tales, they are typically realistic in style and satiric in tone. *My Mortal Enemy* participates in all of the conventions of this early literary form. In the context of that form, for example, the marital infidelities of Myra and Oswald become more integrated with the other events of the story. The use of an eyewitness narrator, in this case Nellie Birdseye, is another common convention of many satiric *novellas*.

Nellie as observer becomes a more significant part of the story when she is viewed as one of the devices of dualism. Her surname, Birdseye, is a blatant clue to Cather's meaning. The bird's telescopic eye, which sees at various distances by moving the lens forward and backward, is quite different from the human eye with its lens that changes its convexity. Nellie's angle of vision demonstrates the shifting planes of reality of Myra's situation according to the younger woman's understanding. Even more relevant is the bird's method of seeing the world about by looking out of one eye and then the other, seeing half of the whole field with each observation. Nellie sees both sides of Myra, but succeeds only at the end in beginning to accomplish any integration of her glimpses of Myra's world. Nellie's is a sensual and emotional account; it is up to the reader to provide a wholly rational structure.

Cather has grafted allegorical meanings onto the simpler novella form. The multiple meaning of nearly every passage provides for irony which, in Frye's definition, means a "technique of saying as little and meaning as much as possible."[59] The whole of Cather's novel cycle has allegorical dimensions, but *My Mortal Enemy* is an allegory that has a continuous second meaning for the incidents and persons in the book. The late sixteenth and the seventeenth centuries produced some of the great allegories of literature--*The Pilgrim's Progress* and *The Fairy Queen* must lead the list as examples of journeys that have one meaning in the earthly realm and another in the spiritual. Myra Henshawe might well be Bunyan's creature in the iron cage of despair, who cries "O eternity! eternity! how shall I grapple with the misery I must meet with in eternity!" The "dark conceit" of Spenser that shows Belphoebe immune from human love in her dedication to Diana finds its way into the first pages of *My Mortal Enemy*. The tradition of Gnostic allegory, however, has even more to offer to the story of Myra.

The use of allegory was widespread in Greek literature as a way to unite philosophy with the power of myth and, after Philo, as a way to use both devices as arguments for his religious tenets. The church fathers borrowed the method for their scriptural allegories to serve the syncretistic purposes of early Christianity. The Christian Gnostics used the same methods often to subvert the meanings of stories, in order to make their point that evil was a force in the world; therefore, they reversed the roles of good and evil, confounding the values originally intended. For example, the Gnostic interpretation of the role of Jesus in the story of Paradise was so firmly established by Mani's time that he could put Jesus in the serpent's place without mentioning the serpent.[60] The same kind of perversion occurs in *My Mortal Enemy* as Oswald and Nellie defend Myra and serve her in spite of jealousies, cruelties, and deceptions. Part of the puzzle of the book is the way the reader accepts Myra as heroine, caring about a woman who deserves little sympathy. But she strikes a Gnostic nerve in all of us.

If Jung is right, the world has left to the Gnostic religion the problem of the role of the unconscious in dealing with evil.[61] Myra is, in fact, a spiritual heroine facing the question of her eternal soul. Her evaluations involve two premises of the Gnostics: first, that sin is not, as the Christians claim, a matter of failing to reach certain moral goals, but rather a question of ignorance--the lack of self knowledge which is insight; and second, that the soul carries within itself the means of salvation, or in terms of psychology, the psyche bears within itself the potential for liberation. Pursuing that gnosis and struggling to liberate the soul, says Pagels, "engages each person in a solitary difficult process," as the Gnostic searches for "interior self-knowledge as the key to understanding universal truths--who we are, where we came from, where we go."[62]

Myra ("Molly") Driscoll Henshawe discloses in a very few sentences a great deal about her understanding of those questions. From the early pages we know only that Myra, as an orphan, was brought up by her great-uncle, a coarse, unlettered, and flamboyant Irish Roman Catholic, and that the "blood tie" was strong. He is the "old Satan"--a force of evil willing to risk ruining himself to crush an enemy and a man of violent prejudices. At the same time he would help a friend, no matter what it cost, and was generous to the church. Myra shares his passionate nature; in her last hours she declares that she would return to him if he were living: "As we grow old we become more and more the stuff our forebears put into us. I can feel his savagery strengthen in me. We think we are so individual and so misunderstood when we are young; but the nature our strain of blood carries is inside there, waiting, like our skeleton" (*MME*,67-68). The strain of blood is so strong that the cultured Myra's elegant language reverts to a rough Irish brogue when she is angry.

The function of the opera *Norma*, so prominent in Nellie's account, gains power in tandem with the passages about Myra's heritage. Two critics have dealt extensively with the parallels between the story of the opera and *My Mortal Enemy*: Richard Giannone focuses on the tone and symbolism, and Harry Eichorn analyzes the plots.[63] Myra repeats Norma's story in falling in love with a man who opposes her religion, in suspecting him of infidelity, in struggling with the conflict of love and religion, and in dying while still claiming the attentions of her lover. An important aria that says much to the story comes at the end of the second act:

> I do not know;--opposing feelings
> Tear my soul: I love, at the same time,
> I hate. . . .[64]

Both Giannone and Eichorn emphasize that mysterious relation that Nellie understands of the *"Casta Diva"* aria to something in Myra's nature. That relation must include the Celtic background of Norma and the Irish heritage of Myra, with the connection to the savagery of their emotions. The very definition of *Celtic* includes both the idea of blood ties and the temperament and imagination that distinguish the people. Myra's wildness as a young woman belongs with these images. The two strands--the underlying theme of the opera and the "strain of blood"--are woven together in the person of Myra as she learns to understand herself.

The Druid background of the opera also reinforces the religious themes of the novel. The Druids were natural philosophers, poets, and teachers who, in spite of their later reputations as savage creatures, had much in common with the Manichaeans--so much so that Michelet treats the two groups as one in the first book of his *History of France*. From Julius Caesar, Pliny, Strabo, and others we learn about the life of the Druids. The primary Druidic doctrine taught the indestructibility of the human soul; other associations with the tenets of the Manichees included moon-worship, inclusion of women even in the priesthood, and the sacred heptad (the number seven). Their reverence for sacred snakes brings to mind Myra's expression at times of stress, and their oral tradition of sacred poetry recalls her chanting memorized passages as she dies. Even her wildness as a young woman refers to her Celtic ancestry. The Druidic theme takes its appropriate place in the historical cycle of Cather's novels: the interest in Celts and Druids was strongest in Roman times and during the Renaissance.

Shakespeare was one of the poets interested in the Celts, and Myra's allusion to Gloucester's cliff from *King Lear* is one of several passages that rely on Shakespearean plays to augment their meanings. Eichorn finds that references allow the reader to know more than Nellie recognizes, or at least acknowledges, in her memoir of Myra. He shows the relation of Gloucester's cliff with death, the connections of Old John of Gaunt from *Richard III* with John Driscoll, and the relevance of the "shooting stars," the "king's highway," and other allusions. Giannone's analysis of the music in *My Mortal Enemy* and Eichorn's careful tracing of the poetic allusions add much to the significance of the novel. Their criticism clarifies another theme that brings together many strands of this work and relates it to Cather's canon--the conflict of art and life.

In *Willa Cather's Imagination*, Stouck discusses this theme in detail as it relates to *The Troll Garden* and other stories about artists, *Youth and the Bright Medusa*, and *The Song of the Lark*. "Willa Cather's vision of life perceived a duality in all human experience," he says, and as an artist she tried to reconcile the opposing claims of art and life.[65] The theme itself is double, as is almost everything else, in *My Mortal Enemy*, as both Nellie and Myra begin by seeing all of life in terms of art. The question of life and art shifts from the claims on the artist to the ability to distinguish what is life and what is art--the seventeenth century literary theme of the difference between appearance and reality. Nellie constructs her images of Myra as the Druid priestess, as the legendary figure of a romantic elopement, and as a magical person who could confer status simply by speaking to someone. Even her hat is a reminder of "pages' caps in old story-books". When Myra speaks with her poet friend she uses a "kind of highly flavoured special language" (*MME*,35); she arranges her party scenes as if they were stage sets; and in talking about her actions says, "I didn't plot anything so neat as this" (*MME*,44). All the world is her stage. The Shakespearean quotations-- they are all references to herself--show her as continuing in that mode until the end of her life. The brilliant wrappings, the candlelight, the ritual tea are all drama, even in her illness. Nellie talks of "episodes" and "watching," as if she were viewing a play. The great dramatic moment, of course, is the death scene with the cedar (the tree of the goddess) and the vast sea as setting.

But it is clear that Myra's reverence for poetry is part of her salvation, as she uses Heine as a sacred text, as she talks about the "new Parnassus" to be found through Whitman, as she quotes Shakespearean passages for consolation, and as she finds that the great poets shine on. As Cather here reaffirms her constant identification of art and religion, the whole experience of reading *My Mortal Enemy* forces a dialogue about the boundaries between art and life.

In *My Mortal Enemy* Cather brings together the conditions of society in a materialistic world full of tension and the psychological problems of the people who try to survive in that world. She adds the appropriate literary forms and myths to create a sense of evil and goodness, of terror and hope. Modern nihilism, Hans Jonas says, means we are living in a crisis. "The beginnings of the crisis reach back into the seventeenth century, where the spiritual situation of modern man takes shape," in part as a result of man's loneliness in the physical universe of modern cosmology.[66] Introducing his study of Gnosticism, Jonas says: "Out of the mist of the beginning of our era there looms a pageant of mythical figures whose vast, superhuman contours might people the walls and ceiling of another Sistine Chapel. . . . Our art and literature and much else would be different, had the Gnostic message prevailed." Gnosticism contributed much to the message that did prevail, yet the tale has found no modern artist or poet to interpret it. Although mythographers have recently begun to point out some relevant passages in Western literature, Willa Cather's story of Myra Henshawe may be one of the purest works of Gnostic fiction to date.

Her cycle has arrived at a materialistic, dualistic, ambiguous state in which only the spiritual answers found in religion and art ("they are the same thing in the end, of course") can provide guidance. At this point of disintegration a culture must begin a new cycle, and as in the Vichian pattern Christianity takes the place of the "frightful religions" of the first age of gods.

5

With Attributes of Gods: *Ricorso*

The Vichian *ricorso* of Willa Cather's novel cycle begins with *Death Comes for the Archbishop*. In this narrative, the development moves from the disintegration of a culture and a general despair to a world of religious figures, powerful myths that control ideas, and the hope of new beginnings. The simplicity of characters and action, coming after the ambiguities of *The Professor's House* and *My Mortal Enemy*, and the slow pace of "sacred time" mark a return to a primitivism which is in itself a rebirth. The events of *Death Comes for the Archbishop* begin in 1848 and end in 1889, a year that figures in each of the first three novels--*O Pioneers!*, *The Song of the Lark*, and *My Ántonia*. *Shadows on the Rock* begins earlier, in 1697, but portrays a somewhat more advanced stage than that of *Death Comes for the Archbishop*, moving the cycle in its inevitable pattern toward more complexity and ambiguity, yet both novels carry the symbols and meanings of Vico's sense of man's creation of civilization. The Vichian signal for a new beginning comes as Father Latour ascends the rock of Ácoma in this new primeval forest and "deafening thunder" breaks overhead; the ensuing storm and distant sunlight make the Bishop think that "the first Creation morning might have looked like this" (*DC*,99). In this new age of gods, recurring after man has created symbols to help him understand the world, the place of the immanent gods is taken by their representatives, the priests that so dominate the stories. These obvious symbols of a new beginning are part of and consistent with the Vichian themes that are important in an emerging civilization in this age of gods--the belief that events are commanded by auspices and oracles; that the natural world is animated by gods; that the religious mystics and poets were the sources of law that should control the "lawless vagrants" living in chaotic times.

In his seminal study, "The Philosophical Ideas of Giambattista Vico," Isaiah Berlin writes of Vico's belief that a dictionary could be composed of basic ideas common to all cultures. Berlin lists these ideas, or the words for them (Vico would not make a distinction between ideas and words): "gods," "family," "heroes," "auspices," "*Patria potestas*" (the authority that Roman citizens had over their descendants), "sacrifices," "rights" (to land), "command," "authority," "conquest," "courage, "fame."[1] A check of the number of times these words, and even more the ideas, are used in *Death Comes for the Archbishop* and *Shadows on the Rock* brings surprising results. The words "gods" and "family" dominate, but all but "fame" and *Patria potestas* appear as words at least several times. These latter two, however, are presented as ideas in both books. "Auspice" and "courage" have especially strong connotations: "Auspice Maria" is not only the inscription on Father Vaillant's ring, but is also the title of a chapter in *Death Comes for the Archbishop*; the pope's parting words to Father Vaillant are "*Coraggio, Americano.*" In *Shadows on the Rock* Auclair's "*Courage, mon bourgeois*" are words of sympathy that he uses for his patients and would like to say even to his bishop. "Sacrifice" and "authority" are two of the words most often used in both novels, but all of these Vichian concepts are included prominently.

Both *Death Comes for the Archbishop* and *Shadows on the Rock* are intensely Christian novels in theme, point of view, use of mythology, and choice of leading characters. Cather, in using the Roman Catholic background in these two final books of her cycle, is extending the continuum of mystery religions begun in her earlier stories. The relation of the Christian religion to the mystery religions in the fourth century of the Roman Empire continues to be open to various interpretations. Three schools of thought are divided among three theories: that there is an actual relation of dependency of Christianity on the mystery religions, especially in the theology of Saint Paul; that ancient mysteries are prototypes which found a "God-given completion" in the Christian mystery; that, although both arose in the same environment of consciousness and syncretistic cults, there are great differences, with Christianity offering to its followers mysteries of revelation, ethical law, and especially salvation by grace that provide a great contrast with the Hellenistic religions.[2] These academic distinctions, however, depend upon recent scholarship and are more complex than earlier ideas about the influences of the mystery cults on emerging Christianity. During the early decades of the twentieth century, the writers who discussed the mysteries were chiefly Christians who would declare with Cumont, "We can understand the Christianity of the fifth century with its greatness and weakness, its spiritual exaltation and its puerile superstitions, if we know the moral antecedents of the world in which it developed." He attempts to show "how the pagan religions from the Orient aided the long continued effort of Roman society, contented for many centuries with a rather insipid idolatry, toward more elevated and more profound forms of worship."[3] Early Christian fathers spoke of the sacraments in terms of the mystery religions: "O truly sacred mysteries! O pure light!" wrote Clement of Alexandria. "In the blaze of the torches I have a vision of heaven and of God. I become holy by initiation."[4] Even articles in the eleventh edition of the *Encyclopaedia Britannica, available to Cather,* stress the rites that Orphism and Christianity practiced in common, and even more the similarities between Neoplatonist and Christian doctrines. Artists, as well, related Christianity to the mystery religions: depictions of Demeter ascending to the heavens and of Christ as Orpheus are among many that made tacit mythological comparisons. Cather might also have found clues in the preface to the third volume of Jacob Grimm's study of Teutonic mythology, where he enumerates the ways in which pagan and Christian practices are alike and shows the interweaving of myth: "New Christian feasts, especially of saints, seem purposely to have been made to fall on heathen holidays. Churches often rose precisely where a heathen god or his sacred tree had been pulled down, and the people trod their old paths to the accustomed site."[5] Both *Death Comes for the Archbishop* and *Shadows on the Rock* focus on beliefs and rites of the early church that can often be compared to more primitive ways of worship.

The conception of worship in the Christian church was influenced by the many contemporary cults, including Gnosticism and Neoplatonism, which brought the ideas of mystery and elaborate rites to religious expression. Christian mysticism, according to Dean Inge at the end of the nineteenth century, developed the secrecy, the symbolism, the idea of the mystical brotherhood that characterize its ceremonies.[6] A further relationship with the earlier mystery religions is the focus in both of these Christian novels on the female as an object of worship or as a religious figure. For Father Vaillant, the month of May is his holy month, to be dedicated to Mary, his patroness. Magdalena, little more than a wild creature when she is introduced to the story, is transformed into a holy vision for the priests. In *Shadows on the Rock* the females are the visionaries for both national survival and religious redemption, while even the archbishop deals only with politics and practicalities until the very end of his life.

Although the Christian beliefs represent the same stage of civilization as that developed in the time of the pagan mysteries, Vico differentiates this cycle by conceiving the whole movement of history as a spiral rather than as a mere sequential repetition of an earlier pattern. For him Christianity takes the place of the mysteries that preceded it in the earlier age and becomes for the Roman Catholic Vico the basis for his attitude of piety in a new beginning of an age of gods. The image in Cather's prologue to *Death Comes for the Archbishop* of congested spiral patterns caused by the sun to quiver over the dinner table of the Cardinals, symbolizing action and "splendid finish," is a suggestion of the Vichian view of the story to come. Yet many correspondences between the Hellenistic religions and Christianity are present in Vico's work as well as in Cather's. In her two novels of this *ricorso* stage of the civilization's cycle, religion becomes both more central to the development of the stories and more satisfying in the lives of the characters. In both novels the power of the seemingly simple narratives resides in the mysteries of faith. The interest in Catholicism is not a new one at this point for Cather. The early novels cast the church in a favorable light, but her emphasis is on the more practical uses of religion. In *O Pioneers!* Marie tells Emil, "I wish you were a Catholic. The Church helps people, indeed it does" (*OP*,92). The music of the church service inspires Emil to crystallize his emotions about Marie. In *My Ántonia* Jalinek's Catholicism is described as a "strong, manly faith."

Death Comes for the Archbishop

Death Comes for the Archbishop is the outstanding example of the fusion of Willa Cather's themes of art, nature, and religion. With its many legends from diverse religions, it might almost be a chapter from a book on comparative mythology. The protagonists of the story, although they are Roman Catholic priests, can easily be translated in terms of comparative mythology as the Twin Heroes of Navajo myth who follow the holy trail, have as their father the sun, and are helped by the Indian counterpart to the Christian Virgin. Bishop Latour and Father Vaillant, who take the same path from France to Ohio and then to the American Southwest, are opposites representing two sides of man: scholarly, well-bred, contemplative Bishop Latour is the *anima*; Father Vaillant, physically active, enthusiastic, friendly, is the *animus*. As schoolboys in France they were instinctively drawn to each other, and their friendship grows during their service in the New World. Each man is the true "other self" like those friends to whom Aristotle, Seneca, and Cicero gave that name. Father Vaillant, a priest of the people, wonders whether or not Bishop Latour's "scholarship, handsome person, and delicate perceptions" were wasted on the frontier, just as Euclide Auclair of *Shadows on the Rock* regrets the martyrdom of a gifted priest in the early Canadian missions. Both doubters decide that God has His reasons. Father Vaillant concludes: "Perhaps it pleased Him to grace the beginning of a new era and a vast new diocese by a fine personality. And perhaps, after all, something would remain through the years to come, some ideal or memory or legend" (*DC*,252).

In their religious quest, the two priests often receive divine assistance from their protectress, the Virgin Mary. They have come from the patriarchal religious environment in France to a new land where they are guided spiritually by the divine female presence. Whether they are saved from dying of thirst in a hidden valley or from an evil American in the desert, a woman appears at the moment of rescue, and in one episode the entire Holy Family appears in the guise of Mexicans to save the life of a priest. Father Vaillant is certain he can tell the color of the Virgin's shawl as she leads a mule to safety. Bishop Latour interprets such miracles as "our perceptions being made finer, so that for a moment our eyes can see and our ears can hear what there is about us always." But Father Vaillant, who has honored the "holy mysteries" of the divine female since early manhood, brings to his worship not only awareness of the power of Mary, but also rituals of the earlier mystery religions: his experiences include a display by an Indian convert of the sacred objects of the Mass that have been kept secret in a deep cave. Ritualistic use of the "golden bough" appears in several scenes. Father Latour, in this same chapter, removes himself for meditation to a sacred grove--"trees of great antiquity" that "seemed to belong to a bygone era" (*DC*,221). This "old, dead, dry wood" has only a few green leaves, but clusters of mistletoe, that symbol of the Druid goddess, are growing among the bare boughs. To this recognition of pagan goddess worship, Father Latour's ruminations on the role of Mary in the Christian sects leads to one of the most powerful syncretistic passages in the novel: "Long before Her years on earth, in the long twilight between the Fall and the Redemption, the pagan sculptors were always trying to achieve the image of a goddess who should yet be a woman" (*DC*,255). Mary thus takes her place in the great panoply of the goddess figures in the background of Cather's novels.

As the two priests go about their tasks, they find that the mingling of Indian, Mexican, and Christian beliefs and rituals seems to enrich all the faiths. There is the lovely Catholic church whose altar is painted with gods of wind, rain, thunder, sun, and moon; whether by Spanish missionaries or Indian converts, it is impossible to tell. A superstitious priest raises parrots for the feathers used in Indian ceremonial robes and keeps a parrot idol in his house; the Indians, in turn, use a portrait of Saint Joseph in their rain-making rituals. The bishop acquires deep respect for the traditions of other cultures, and regretting his former delay he begins in his old age to record the legends he has learned in the New World. Often, *Death Comes for the Archbishop* reads like a poetic version of William James's *Variety of Religious Experiences*.

The one form of the Indian religion that distresses the bishop is serpent worship, generating in him not intellectual disapproval, but irrational fear. The Gothic chapel form of the cavern where the bishop and an Indian guide take refuge during the storm emphasizes its ceremonial use. The glacial air, the fetid odor, the great vibration combine to evoke repugnance on the bishop's part. The sound of the underground river--"one of the oldest voices of the earth"--fails to explain the feeling of horror of the cave. The vibrations of the underground stream, which were a symbol of sexual desire in those early novels that emphasize pagan religious responses, are "terrible" for the priest; the stone lips of an orifice of the cave are a mystery. The sexual symbolism of the cavern scene, like the earlier forest scene in which the cone-shaped trees wearied his eyes, is significant to the celibate priest. Cather is both subtle and paradoxical: the Indians worship a force and its serpentine symbol while the Christians consider these to be representative of greatest evil. This juxtaposition provides one of the strongest points of contrast of religions in the book; yet the bishop involuntarily responds to the power of the Indian god. Joseph Campbell, discussing the attitudes of Roman Catholics toward the American natives, reminds us of the constant archetypes of mythology. The Europeans, who were firmly trained in their own symbology, he says, "regarded the myths and images, sacraments and temples of the

New World as diabolical mockeries of the one True Church."[7] Cather's archbishop conveys this attitude even as he strives for an appreciation of the cultures that he encounters.

From the beginning of the book, the syncretism of religions is emphasized. In a charming exchange, Father Joseph objects when Father Latour relates the tone and design of a church bell to bells made of Moorish silver. The Bishop explains, "A learned Scotch Jesuit in Montreal told me that our first bell, and the introduction of the bell in the service all over Europe, originally came from the East. He said the Templars brought the Angelus back from the Crusades, and it is really an adaptation of a Moslem custom." He adds that the Spaniards handed on this Moorish skill to the Mexicans, and the Mexicans taught the Navajos to work the silver (*DC*,45). That passage might well be a gloss on the meaning of much of the novel. And yet the ambiguities of Cather's view make the message more complex. In spite of the admirable qualities of the individual Indians, Jacinto and Eusabio, the Indian people are "antediluvian creatures" with a "low life force" who are incapable of understanding the Christian sacrifice. Their priests have their own mysteries, whose symbols of the eternal fire and snake worship are both incomprehensible and distasteful to Father Latour. Yet, as A. S. Byatt says, "he is content to rest with the mystery,"[8] even though he despairs at one point of accomplishing anything in this land: "The Indians travelled their old road of fear and darkness, battling with evil omens and ancient shadows. The Mexicans were children who played with their religion" (*DC*,211). His feeling that he is back in the stone age and that no one can understand the Indian mind reinforces the idea of the spiral in the cyclical pattern of civilization. In *Death Comes for the Archbishop* it is clearly the Christian spirituality that creates the superior human condition whose exemplars here are the two priests.

The form of the book has intrigued many scholars who have found many sources for Cather's inspiration: saints legends, biblical passages, Dante, Puvis de Chavannes, Holbein's *Dance of Death*, and the nine-part sound of the Angelus among them. Her reading for the historical information she used has been documented by Edward and Lillian Bloom in *The Gift of Sympathy*, and John Murphy has traced her debts to classical and Western American literature.[9] Acknowledging Cather's accretion of background and structure for all of her novels, there is no reason to dismiss any of these ideas. Cather provided much of this information in her letter to *The Commonweal* about her sources for *Death Comes for the Archbishop* (*OW*,3-13). She chose to call this book a narrative, not a novel. In the progression of genres that accompanies the cycles of civilizations, nevertheless, the structure and content of *Death Comes for the Archbishop* very frequently and consistently point to the chronicles that were so important as the primary sources of Roman and Anglo-Saxon history. They were especially significant for the church, serving as the calendar for the liturgical year and as depository for local records. These chronicles fit best the cyclical stage of this novel, although the biblical chronicles and the adaptation by Shakespeare of the Anglo-Saxon histories certainly were part of Cather's literary consciousness.

Some of the qualities of the chronicle that influence the form of *Death Comes for the Archbishop* include the concise language, the importance of dates, the recounting of parallel events in various parts of the world, and the interspersion of matters of grave importance with frivolous stories. The first sentence of the prologue to the novel, "At Rome," begins with a date--"One summer evening in the year 1848"--and this brief introduction is a kind of chronicle in miniature, talking of France and Italy, Spain and North America, referring to the reign of Gregory XVI, discussing a painting by El Greco, a new opera by Verdi, and the case of a Spanish dancing-girl who was working miracles in Andalusia. From that point nearly every chapter begins with a reference to the date, as if the storyteller is tracking time; Book 1 begins, "One afternoon in the autumn of 1851"; Book 2, "In mid-March"; Book 3, "During the first year after his arrival in Santa Fe"; Book 4, "A month after the Bishop's visit." Somewhere early in each of the other books of the narrative is a reference to a date or a specific historical event to place the time of the action. The final book begins with letters dated December 1888 to establish the time of the Archbishop's death. The books are remarkably uniform in length, without regard for the importance of the subject to the story as a whole, just as the chronicles, recorded on the calendars, had a prescribed space in which to write accounts of events, significant or not. The books are, in turn, divided into very short segments. One of the more interesting examples in *Death Comes for the Archbishop* is the juxtaposition of the story of Doña Isabella, the vain woman willing to forgo her inheritance after the death of her husband (dated in true chronicle style as "Septuagesima Sunday") to maintain a lie about her age, with the story of "The Great Diocese," which includes the month of Father Vaillant's consecration to the Virgin Mary. Doña Isabella's story is slightly longer than that of the spiritual events of the following chapter. Just as Doña Isabella's superficial behavior deepens Father Joseph's appreciation for the nuns of France, her story heightens in the next chapter the meaning of the devotion to the Virgin.

As the Archbishop begins at the end of his life to record the old legends that were already dying out, the miscellany of memories at the conclusion of his life, as he is about to dispense with "calendared time," has the same lack of perspective displayed by the chronicle. Perhaps the most persuasive argument for including the chronicle as a source of Cather's structure here is that the emphasis on single, isolated events in the chronicle explains the episodic, sometimes seemingly unrelated, chapters of this novel, as well as the many parallel stories of the religious beliefs and practices, all without comment or attempt at unification by the author. The work and pleasures of comparison are left to the informed reader.

Shadows on the Rock

Shadows on the Rock continues Cather's examination of the cycles of civilization, expressing the same interest in new beginnings that is evident in *Death Comes for the Archbishop*. In the earlier book the "new era" and its contrast with the "bygone age" occupies the attention of the two priests, and the need to succeed the "old order" is a great part of their mission. This last book of the cycle pays even more attention to the ideas of a new order, with the establishment of a Christian culture on the rock of Quebec. In Western history one of the greatest changes to initiate a new era comes after the fall of the Roman Empire when Christianity brings new thought and a new sense of the place of man in the world. Vico sees this moment as the beginning of the spiral of a *ricorso*, a start of a new cycle. The new currents of thought, signalled by the philosophy of Augustine, looked back at the pagan world and forward to a new order, with all the potentialities that the Christian dogma promised. The pagan inheritance and the Christian view together paved the way for a new rise of Western civilization.

There are significant differences between the manifestations of the new order in *Death Comes for the Archbishop* and those in *Shadows on the Rock*. For the archbishop, the new world makes him feel that he is always young, and he considers the very air of new countries different from that where man has plowed the land: "Something soft and wild and free, something that whispered to the ear on the pillow, lightened the heart, softly, softly picked the lock, slid the bolts, and released the prisoned spirit of man into the wind, into the blue and gold, into the morning, into the morning!" (*DC*,273). The picture changes in *Shadows on the Rock*: no such lyrical description is forthcoming of the effects of the Canadian land on its inhabitants; for Padre Martinez was right-- religion grows out of the soil of the country. This Canadian world demands endurance, as Cather suggested in her letter to Governor Cross, rather than offering the release of the spirit. Much of the story of *Death Comes for the Archbishop* occurs in the lovely fall months of the American Southwest; *Shadows on the Rock* is a winter's tale. The most poetic of descriptions here is of the sky, rather than of the land: "All the western sky, which had been hard and clear when the sun sank, was now throbbing with fiery vapours, like rapids of clouds; and between, the sky shone with a blue to ravish the heart,--that limpid, celestial, holy blue that is only seen when the light is golden" (*SR*,104). Cather's skill in descriptions of the sun, rising and setting, is at its height in this novel, especially in moments of psychological transformation. But even the most civilized part of this country is a fortress-like abode. The difficulties of the physical structure of the city, the frightening vegetative world outside the inhabited area, the brutal climate, and the class struggles all play a part. The stagnation of customs and ideas, only infrequently challenged, provides a troubling undercurrent that makes this novel a more complex work than is generally recognized, although that theme is less obvious than it is in *Death Comes for the Archbishop*.

The balancing of stability and change, of honoring the Old World and deifying the New, of admiring the past and looking toward the future-- ambivalences that pervade Cather's work--are all very much a part of her examination in this stage of her cycle. As in *Death Comes for the Archbishop*, the last scene of this book looks backward and forward at the "changes in the nations," weighing the benefits of the past, the present, and the future. The rock as a symbol of indestructibility and permanence can become, "without shadow of change," the sign of the literalness of Indian life, "often shocking and disconcerting" (*DC*,97). Both Bishop Latour and Auclair are transitional figures in this movement between worlds, between permanence and transformation.

Auclair himself had been uncertain that he could survive the voyage from France. Yet once in the New World, he serves a valuable function as an intermediary in the social as well as the medical milieu. In spite of his scientific approach to medicine, he recognizes the value of what has gone before: "I think the methods of the last century better than those of the present," he says, and in a phrase reminiscent of Vico, "Change is not always progress." He searches the Latin books in the Paris libraries for histories of medicine.[10] The location of his house in Quebec midway between the upper city with its religious atmosphere and the lower town with its daily commerce perhaps best symbolizes his middle-of-the-road approach. The goal of life for Auclair is not to subdue a vast wilderness, but to find a refuge that offers "the spirit of peace, the acceptance of fate." Yet much of the emphasis in *Shadows on the Rock*, as in *Death Comes for the Archbishop*, is on the future and the importance of continuing the culture. The very different qualities demanded by the New World from those of the Catholic faith are stressed here. Catherine, the European mother superior of the convent at Quebec, is brilliant, but slight, nervous, and sickly from childhood. Her choice of her successor, aided by her visions of the Canadian martyr Father Brebeuf, seems strange to many. It is Jeanne Juschereau-- "hardy, sagacious, practical,--a *Canadienne*, and the woman for Canada," who is strong enough to lead the way into the future. In the epilogue, Cécile's four sons are also described as the "Canadians of the future" who, the bishop predicts, will live to see better times. Yet the story emphasizes the relationship of men and women to this new land; even Cécile's thoughts of her future husband are a recognition that his real strength comes because he has authority, and "a power which came from knowledge of the country and its people; from knowledge, and from a kind of passion" (*SR*,268). His qualities are identical to those of Alexandra in the first book of this cycle. Willa Cather's reverence for man's creation of a culture is the heart of *Shadows on the Rock*, as the religious language in her letter to Governor Cross makes clear: "Those people brought a kind of French culture there and somehow kept it alive on that rock, sheltered it and tended it and on occasion died for it, as if it really were a sacred fire" (*OW*,16).

The Vichian concept that man can understand truly only what he creates is significant in the culture explored in *Shadows on the Rock*: the importance of well-made meals, the artificial flowers, Auclair's alligator, the bowl of glass fruit bequeathed to Cécile by the count, the tools of housekeeping--all create the order that is so central to Cather's idea of civilization. Auclair thinks of even his city as

one of those little artificial mountains which were made in the churches at home to present a theatric scene of the Nativity; cardboard mountains, broken up into cliffs and ledges and hollows to accommodate groups of figures on their way to the manger; angels and shepherds and horsemen and camels, set on peaks, sheltered in grottoes, clustered about the base (*SR*,5).

It is Cécile, however, who best sums up the Vichian principle: "One made a climate within a climate; one made the days,--the complexion, the special flavour, the special happiness of each day as it passed; one made life." Michelet interpreted this principle as meaning that man is his own Prometheus, and the dialogue that continues Cécile's thoughts and ends Book IV supports the idea. Auclair asks why Cécile has not called him to make the fire, and she replies, "It is no trouble to make a fire. Oh, Father, I think our house is so beautiful!" (*SR*,198). The sacred fire of the pagan caves has moved to the household and sometimes to the sanctuary in this stage of man's development.

Cather was interested in Quebec, she said in her letter to Governor Cross, because "there another age persists," and there she found a "mental complexion inherited, left over from the past." The paradox that runs throughout her earlier novels comes to its conclusion here. She admired those pioneers who were strong enough to create a new life in America; yet they seemed to her only barbarians if they discarded their national heritage. The characters in her stories who succeed are invariably those who maintain in their New World quest their age-old traditions--the "feeling about life that comes down through so many centuries." For Cather, respect for tradition not only imposed that order so dear to her, but it also provided a unified background out of which individualism could spring. With no common tradition, the settlers in her early stories could create a society in which they only imitated each other, a habit that Cather examines in the three novels of the first stage of her cycle. At the same time, individualism, she thought, could receive a certain sanction from a heritage in common with others, and both were necessary in her scheme. Alexandra's brothers, denying all links with their past, are shallow and worthless; the Indians of Ácoma, on the other hand, rooted in long tradition but refusing new experience, are undeveloped antediluvian creatures. What is needed is the proper balance of tradition and the pioneer spirit: "When an adventurer carries his gods with him into a remote and savage country, the colony he founds will, from the beginning, have graces, tradition, riches of mind and spirit" (*SR*,98). Not many of the pioneers were able to attain this balance. After the pioneering age, there remained few whom Cather could admire, and none whom she could deify except the gods themselves. Her warning to her generation was, as Henry Adams' had been, that the prevailing scientific, mechanistic view of the world could not substitute for the concepts of the cycles of nature, the values of tradition, and individual responsibility. Vico had faced the same question in the new scientific age of the eighteenth century and had replied that philosophers should study less of the physical order and more of the divine; "that is, to understand what is hidden from men, the future, or what is hidden in them, their consciousness."[11] Cather echoes this in the words of the dying Count Frontenac:

> There was something in himself and in other men that this world did not explain. Even the Indians had to make a story to account for something in their lives that did not come out of their appetites: conceptions of courage, duty, honour. The Indians had these, in their own fashion. These ideas came from some unknown source, and they were not the least part of life (*SR*,247).

The myths and miracles in Cather's novels, as in Vico's system, are attempts to explain these ideas.

In this representation of the early Christian era, the references to the classical period, although fewer and less obvious than in the earlier stories of the frontier, still appear, as they have continued to appear throughout Western culture. A French Canadian priest, for example, substitutes a secular Latin poem for a prayer in a moment of danger, emphasizing Cather's belief in the close identity of religion and art and at the same time revealing a frequent practice in the early church. The nuns in Quebec believe in the possibility of acquiring the qualities of saints by eating their ground bones, just as the early rulers in Christian Rome maintained caves with pagan relics, including bones, for the populace to visit.

Even Cather's choice of form in this work is related to the stories within the novel as expressions of the national spirit. Stouck and Sergeant both describe the work as a historical novel, but if it is viewed in the context of its early medieval representations, it clearly seems to be more history than novel. First, the book lacks important elements of the novel--a deliberate device on Cather's part. She told Mary Ellen Chase that the book would truly be shadows, which meant more to her than substance: "It won't have a trace of what is called *movement* or *suspense*. It will just have people and a lot of *things*."[12] The characters are more medieval representations of human qualities than they are modern novelistic figures that show some development in the course of their story. In fact a shadow, in addition to being that lack of substance mentioned by Cather, can also mean an adumbration, a type or symbol. It would seem that by the author's design her characters, as the shadows of the title, serve the medieval role of representing one-dimensional moral qualities. John Murphy points out the medieval dimensions of the novel in his essay, "*Shadows on the Rock*: Cather's Medieval Refuge."[13]

Much of the literature of the Middle Ages came in the form of history, with heroes drawn from the figures of the aristocracy, exploration, and religious life. The medieval chronicles, perhaps best represented by Geoffrey of Monmouth, transmitted much of the historical lore, real and imagined, that described the racial character. During the twelfth century there arose an urge to write historical narrative; it demanded an open mind, ready to reflect on a wealth of experience, as Heer says. The most important chroniclers of the time, among them the Frenchmen, took as their mission the explanation of the rise in influence of their peoples and the internal conflicts that interfered in that rise.[14] The mixture of political and religious information offered by *Shadows on the Rock* is typical of the histories of the Middle Ages.

Religious history in this novel takes the forms of both narrative about contemporary ecclesiastical matters and repetitions of the legends of local saintly figures. The saints tales in *Shadows on the Rock* are strung together through oral repetition, with as little emphasis or structure as the stories in *Death Comes for the Archbishop*. The religious tone is further sustained by everyday experiences that are related in terms of religious and historical themes; every thought and action takes on a spiritual significance. Even for the adventurer Pierre Charron, the idea of family is "engrafted with religion," Cather says. The attitude that finds the religious and the secular life inseparable belongs to an early stage of man's development, indeed. In the Vichian cycle the new stage of the *ricorso* is a profoundly religious period. Its heroes, aside from the pioneer Charron, are chiefly the leaders and the saints of the church, whose stories, although interspersed among mundane events, have the qualities of legend--they are larger than life, removed in time and space, yet are told as part of the history of the nation.

One unforgettable story in *Shadows on the Rock* is that of Jeanne Le Ber, daughter of the richest merchant of Montreal and former lover of Pierre Charron. Her renunciation of the world is at first unremarkable; but soon she retires to a cell behind the chapel she has built for the

Sisters of the Congregation of the Blessed Virgin. The story of the angels who repair her spinning wheel brings joy to Cécile and a gift to the people of Quebec in its affirmation of the possibility of miracles. The cost of Le Ber's contribution to the religious life of Quebec, however, for at least two people, is the dark side of the tale, revealed in a powerful passage. Charron, who counts as dead the woman who has been a recluse for twenty years, sees Le Ber's face at the altar:

> It was like a stone face; it had been through every sorrow. . . . When she prayed in silence, such sighs broke from her. And once a groan, such as I have never heard; such despair--such resignation and despair! It froze everything in me. I felt that I would never be the same man again. I only wanted to die and forget that I had ever hoped for anything in this world" (*SR*,182-83).

In telling of the contrary effects of Le Ber's self-discipline, Cather may have borrowed some of her description from the autobiography of the daughter of the mayor of Lynn, Margery Kempe, a fourteenth-century British mystic whose behavior in the church included weeping, writhing on the ground, and loud cries of "I die, I die." Baugh in *A Literary History of England* says that the *Book of Margery Kempe* has great interest as a human document with a broad view of medieval life, but he claims that only an eight-page quarto printed in 1501 was available before the discovery of a complete copy in 1934. However, Evelyn Underhill in her 1911 *Mysticism* cites a 1910 reprint by F. Gardner in *The Cell of Self-Knowledge*. The works of both Underhill and Gardner would have been available to Cather.[15]

She read many books in preparation for *Shadows on the Rock*: Edith Lewis lists the *Jesuit Relations*, Lahontan's *Voyages*, and Saint-Simon's *Memoirs*. E. K. Brown adds Juchereau's history of Quebec, the letters of Mother Marie de l'Incarnation, and especially the chronicles of Parkman. A scholarly abbé who had written of the life of Laval for the *Makers of Canada* contributed to her knowledge of Quebec history. She borrowed much, from the historian Juchereau's name (spelling slightly changed) for her Reverend Mother to Abbé Scott's interpretation of the life of Laval. This list reveals a composite of historical and religious sources, an admixture that closely parallels the structure of *Shadows on the Rock*.

The tone of the book is indebted in several ways to another art--tapestry. Stouck cites Cather's letter to Dorothy Canfield Fisher, in which she compares the writing process of *Shadows on the Rock* to work on a tapestry, which can be interrupted without loss to a design. The idea of a tapestry is suggestive, Stouck says, "not only of a static quality in *Shadows on the Rock*, but of a fundamental element of structure--an intricate design wrought through the comparison and contrast of figures and colors. As in a tapestry the characters and events of the novel are not related to each other through sequential dramatic action, but through juxtaposition in parallel and contrasting scenes."[16] His extended analysis is insightful. Some of the medieval tone of the novel may be related to the tapestry form, as well. During the writing of *Shadows on the Rock* Cather placed at the foot of her bed full-size copies of *The Lady with the Unicorn*, medieval tapestries that hang in the Cluny Museum in Paris. The representations of the natural and the animal world are clearly only symbols of the ideal world that is unseen. The language of a motto prominently displayed must have pleased Cather--"*A mon seul désir.*"

Another of Cather's many explanations to Governor Cross of her methods in writing this novel is that "the text was mainly anacoluthon, so to speak, but the meaning was clear." Most interpretations by the critics of the term "anacoluthon" are taken from the grammar books, which define it as a change in midsentence to another grammatical construction; that definition, however, is unsatisfactory in the discussion of an entire novel. The Latin term is from the Greek word meaning simply "want of sequence." A better interpretation of Cather's use of the word would be from the Thrall and Hibbard *Handbook to Literature*: in units of composition larger than the sentence, the term refers to an obvious incoherency among the parts. Using that definition, it seems appropriate to call *Death Comes for the Archbishop* as well as *Shadows on the Rock* anacoluthic. If the form for the first is the chronicle and for the second, the medieval history, the disconnected structure in each case seems not only apt, but inevitable. Still another relation to early historical forms partly accounts for the stilted dialogue in *Shadows on the Rock*. E. K. Brown explains that this was Cather's intention; indeed, she translated conversations into French in order to achieve the effect of the language of Quebec.[17] This would approximate the sense of translating the early medieval histories from the Latin.

The relation of the writing of the early Middle Ages to *Shadows on the Rock* is illuminated by Auerbach's discussion of the period in *Mimesis*. The language of Gregory of Tours in his *History of the Franks*, Auerbach says, organizes badly or not all. It "lives in the concrete side of events, it speaks with and in the people who figure in them." Cather's deliberate attempt to create the world in this book with just people and a "lot of things" in a composition that is anacoluthic would seem to mimic the histories of Gregory and his time. Her story, like his, has room for "everything that can impress the people--legends of the saints, relics, and miracles to feed the imagination, protection against violence and oppression, simple moral lessons made palatable by promises of future rewards. The people among whom he lived understood nothing about dogma and had but a very crude idea of the mysteries of the faith."[18] Auerbach, whose book traces the literary interpretation of reality through the ages, uses the term "figural" to describe the view expressed in the Christian works of the late classical period and the early Middle Ages. In this view an earthly event signifies at the same time itself and another occurrence within the divine plan, which has no causal or chronological connection. It was, Auerbach says, the story of Christ, with its mixture of reality and sublime tragedy, that created the possibility of this conception.

In *Shadows on the Rock* the symbols of the immediate present are the gray rock and the Canadian wilderness--"dead," "sealed," "suffocating." The very first page talks of the "stern realities of life." Yet the religious theme is reached quickly. Atop the rock are a cathedral, a convent, and a seminary, around which revolve many of the legends in the novel. As in *Death Comes for the Archbishop*, the holy family plays in important symbolic role, and there is even a scene in which an infant is transfigured into the Divine Child in the presence of the old bishop. The predominating myth of these two later novels, then, is the Christian story as interpreted by the Roman Catholic Church; the emphasis is again on the mysteries and miracles:

> The people have loved miracles for so many hundred years, not as proof or evidence, but because they are the actual flowering of desire. In them the vague worship and devotion of the simple-hearted assumes a form. From being a shapeless longing, it becomes a beautiful image; a dumb rapture becomes a melody that can be remembered and repeated; and the experience of a moment, which might have been a lost ecstasy, is made an actual possession and can be bequeathed to another (*SR*,137).[19]

This description is as much about the process of literary creation as it is about religious symbolism. Cather has bequeathed to her readers that melody to be remembered, that satisfying of their own desire to understand themselves and their world. Although Daiches finds a loss of vitality in this book and in *Death Comes for the Archbishop*,[20] Cather's statements about these novels makes clear her intention in *Death Comes for the Archbishop* to write a narrative without drama and in *Shadows on the Rock* to reveal lives lacking in robustness and full of pious resignation. Christianity as a revealed mystery has a literary power different from "the inexplicable presence of the thing not named" (*OW*,41) of the mystery religions. With *Shadows on the Rock* Cather had finished her religious and historical cycle. Her picture of the rise and fall of the American West was complete, and her evocation of our spiritual heritage had reverberated in the American psyche.

6

Something Complete and Great

Willa Cather may have taken great pains to conceal her sophistication, as Wallace Stevens once wrote,[1] but studied as a whole her novels yield information about the wide range of her reading, her familiarity with the places she wrote about, her broad experience with people from all strata of society, and--most of all--the quality of the mind interpreting the whole. Maxwell Geismar's evaluation of nearly fifty years ago seems apt today: "As a matter of fact, Willa Cather's is one of the most complex, if not difficult and contradictory, minds in our letters."[2] In addition to the complexity of her work, it is important to note her scope; she could be speaking for herself as writer when she has Alexandra say, "If the world were no wider than my cornfield, if there were not something beside this, I wouldn't feel that it was much worth while to work" (*OP*,124). Complaining that other American authors were not large enough and expressing disdain for poets who renounced old themes, she took on the tasks assumed by the great writers preceding her who, by their boldness, imagination, and skill, had captured the myths of nations at turning points in their cultural development. And so the critics find in her work traces of Virgil, Dante, Milton, Shakespeare, Keats, Flaubert, and many others--the list is long.

Her depiction of the American West revealed insights into the structure of history that few novelists have offered. In using a universal scheme such as the one formulated by Vico, she was able to place the West into a framework for interpretation. Her art, in the novels of her cycle, realizes what Berlin describes as the heart of Vico's thought:

> In the individual and society alike, phase follows phase not haphazardly,
> . . . nor in a sequence of mechanical causes or effects, . . . but as stages

in the pursuit of an intelligible purpose--man's effort to understand himself
and his world, and to realize his capacities in it. History for him is the
orderly procession (guided by Providence, working through men's
capacities) of ever deepening types of apprehension of the world, of ways
of feeling, acting, expressing, each of which grows out of, and supersedes,
its predecessor.[3]

In the final book of her cycle, Cather alludes often to this philosophy,
as in the bishop's final monologue: "Monsieur, we are in the beginning
of a new century, but periods do not always correspond with centuries.
At home the old age is dying, but the new is still hidden. I felt the same
condition in England, during my long captivity there. . . . The changes
in the nations are all those of the old growing older" (*SR*,277). To the
mind that thinks in Vichian terms, the body politic everywhere lives its
cycle like the human body and can be understood in terms of what has
gone before.

This "rhythm of cultural aging," now proposed by many of the
modern philosophical historians and often labeled "Spenglerian," is in
practice "taken for granted by everyone today, and seems to be one of
the inevitable categories of the contemporary outlook," as Northrop Frye
said in 1957.[4] Cather's vision in the nine novels represented in this study
constitutes a view of the cultural development of the United States that
is one of the most comprehensive undertaken by any writer of American
fiction. Her comparisons between ancient and contemporary civilizations
were frequent even in her early Nebraska writing, as shown in *The
World and the Parish* and *The Kingdom of Art*. By the time Cather
began her novels, the habit of seeing the events of one era in terms of
another had become a method of her mind and a primary source of her
mature art. As Vico said of Homer's works, they are the "self-
revelations of a race," and the "spiritual creations of an epoch."[5]

The spiritual component of a Vichian pattern of history is critical to
its exposition: Vico emphasizes myth, art, and language as the creations
that have empowered the human mind to understand the world. In her
use of myth, Cather moves beyond the contemporary spiritual myths to
others long buried in the consciousness of the race. From the beginning,
Cather's heroines represent the early goddesses who are the focus of
worship in the mystery religions. Alexandra and Ántonia display the
precognition of the female in relation to the land; Thea's intuition relates
to her art. Nature and art are the basis for the religious emotions that
pervade all of the novels of the cycle. Like many scholars of religion,

Cather finds an intellectual and spiritual source in the myths and rituals of agriculture that gave rise to the mysteries. Here she captures the religious impulse of her own time and place, much as Virgil, according to one early critic, gave expression to the best religious feeling of the Roman mind.[6] There is little in her novels that does not have some relation to religion as she defines it, and many of her most memorable passages describe moments of transformation and transcendence. Howard Mumford Jones, reviewing *The Song of the Lark*, contrasts the pagan mysticism of Henry James and Willa Cather in their stories of an artist's development: "The one pays homage to Apollo, the other to Dionysius, and though both agree that the artist is possessed of a secret and superior truth, for James the problem is Platonic, whereas Miss Cather narrates the unfolding of her singer in terms of Orphic initiation. . . . Art for the one is wisdom; for the other it is radiance."[7] The religious background that Cather weaves into her novels lifts her prose to a plane that fascinates and compels the reader, even when the reason for that response is not fully understood. "What is the secret?" Umberto Eco asks in *Foucault's Pendulum*. He answers, "What the revealed religions have been unable to reveal. The secret lies beyond."

Like the historical and cultural path of religious understanding and acceptance, Cather's books move from pagan to Christian modes of redemption. The pious certainties of Mahailey in *One of Ours* and Augusta in *The Professor's House* offer succor; the professor and Myra Henshawe accept the answers of Christianity, even though they seem not fully satisfying to them. But in *Death Comes for the Archbishop* and *Shadows on the Rock* the Christian faith becomes the dominant experience, the controlling philosophy, as Cather recapitulates the religious history of man in the Western world. Elizabeth Sergeant finds the significance of the novels of Cather's fifties, from *The Professor's House* to *Shadows on the Rock* to be religious; but in fact all nine books of her cycle have profound religious meaning, if the reader follows Cather's comprehensive sense of the sacred. She uses her myths and mysteries not as mere literary decoration, or even as structural elements, but to achieve the dramatic, imaginative force and spiritual power that they provide.

The sequence followed by religious change in the stages of history is loosely paralleled by literature and its language. What Frye calls the "progression of modes" is applicable to the novels of Cather's cycle. In speaking of her manipulation of types of literature, or what critics like to call *genres*, it probably is most useful in studying her work to remember Frye's warning that although a work of literature has form, many critical efforts to grapple with genre are "chiefly interesting as examples of the psychology of rumor."[8] In addition, it seems certain that Cather allowed her material to shape her novels, drawing from multiple models to create a new form. Some early critics, finding it hard to classify her work, seemed to devalue it for that reason; in turn, she dismissed her colleagues who, in her view, experimented too little. And yet there is discernible in her novels a sequence, a pattern, a participation in the appropriate forms that enhance the historical, social, and religious material she is dealing with at any stage of her cycle.

Cather may be typical in one way: according to Frye, poets have generally perceived civilized life to be assimilated to the organic cycle of growth, maturity, decline, death, and rebirth. Yet few American writers have produced a whole body of work that so fully captures the cycle for their own civilization. Part of the achievement of Willa Cather's novels viewed collectively is their completeness in their vision. The result is an allegory of the American West in the best sense of that term.

The tendency toward allegory, like much of the whole process of creativity, may be conscious or unconscious. The reports of two of Cather's confidantes, Elizabeth Sergeant and Edith Lewis, support the idea that her conception for her novels came as a whole, and there seems no reason to doubt them; Sergeant and Cather herself frequently use mystical language to describe her method of composition. It is likely that the same kind of revelation took place in the Southwest in 1912 as she began her novel cycle; the elements necessary for a creative breakthrough were all present--the unconscious idea comes to displace a previously-held belief; a state of heightened consciousness intensifies the experience; the insight completes a commitment that the unconscious is waiting to make; the insight comes at a moment of transition from work to relaxation.[9] In addition, many psychologists and mythographers--Neumann, Jung, Frye, and Campbell among them--insist that unconscious responses take over when myth is at play in the creative process, and the voice of genuine individual genius bcomes that of collective genius.[10] Psychologist Erich Neumann explains further that in the creative individual the content of the unconscious spontaneously combines with consciousness and expresses itself in creativity.[11] The probability that Cather conceived ideas for her novels in flashes of insight, as she and a few of her biographers claim, therefore does not detract from her large stock of information or her careful craftsmanship.

In writing her novel cycle, Cather joined a vast store of material, acquired through nearly forty years of observing and reading, to her intuition, which understood the cultural directions of her country. She amassed a remarkable amount of history, literature, art, and myth in each work of fiction, providing enough connections with every reader to elicit reverberations of response. Her method is a kind of *bricolage*, defined by the anthropologist Lévi-Strauss as a "putting together of bits and pieces of whatever comes to hand." Cather's is truly a method of composition, in the sense of the meaning of the Latin root, "to put together." In her case, there is more material than usual that is brought into play in her fiction, and every word must be considered to be invested with meaning or meanings relevant to the whole of each novel and eventually to the entire body of her major work.

Some of what she intended to achieve may be found in the language of her own later essays and introductions, which have been collected in *Willa Cather on Writing* and *Not under Forty*. The qualities that she admires in other writers are, not surprisingly, those that represent both the goals she thinks literature should strive for and the purposes of her own mature art. Her historical sense of the repetition of cycles as well as her mystical approach to poetry and human are both revealed in these collections. In "Escapism," for example, she decries the contempt for the old: "The themes of true poetry, of great poetry, will be the same until all the values of human life have changed and all the strongest emotional responses have become different--which can hardly occur until the physical body itself has fundamentally changed" (*OW*,28). As Vico said, in all lands and ages human nature is essentially the same.[12] The relation of literature to history is delineated by what seems to be Cather's paraphrase of Vico's ideas: "The 'sayings' of a community, its proverbs, are its characteristic comment upon life; they imply its history, suggest its attitude toward the world and its way of accepting life. Such an idiom makes the finest language any writer can have" (*OW*,56-57). Further, the imaginative novel must deal with the "eternal material of art" (*OW*,40); indeed, the admired authors about whom she wrote in *Not under Forty* "slid back into yesterday's seven thousand years," as she said in the prefatory note. She counted herself among them. She wanted her novels, like Mann's *Joseph and His Brothers*, to waken the "deep vibrations of the human soul" (*NUF*,122).

Some interpreters of Cather, in turn, echo her own language when writing about her work. Elizabeth Sergeant talks about the critical turning point when Cather "took the veil of final dedication to the art of fiction," the "literary fate she harbored," the moment in which "she had made the turn, as if unconsciously, and found herself at a new level of the spiral of work and living."[13] Dorothy Van Ghent, in her brief but powerful evaluation of Cather's art, reaches for even more mystical phrases: Cather's best work "reaches into human truths immeasurably older than the historical American past from which she drew her factual materials, truths that provide the essential forms of experience. . . . She was able to speak in a way that often reveals to the reader something extraordinarily valuable that seems to have been in his mind always."[14]

In many ways all of her novels can be approached as a fascinating puzzle, with many facets to be examined, many hidden clues, and ambivalences and ambiguities that are necessary to an unravelling toward the truth. And if, as Stevens points out, there are thirteen ways of merely looking at a blackbird, how many more ways of looking there must be in viewing the major work of an author who sought not just the truth, but the "truth under all truths." Her "structure of reality," in Stevens' term, may always remain in part an enigma; and it may be true, as one critic says, that "all works of art which are the products of imaginative genius are mystical enigmas akin in character and significance to the religious mysteries."[15] Cather's work demands a great deal from those who seek to understand its significance. That understanding is expanded and illuminated by an awareness of the sacred fire that burned intensely in her imagination and in her art.

Notes

(Page references are from the most recent editions in bibliography entries)

Part 1. The Law Behind the Veil

1. Bloom and Bloom, *Willa Cather's Gift of Sympathy*, 114.
2. R. W. B. Lewis, *The American Adam*, 1.
3. In Murphy, *Five Essays on Willa Cather*, 1-19.
4. *The Kingdom of Art* contains Cather's Lincoln criticism and a valuable introduction by Bernice Slote that includes a summary of Cather's early reading.
5. Alfred Knopf to Evelyn Helmick, 26 July 1983.
6. Sergeant, *Willa Cather: A Memoir*, 6.
7. Interview, 20 November 1925, in Bohlke, *Willa Cather in Person*.
8. *American Quarterly* (Winter 1964-65); *Prairie Schooner* (Summer 1967).
9. *Western American Literature* (Cather issue 1972); doctoral dissertation, University of California, 1979.
10. Skaggs, *After the World Broke in Two*.
11. Brown, *Willa Cather: A Critical Biography*, 58.
12. Dillard, *Living by Fiction*, 179.
13. Dewey, *Art as Experience*, 65.
14. Yeats, *Essays and Introductions*, 171.
15. Sergeant, 203; Cather to Sergeant, 12 September 1912, Pierpont Morgan Library, New York City.
16. Wilson, *To the Finland Station*, 34.
17. Berlin, *Vico and Herder*, 93. I am indebted to that volume and to Bergin and Fisch, *The New Science of Giambattista Vico*, for information on Vico.
18. The earlier is George L. White, "Willa Cather," *Sewanee Review*, 50 January 1942), 18-25.
19. The speech is reproduced in its entirety in Woodress, *Willa Cather: A Literary Life*, 60-62.
20. O'Brien, *Willa Cather: The Emerging Voice*, 424.
21. Frye, *The Critical Path*, 34.
22. Berlin, *Vico and Herder*, 93.
23. In Tagliacozzo and White, *Giambattista Vico*, 125.
24. Ellmann, *James Joyce*, 565, 706.
25. Tagliacozzo and White, 577-78.
26. Jung, "The Stages of Life," in *The Portable Jung*, 8.
27. A discussion of Bergson's influence on Cather is found in Loretta Wasserman, "The Music of Time," *American Literature* (May 1985). Tom Quirk, *Bergson and American Culture*, shows Bergson's impact on the intellectual climate of the early twentieth century, as well as its influence on the work of Willa Cather and Wallace Stevens.

28. The question of the conflict of opposites in Cather's life and work is explored fully in Lee, *Willa Cather: Double Lives*, and Rosowski, *The Voyage Perilous.*

29. Quoted in Wilson, 4.

30. Wilson, 14.

31. In Slote and Faulkner, *The Art of Willa Cather*, 238-47.

32. Lewis, *Willa Cather Living*, 47-48.

33. Daiches, *Willa Cather: A Critical Biography*, 94.

34. David Stouck writes that he has searched Michelet's histories in vain to find the phrase and that Leon Edel has found only a slightly similar phrase in Mallarmé. I have read most of Michelet without encountering it.

35. Jones, *The Bright Medusa*, 22-23.

36. Geismar, *The Last of the Provincials*, 187-78. Sister Peter Damian Charles repeats that idea in *"The Professor's House*; An Abode of Love and Death," *Colby Library Quarterly* (June 1968).

37. Frye, *The Critical Path*, 36.

38. Slote and Faulkner, 156-79.

39. Willoughby, *A Study of Mystery Initiations in the Graeco-Roman World*, 26.

40. Gibbon, *Memoirs of My Life*, 145-46, carries on a dispute with Bishop Warburton over whether Virgil had revealed his initiation into the Eleusinian mysteries in his description of Aeneas's descent into hell: "If Virgil was not initiated he could not, if he were, he would not, reveal the secrets."

41. Cather to Zoë Akins, 20 May 1939.

42. Cather to Dorothy Canfield, 10 October 1899.

43. Sergeant, 9.

44. In Harrison, *Themis*, 272.

45. MacMullen, *Paganism in the Roman Empire*, xi.

46. Grant, *The World of Rome*, 227-28.

47. Angus, *The Mystery-Religions*, 34, 213.

48. Eliade, *The Sacred and the Profane*, 189.

49. Cumont, *Oriental Religions in Roman Paganism*, 28.

50. MacMullen, 92.

51. Meyer, *The Ancient Mysteries*, 102.

52. Grant, *Ancient Roman Religion*, xxv.

53. Cumont, *Oriental Religions*, 34.

54. Angus, 109.

55. Meyer, 243.

56. Meyer, Inscription.

57. In Schroeter, *Willa Cather and Her Critics*, 148-56.

58. The initiation ceremonies of the cult of Isis, following those of the *Book of the Dead*, have been found in *The Pilgrim's Progress*, and following Plutarch and Lucian, in the fifth book of Spenser's *Fairy Queen*.

59. Burkert, *Ancient Mystery Cults*, 78-84.
60. Bloom and Bloom, "Willa Cather's Novels of the Frontier," *American Literature*, 21 (March 1949), 71-93.
61. Frye, *The Educated Imagination*, 123.
62. Brown, 171-72.

Part 2. Prairie Dawn: The Age of Gods

1. Stouck, in *Willa Cather's Imagination*, 47-58, and Randall, in Murphy, *Five Essays*, 51-74, discuss Cather's use of the pastoral in the early novels. *Sacred Fire* focuses on the pastoral only in its relation to myth and the mystery religions.
2. Segal, *Poetry and Myth in Ancient Pastoral*. I am indebted to these essays for several connections between myth and the pastoral form.
3. Segal, 7.
4. Flint, *Vico*, 219.
5. Porterfield, "An English Opinion," *The London Mercury* (March 1926).
6. Auerbach, *Mimesis*, 155.
7. The plow, so important to this first stage for Cather, figures as a sacred symbol in Herodotus, in Vico (the frontispiece of his *Scienza Nuova* prominently features the plow), and in Celtic histories.
8. Stouck, "Willa Cather and the Epic Tradition," *Prairie Schooner* 46 (Spring 1972) calls Alexandra "the Eternal Mother"; Daiches, *Willa Cather: A Critical Introduction*, identifies her as a corn goddess.
9. Those qualities help to explain the impact of Alexandra on the modern reader: Gimbutas, in *The Language of the Goddess*, says, "The Goddess-centered religion existed for a very long time, . . . leaving an indelible imprint on the Western psyche."
10. Neumann, *The Origins and History of Consciousness*, 377.
11. Frazer, *The New Golden Bough*, 204, explains the symbolism of the poppy by comparing its shape to the earth's, its uneven edges to mountains and valley; a sunflower's edges are more suggestive of the "shaggy ridges" of the Divide.
12. Scully, *The Earth, the Temple, and the Gods*, 3. Cather's feminine landscape is discussed in Fryer, *Felicitous Space*.
13. Jacks, "Willa Cather and the Classics," *Prairie Schooner*, 25 (Winter 1961-62).
14. Murphy, in *My Ántonia*, finds a connection between biblical and pastoral themes. This volume contains a very useful chronology of Cather's life.
15. Jung, *Man and His Symbols*, 280.
16. Segal, 235
17. In Schroeter, 7-8.

18. Brown, 247.
19. Sergeant, 49.
20. Jung, *The Undiscovered Self*, 122.
21. Scully, *Pueblo*, 10-11.
22. Ramsey, "From 'Mythic' to 'Fictive' in a Nez Perce Orpheus Myth," *Western American Literature* 13 (Summer 1978), 119-31.
23. Neumann, 48.
24. Grimm, *Teutonic Mythology*, 2:442-4, 455, 470, 508.
25. Grimm, 3:xxxiv; 1:557; 2:570; 1:138.
26. Sergeant, 80.
27. Stouck, *Imagination*, 183-98.
28. Tylor, *Primitive Culture*, 2:304.
29. Rohde, *Psyche: The Cult of Soul and Belief in Immortality among the Greeks*, 223-24.
30. Neumann, *The Great Mother*, 204, 253.
31. Harrison, *Prolegomena to the Study of Greek Religion*, 271.
32. Stouck, "Perspective as Structure and Theme in *My Ántonia, Texas Quarterly* 12 (Summer 1970), 285-94.

Part 3. The Memory of Our Vanished Kingdom: The Age of Heroes

1. *The Nation* 1923, 238.
2. Sergeant, 121.
3. Heer, *The Medieval World*. The historical information in this chapter owes much to Heer.
4. This assessment of Chrétien's intent is from Heer, 183.
5. One more interesting parallel: the tasks that Claude sets for himself, the obstacles that he overcomes, his steadfast faith in his beliefs, all recall a favorite story of the young Willa Cather--*The Pilgrim's Progress*. Although the five chapters of *One of Ours* do not divide in the same way as Bunyan's story, the City of Destruction describes Frankfort; the Slough of Despond is Claude's life on the farm; the Valley of Humiliation is marriage to Enid; the Land of Beulah, the lower paradise, is France; and Heavenly Jerusalem, the celestial paradise, is the salvation he finds in battle. The outline of Claude's story resembles part of Christian's, but Claude is an ironic Christian indeed. The engraved scenes from *The Pilgrim's Progress* hanging in the Wheeler living room encourage the connection.
6. Campbell, *The Power of Myth*, 59.
7. Some of the ideas in the discussion of the Parsifal story were generated in a seminar led by Joseph Campbell in the fall of 1986.

8. A major source for this discussion of Neoplatonism is *The Essential Plotinus*, translated by Elmer O'Brien, S.J.
9. *The Essential Plotinus* 39-40
10. Rachel Bespaloff, *On the Iliad*, 93.
11. This interview, from the book section of the *New York Herald* of 24 December 1922, is reprinted in Sergeant, 174-80.
12. *The Essential Plotinus*, 122.
13. Baugh, *A Literary History of England*, 1245.
14. Stouck has pointed our the relationship between Neoplatonism and Christian Science, and the interesting revelations of Cather's role in writing Mary Baker Eddy's "autobiography." The volume has been recently reissued by the University of Nebraska Press.
15. Campbell, *The Masks of God: Occidental Mythology*, 509.
16. Oliver Huckel, *Parsifal*, published in 1903, xii.
17. This essay is reprinted in *On Writing*, 60-66.
18. Quoted in Howard Duffield, *Parsifal, the Blameless Fool*, published in 1904, 72.
19. The later conventions dictated by the Renaissance critics do not apply: i.e., that the epic must begin *in media res*, must contain supernatural elements, and must end with the hero victorious.
20. Sergeant, 121.
21. Jung, *The Psychology of the Unconscious*, Collected Works. vol 7, 386.
22. Neumann, *Origins and History*, 27.
23. Heer, 106.
24. Heer, 181.
25. Auerbach and Heer choose romance to describe the form of the *Satyricon*; Frye and others restrict the genre to tales of a hero's quest and would call the *Satyricon* a satirical novel. Although there may be fine distinctions possible among romance, heroic poem, epic, and *chanson de geste*, Cather's eclectic combinations of stories and forms make a discussion of very precise labels of her forms meaningless. The forms, in fact, had already become confused in the Middle Ages.
26. Heer, 181.
27. Angus, 109.
28. Starr, *Civilization and the Caesars*, 58.

Part 4. *In Media Vita*: The Age of Men

1. Skaggs, *After the World Broke in Two*.
2. Jung, *The Spirit in Man, Art, and Literature*, 119.
3. Artz, *From the Renaissance to Romanticism*, 15.
4. Murray, *Four Stages of Greek Religion*, 103.

5. Stouck, 100-112; Murphy, *Critical Essays*, 217-27; Brown, 236-51.

6. Byatt, *Passions of the Mind*, 204.

7. Sypher, *Four Stages of Renaissance Style*, 100.

8. Murphy in *Cather Studies I*, 21-35, has elaborated on Cather's debt to Dante in *My Mortal Enemy*, *Death Comes for the Archbishop*, and *Shadows on the Rock*.

9. Bergin and Fisch, 131.

10. In Schroeter, 363-81.

11. Daiches, 67.

12. Woodward in a speech given at the Smithsonian Institution in May 1983.

13. The preface to *The Journals of Francis Parkman*, ed. Mason Wade.

14. In Baugh, 537.

15. Wilson, 7.

16. Flint, 24.

17. In Baugh, 1216.

18. Murphy, *Critical Essays*, 198-200.

19. *The Portable Jung*, 19-22.

20. The second book of *The Professor's House* does have seven chapters, although in the Grossett & Dunlap 1925 edition and the Vintage reprint of 1973 there are two chapters numbered six. The William Heinemann edition in England and the 1990 Vintage Classic edition are numbered correctly.

21. Cumont, *Astrology and Religion*, 199. This chapter owes much to this book and to Cumont's *Mysteries of Mithra*.

22. Farnell, *Evolution of Religion*, quoted in Cumont, *Oriental Religions*, 156.

23. Burkert, 103.

24. Campbell, *Occidental Mythology*, 257-58.

25. Skaggs, 84, connects the name of the ship the *Berengaria* with the followers of Berenger of Tours, a heretic who denied transubstantiation. The allusion, she says, is to St Peter's family, so immersed in worldly pleasures.

26. Cumont, *Mysteries of Mithra*, 111.

27. Campbell, *Occidental Mythology*, 258.

28. Cumont, *Mysteries of Mithra*, 143.

29. Burkert, 86.

30. Jung, *Civilization in Transition*, 21.

31. Neumann, *Origins and History*, 378-99.

32. Lewis, xvii.

33. *The Portable Jung*, 17.

34. Brown and Crone, *Only One Point of the Compass*. The 1980 edition is quoted in O'Brien, 241. The letters of Isabelle using this name do not appear in the 1970 Scribner edition.

35. Cather to Sarah Orne Jewett, 18 December 1908.

36. Clark, *Civilization*, 149-50.

37. Jones, *O Strange New World*, 169.

38. Madigan in his article on Cather and Dorothy Canfield Fisher in *Cather Studies I* says that Cather was an outsider in the world of the Canfields, and Yongue in "Willa Cather's Aristocrats," *Southern Humanities Review* 14 (Winter and Spring 1980), describes her ambivalence toward the aristocratic life.

39. Sypher, 100.

40. Sypher, 33.

41. Pagels, *The Gnostic Gospels*. This study notes many connections between Gnosticism and psychoanalysis.

42. Jung, *Civilization in Transition*, 83.

43. Jonas, *The Gnostic Religion* 3-4.

44. Willoughby, 211-20.

45. Boyce, *Manichaean Hymn Cycles in Parthian*, 8.

46. Jonas, 73.

47. Widengran, *Mani and Manichaeism*, 47.

48. Asmussen, *Studies*, 12-13.

49. Jonas, 68.

50. Skaggs, 92, recognizes the three phases of Myra as goddess. As Molly Driscoll, the mature priestess of Part 2, and the old Irish woman she represents the Virgin, the Mother, and the Crone.

51. Jonas, 73.

52. In this sense, George Seibel won his argument (supported by Cather) when he said that Oswald is the enemy, not Myra. That is probably so, if those are the two choices. But Cather added that there wasn't much to the story unless one gets the point, and that there was not much to it *but* the point. Seibel does not try to wade into those waters, even though Cather's letter says he would understand *My Mortal Enemy*, and most people would not. This information is from "Miss Willa Cather of Nebraska" in *The New Colophon* 2 (1949), 195-208. Seibel may have been able to tell more; the Pittsburgh scene as he describes it has many parallels in the novel.

53. Cremation was popular in Rome until the ascendancy of Christianity and has only recently been acceptable to the Roman Catholic church.

54. Only in his later years did Augustine find Manichees to be "poisonous heretics," and in the Middle Ages the strongest Manichaean sect, the Cathars, were annihilated in France for their beliefs. Campbell and Jung trace the Manichaean philosophy forward to the alchemists of the seventeenth century, as well as to twentieth century thought.

55. Campbell, *The Inner Reaches of Outer Space*, 127.

56. Sypher, 171.

57. Sypher, 106.

58. Sypher, 151.

59. Frye, *Anatomy of Criticism*, 40.

60. Jonas, 92.
61. Jung, *Civilization in Transition*, 356-8.
62. Pagels, 150-62.
63. Giannone, 169-83; Eichorn, in Murphy, *Critical Essays*, 230-43.
64. This is Giannone's translation of the score, 181.
65. Stouck, 174.
66. Jonas, 322.

Part 5. With Attributes of Gods: *Ricorso*

1. Berlin, *Vico and Herder*, 48.
2. Rahner, "The Christian Mystery and the Pagan Mysteries," in Campbell, *The Mysteries*, 337-401.
3. Cumont, *Oriental Religions*, xxiv.
4. Quoted in Campbell, *The Mysteries*, 369.
5. Grimm, 3:xxxv.
6. Inge, *Christian Mysticism*, 1899, cited in Angus, vii.
7. In Wilbur and Muensterberger, *Psychoanalysis and Culture*, 329.
8. Byatt, 216, adds that "Willa Cather's composed acceptance of mystery is a major, and rare, artistic achievement."
9. The Bloom essay is in Schroeter, 323-55; the second essay is in Murphy, *Critical Essays*, 258-65.
10. There is a suggestion in Auclair of the seventeenth-century alchemist, who, as Jung says, carries on some of the search of the Renaissance Manichee.
11. Bergin and Fisch, 91.
12. Chase, "Five Literary Portraits," *Massachusetts Review* 3 (Spring 1962), 511-16.
13. Murphy, in *Renascence* 15 (Winter 1963), 76-78.
14. Heer, 278.
15. Romines, in *Cather Studies I*, 147-58, points to the parallels between Jeanne Le Ber and Joanna Todd, the hermit of *The Country of the Pointed Firs*.
16. Stouck, 153-56.
17. Brown, 327.
18. Auerbach, 78-80.
19. Skaggs, 24, says, "*Miracle* is one of Cather's strongest words and a word she *never* uses loosely." Only the word *desire* carries a heavier burden of emotion throughout the novels examined in this cycle.
20. Daiches, 91-92.

Part 6. Something Complete and Great

1. *The Letters of Wallace Stevens*, 381.
2. In Schroeter, 171-202.
3. Berlin, *Vico and Herder*, 34-35.
4. Frye, *Anatomy of Criticism*, 343.
5. Flint, 177.
6. Fowler, *The Religious Experience of the Roman People*, 403.
7. In Schroeter, 248.
8. Frye, *Fables of Identity*, 11.
9. This typical breakthrough is described by May in *The Courage to Create*, 61-68.
10. Still, *The Timeless Theme*, 18.
11. Neumann, *Origins and History*, 343.
12. Flint, 199.
13. Sergeant, 9, 85, 87.
14. Van Ghent, *Willa Cather*, 44.
15. Still, 18.

Bibliography

Works by Willa Cather:

AB   *Alexander's Bridge*. Boston: Houghton Mifflin, 1912. New York: Bantam Books, 1922.

AT   *April Twilights (1903)*. Boston: Gorham Press, 1903. Reprint. Edited by Bernice Slote. Lincoln: University of Nebraska Press, 1964.

CSF   *Willa Cather's Collected Short Fiction, 1892-1912*. Lincoln: University of Nebraska Press, 1965. Rev. ed. Edited by Virginia Faulkner, 1970.

DCA   *Death Comes for the Archbishop*. New York: Alfred A. Knopf, 1927. Reprint. Vintage Books, 1971.

KA   *The Kingdom of Art: Willa Cather's First Principles and Critical Statements, 1883-1896*. Edited by Bernice Slote. Lincoln: University of Nebraska Press, 1966.

LG   *Lucy Gayheart*. New York: Alfred A. Knopf, 1935. Reprint. Vintage Books, 1976.

LL   *A Lost Lady*. New York: Alfred A. Knopf, 1923. Reprint. Vintage Books, 1990.

MA   *My Ántonia*. Boston: Houghton Mifflin, 1918. Reprint, with foreword by Doris Grumbach, 1977.

MME   *My Mortal Enemy*. New York: Alfred A. Knopf, 1926. Reprint. Vintage Books, 1961.

NUF   *Not Under Forty*. New York: Alfred A. Knopf, 1936.

OB   *The Old Beauty and Others*. New York: Alfred A. Knopf, 1948. Reprint. Vintage Books, 1976.

OD   *Obscure Destinies*. New York: Alfred A. Knopf, 1932. Reprint. Vintage Books, 1974.

OO   *One of Ours*. New York: Alfred A. Knopf, 1922. Reprint. Vintage Books, 1991.

OP   *O Pioneers!*. Boston: Houghton Mifflin, 1913. Reprint, with foreword by Doris Grumbach, 1987.

OW   *Willa Cather on Writing*. New York: Alfred A. Knopf, 1949.

PH   *The Professor's House*. New York: Alfred A. Knopf, 1925. Reprint. Vintage Books, 1973.

SL   *The Song of the Lark*. Boston: Houghton Mifflin, 1915. Reprint, with foreword by Doris Grumbach, 1987.

SR   *Shadows on the Rock*. New York: Alfred A. Knopf, 1931. Reprint. Vintage Books, 1971.

SSG   *Sapphira and the Slave Girl*. New York: Alfred A. Knopf, 1940. Reprint. Vintage Books, 1975.

TG   *The Troll Garden.* New York: McLure, Phillips, 1905. Reprint, with
        afterword by Katherine Anne Porter. New York: Signet Classics,
        1961.

UV   *Uncle Valentine and Other Stories: Willa Cather's Uncollected
        Fiction, 1915-1929.* Edited by Bernice Slote. Lincoln: University
        of Nebraska Press, 1973.

WP   *The World and the Parish: Willa Cather's Articles and Reviews, 1893-
        1902.* Edited by William M. Curtin. 2 vols. Lincoln: University of
        Nebraska Press, 1970.

YBM   *Youth and the Bright Medusa.* New York: Alfred A. Knopf, 1920.
        Reprint. Vintage Books, 1975.

Books about Willa Cather:

Bennett, Mildred. *The World of Willa Cather.* New York: Dodd, Mead & Co,
    1951. Lincoln: University of Nebraska Press. Bison Edition, 1961.

Bloom, Edward A., and Lillian D. Bloom. *Willa Cather's Gift of Sympathy.*
    Carbondale: Southern Illinois University Press, 1962.

Bohlke, L. Brent, ed. *Willa Cather in Person: Interviews, Speeches and Letters.*
    Lincoln: University of Nebraska Press, 1987.

Brown, E. K. *Willa Cather: A Critical Biography.* New York: Alfred A. Knopf,
    1953.

Byatt, A. S. *Passions of the Mind.* New York: Vintage International, 1993.

Daiches, David. *Willa Cather: A Critical Introduction.* Ithaca: Cornell
    University Press, 1951.

Edel, Leon. *The Paradox of Success.* Washington: Library of Congress, 1960.

Giannone, Richard. *Music in Willa Cather's Fiction.* Lincoln: University of
    Nebraska Press, 1968.

Lee, Hermione. *Willa Cather: Double Lives.* London: Virago Press, 1989. New
    York: Pantheon Books, 1990.

Lewis, Edith. *Willa Cather Living.* New York: Alfred A. Knopf, 1953.

Middleton, Jo Ann. *Willa Cather's Modernism: A Study of Style and Technique.*
    Rutherford: Fairleigh Dickinson University Press, 1990.

Moers, Ellen. *Literary Women: The Great Writers.* New York: Oxford University
    Press, 1977.

Murphy, John J. *Critical Essays on Willa Cather.* Boston: G. K. Hall & Co,
    1984.

------. *Five Essays on Willa Cather: The Merrimack Symposium.* North
    Andover: Merrimack College, 1974.

O'Brien, Sharon. *Willa Cather: The Emerging Voice.* New York and Oxford:
    Oxford University Press, 1987.

Quirk, Tom. *Bergson and American Culture: The Worlds of Willa Cather and Wallace Stevens*. Chapel Hill: The University of North Carolina Press, 1990.

Rose, Phyllis. *Writing of Women: Essays in a Renaissance*. Middletown, Connecticut: Wesleyan University Press, 1985.

Rosowski, Susan, ed. *Cather Studies*. Vol 1. Lincoln: University of Nebraska Press, 1990.

------. *The Voyage Perilous: Willa Cather's Romanticism*. Lincoln: University of Nebraska Press, 1966.

Ryder, Mary Ruth. *Willa Cather and Classical Myth*. Lewiston: The Edwin Mellen Press, 1990.

Schroeter, James. *Willa Cather and Her Critics*. Ithaca: Cornell University Press, 1967.

Sergeant, Elizabeth Shepley. *Willa Cather: A Memoir*. Philadelphia: J. B. Lippincott Co, 1953. Lincoln: University of Nebraska Press. Bison Edition, 1963.

Skaggs, Merrill Maguire. *After the World Broke in Two: The Later Novels of Willa Cather*. Charlottesville: University Press of Virginia, 1990.

Slote, Bernice, and Virginia Faulkner, eds. *The Art of Willa Cather*. Lincoln: University of Nebraska Press, 1974.

Stouck, David. *Willa Cather's Imagination*. Lincoln: University of Nebraska Press, 1975.

Van Ghent, Dorothy. *Willa Cather*. Minneapolis: University of Minnesota Press, 1964.

Woodress, James. *Willa Cather: A Literary Life*. Lincoln and London: University of Nebraska Press, 1987. Bison Edition, 1989.

------. *Willa Cather: Her Life and Art*. New York: Pegasus, 1970.

Other works cited:

Angus, Samuel. *The Mystery-Religions and Christianity*. London: John Murray, 1928. Reprinted as *The Mystery-Religions*. New York: Dover Publications, 1975.

Artz, Frederick B. *From the Renaissance to Romanticism*. Chicago: The University of Chicago Press, 1962.

Asmussen, Jes. P. *Studies in Manichaeism*. Copenhagen, 1965.

Auerbach, Erich. *Mimesis: The Representation of Reality in Western Literature*. Translated by Willard Trask. Princeton: Princeton University Press, 1953; Anchor Books, 1957.

Bergson, Henri. *Creative Evolution*. Translated by Arthur Mitchell. New York: Henry Holt, 1911.

Bergin, Thomas and Max H. Fisch, trans. *The New Science of Giambattista Vico*. Ithaca: Cornell University Press, 1948; Anchor Books, 1968.

Berlin, Isaiah. *Against the Current: Essays in the History of Ideas*. New York: The Viking Press, 1980.

------. *Vico and Herder: Two Studies in the History of Ideas*. New York: Viking Press, 1976. Vintage Books, 1977.

Bespaloff, Rachel. *On the Iliad*. Translated by Mary McCarthy; Introduction by Hermann Broch. Princeton: Princeton University Press, 1947; Bollingen Series IX, 1970.

Bloom, Harold. *The American Religion: The Emergence of the Post-Christian Nation*. New York: Simon and Schuster, 1992.

Boyce, Mary. *Manichaean Hymn Cycles in Parthian*. Oxford: Oxford University Press 1954.

Burkert, Walter *Ancient Mystery Cults*. Cambridge, MA, and London: Harvard University Press, 1987.

Campbell, Joseph. *The Masks of God: Occidental Mythology*. New York: The Viking Press, 1964; Viking Compass Edition, 1970.

------. ed. *The Mysteries: Papers from the Eranos Yearbooks*. Princeton: Princeton University Press, 1955. Reprint. Princeton/Bollingen, 1978.

------. *The Flight of the Wild Gander*. South Bend: Regnery/Gateway, 1979.

Croce, Benedetto. *The Philosophy of Giambattista Vico*. Translated by R. G. Collingwood. London: 1913. Reprint. New York: Russell & Russell, 1964

Cumont, Franz. *Astrology and Religion among the Greeks and Romans*. Translated by J. B. Baker. New York and London: G. P. Putnam's Sons, 1912. Reprint. Dover Publications, 1960.

------. *The Mysteries of Mithra*. Translated by Thomas J. McCormack. New York: The Open Court Publishing Co, 1903. Reprint. Dover Publications, 1956.

------. *Oriental Religions in Roman Paganism*. London: G. Routledge & Sons, 1911. Reprint. New York: Dover Publications, 1956.

Eliade, Mircea. *The Sacred and the Profane: The Nature of Religion*. Translated by Willard R. Trask. New York and London: Harcourt Brace Jovanovich. Reprint. Harvest/HBJ, 1959.

Ellmann, Richard. *James Joyce*. New York: Oxford University Press, 1959. Galaxy, 1965.

Flint, Robert. *Vico*. Edinburgh and London: William Blackwood and Sons, 1884. Reprint. Ann Arbor: University Microfilms International, 1990.

Fowler, W. Warde. *The Religious Experience of the Roman People: From the Earliest Times to the Age of Augustus*. London: Edinburgh University, 1911. Reprint. New York: Cooper Square Publishers, 1971.

Frazer, Sir James. *The Golden Bough*. 12 vols. London: Macmillan, 1907-1915. Published as *The New Golden Bough*. New York: Criterion Books, 1959; Mentor, 1964.

Frye, Northrop. *Anatomy of Criticism*. Princeton: Princeton University Press, 1957. Reprint. New York: Atheneum, 1965.

------. *The Critical Path*. Bloomington: Indiana University Press, 1971. Midland Books, 1973.

------. *The Educated Imagination*. Bloomington: Indiana University Press, 1964.

------. *Fables of Identity: Studies in Poetic Mythology*. New York: Harcourt, Brace & World, 1963.

Geismar, Maxwell. *The Last of the Provincials: The American Novel, 1915-1925*. Boston: Houghton Mifflin, 1947.

Gimbutas, Marija. *The Language of the Goddess: Unearthing the Hidden Symbols of Western Civilization*. Foreword by Joseph Campbell. San Francisco: Harper, 1989.

Grant, Frederick C., ed. *Ancient Roman Religion*. New York: Bobbs Merrill, 1957.

Grant, Michael. *The World of Rome*. New York: World Publishing Co., 1960. Mentor Books, 1961.

Graves, Robert. *The White Goddess: A Historical Grammar of Poetic Myth*. New York: The Noonday Press, 1988.

Grimm, Jacob. *Teutonic Mythology*, 4 vols. London: George Bell and Sons, 1883-87; New York: Dover Publications, 1966.

Harrison, Jane Ellen. *Ancient Art and Ritual*. Oxford: Oxford University Press, 1913. Reprint. New York: Greenwood Press, 1969.

------. *Prolegomena to the Study of Greek Religion*. Cambridge: Cambridge University Press, 1903. Reprint. New York: Arno Press, 1975.

------. *Themis: A Study of the Social Origins of Greek Religion*. Cambridge: Cambridge University Press, 1912; New Hyde Park, N. Y.: Meridian Books, 1962.

Heer, Friedrich. *The Medieval World*. New York: The World Publishing Company; Mentor Books, 1963.

Jonas, Hans. *The Gnostic Religion: The Message of the Alien God and the Beginnings of Christianity*. Boston: Beacon Press, 1958. Expanded edition. Beacon Paperback, 1963.

Jones, Howard Mumford. *The Bright Medusa*. Urbana: University of Illinois Press, 1952.

Jung, C. G. *Civilization in Transition*. The Collected Works, 10. Princeton: Princeton University Press, 1964

------. *The Portable Jung*. New York: Viking Press, 1971.

------. *The Spirit in Man, Art, and Literature*. The Collected Works, 15. Princeton: Princeton University Press, 1966; Bollingen Series, 1972.

Lewis, R. W. B. *The American Adam: Innocence and Tragedy and Tradition in the Nineteenth Century*. Chicago: The University of Chicago Press, 1955.

MacMullen, Ramsay. *Paganism in the Roman Empire*. New Haven and London: Yale University Press, 1981.

Mazlish, Bruce. *The Riddle of History: The Great Speculators from Vico to Freud*. New York and London: Harper & Row, 1966.

Meyer, Marvin W., ed. *The Ancient Mysteries, A Sourcebook: Sacred Texts of the Mystery Religions of the Ancient Mediterranean World*. San Francisco: Harper & Row, 1987.

Michelet, Jules. *History of the French Revolution*. 7 vols. Translated by Charles Cocks. Chicago: University of Chicago Press, 1967.

------. *Joan of Arc*. Ann Arbor: University of Michigan Press, 1957; Ann Arbor Paperback, 1967.

------. *Oeuvres choisies de Vico*. Paris, 1835.

------. *Principes de la philosophie de l'histoire*. Paris, 1827.

Murray, Gilbert. *Four Stages of Greek Religion*. New York, 1912. Published as *Five Stages of Greek Religion*. New York, 1925; Anchor Books, 1955.

Neumann, Erich. *The Origins and History of Consciousness*. Princeton: Princeton University Press, Bollingen Series XLII, 1970.

O'Brien, Elmer, S. J., trans. *The Essential Plotinus*. New York: New American Library, 1964. Reprint. Hackett Publishing, 1975.

Pagels, Elaine. *The Gnostic Gospels*. New York: Random House, 1979. Vintage Books, 1981.

Scully, Vincent. *The Earth, the Temple and the Gods: Greek Sacred Architecture*. New Haven and London: Yale University Press, 1962. Revised ed., 1979.

------. *Pueblo*. New York: Viking Press, 1975.

Segal, Charles. *Poetry and Myth in Ancient Pastoral: Essays on Theocritus and Virgil*. Princeton: Princeton University Press, 1981.

Still, Colin. *The Timeless Theme*. London: Ivor, Nicholson & Watson, Ltd., 1936.

Sypher, Wylie. *Four Stages of Renaissance Style: Transformations in Art and Literature, 1400-1700*. Garden City, N. Y.: Doubleday, 1955.

Tagliacozzo, Giorgio, and Hayden V. White, eds. *Giambattista Vico: An International Symposium*. Baltimore: Johns Hopkins Press, 1969.

Tylor, Edward. *Primitive Culture: Researches into the Development of Mythology, Philosophy, Religion, Language, Art, and Custom*. 2 vols. London: John Murray, 1903.

Widengren, George. *Mani and Manichaeism*. Translated by Charles Kessler. New York: Praeger, 1966.

Willoughby, Harold R. *A Study of Mystery Initiations in the Graeco-Roman World*. Chicago: University of Chicago Press, 1929; Revised edition, 1960.

Wilson, Edmund. *To the Finland Station*. New York: Harcourt Brace, 1940; Anchor Books, 1953.

Index